DO YOU KNOW WHAT IT'S LIKE TO:

- Bust your butt to do a good job and have the boss take all the credit?
- Work for a boss who's so moody you never know whom you're going to have to deal with, Dr. Jekyll or Mr. Hyde?
- Work for a boss who's more interested in your body than your knowledge or ideas?
- Work for a boss who doesn't give a hoot about who you are and what you want out of life?
- Work in a family-owned business where your boss has no business being a boss except that he's part of the family?
- Have a boss who's so authoritarian that you're actually afraid of him?
- Feel like you may be pushed out of your job by a boss who's threatened by your competence?

IF YOU ANSWERED "YES" TO ANY OF THESE QUESTIONS—THEN *PROBLEM BOSSES* IS THE ANSWER TO *YOUR* PROBLEM.

PROBLEM BOSSES

Who They Are And How To Deal With Them

Dr. Mardy Grothe and Dr. Peter Wylie

FAWCETT CREST • NEW YORK

MG: *To Hilary, Jordan, Lorna, and the memory of Ted*
PW: *To two very special women—*
Ruth Christie Wylie, and Linda Margolis Wylie

A Fawcett Crest Book
Published by Ballantine Books
Copyright © 1987 by Mardy Grothe and Peter Wylie

The excerpt from "Take This Job and Shove It" on page 338

The characters in this book are all fictitious, although the events and people are created as composites from our experience as counsellors.

Library of Congress Catalog Card Number: 86-9009

ISBN 0-449-21486-9

This edition published by arrangement with Facts on File Publications

Manufactured in the United States of America

First Ballantine Books Edition: January 1988

•••••••••••••••••••••

ACKNOWLEDGMENTS

Thanks to Bill, Carleton, Carol, Cherie, Dee, Faye, Floyd, George, Kate, Lisa, Marty, Pam, Serene, Smee, Susan, and the hundreds of people who've shared their stories with us.

CONTENTS

PREFACE

Several years ago, on a flight home from the West Coast, we found ourselves sitting next to a distinguished-looking older gentleman. He cut an impressive figure—a handsome fellow with a thoughtful face and wavy gray hair that matched the pinstripes on his vested suit. He looked like a Real Boss. You know, like those top-flight executives you see in television and magazine ads.

We had just finished writing our first book, a "how-to" book called *Problem Employees: How to Improve Their Performance.* We were doting over a copy of it as if it were our first child. The older gentleman noticed our excitement, and his curiosity got the best of him.

He leaned over and said, "Problem employees, eh?"

"That's right," one of us replied.

"I've had my share of them over the years!" he laughed.

"So have we!" we echoed and gave him that knowing look that managers give when they trade stories about employees.

"I've had my share of problem bosses, too," he volunteered thoughtfully.

We were used to hearing employees complain about problem bosses. But it was a little surprising to hear these words coming from a boss. We glanced quickly at each other. "So have we!" we said in one voice.

We spent the next several hours interviewing our new friend about the problem bosses he'd worked for. Without rancor, but with much emotion, he laid out a rogue's gallery of problem bosses: an alcoholic boss, several indecisive bosses, a couple of tyrants, one imcompetent boss, a con artist, a few womanizers, a bunch of credit takers, and more. He recalled each one in vivid detail, even some that went back thirty years and more. Each had left a special mark. Some had left scars.

As the plane started down, we commented on how different his view of bosses was from the way bosses are portrayed in the best-selling business books and in magazines like *Fortune* and *Inc*.

He laughed heartily and said:

Well, to me it's a little bit like the fable of the emperor and his new clothes. All these people "ooing" and "aahing" about how wonderfully skilled the bosses are. But to me most of 'em look pretty naked. Maybe my view is a little jaundiced. But when I see all these managerial types reading books like *In Search of Excellence*, I find myself thinking that most of 'em would be a helluva lot better off if they were reading *In Search of Basic Competence*.

We all laughed so heartily that the people in the adjoining seats were craning their necks to see what was so funny. He continued:

When it comes to management, I read everything I can get my hands on. But, unfortunately, when I compare what I read in most business books and magazines to what I really know about bosses, I find that a lot of them are pretty naive. If anything, I think they've helped to create a myth. You might call it "The Great American Management Myth."

We glanced briefly at each other. He was making a lot of sense.

The plane touched down. Realizing we didn't have much time, one of us blurted out, "Okay. What kind of problem boss are you?"

He looked at us, paused for a moment, and laughed. "You should probably get that information from the people who've worked for me," he said. "They see me a whole lot differently than I see myself." He added, "And maybe more accurately!" Then he leaned over and said in a soft, serious voice:

Everything I said earlier about bosses applies just as much to me. Over the years I've done much that I'm proud of. But I'm far from perfect, and I've made some terrible mistakes when it comes to managing people. I don't like to admit it, but I've destroyed the careers of some people and I've been a royal pain-in-the-butt to countless others. You might not think so from talking to me now, but I've been as much as a problem boss to my employees as any of my bosses have been to me.

With that, he stood and grabbed his raincoat from the overhead. As he edged toward the aisle, he leaned back over the seat in front of us and said, "Hey, maybe you guys should write a book on problem bosses."

••••••••••••••••••••

INTRODUCTION:
THE PROBLEM OF PROBLEM
BOSSES

Over the past ten years we've spent thousands of hours thinking about, talking about, reading about, and looking at bosses. We've remembered our own problem bosses. We've even searched our souls about the kinds of bosses we were and have concluded that we were big problems to our employees, too.

We've listened wide-eyed to hundreds and hundreds of employees who've told us about their bosses. We've heard stories that made us laugh and stories that made us cry. Stories that were so outrageous (or unjust) we didn't believe them—until we heard them again from other employees. We've seen employees feel a tremendous sense of relief after revealing horror stories they'd never told anyone else before.

In our seminars, we've listened carefully to scores of managers talk about their employees *and* their bosses. Most of the bosses we've talked to have been decent, conscientious people struggling in a job that demanded much—sometimes too much—of them. We've also talked with many people who had no business being bosses: people who were so ill-fitted to be in positions of power and authority that they made us shudder.

We've also looked carefully at the kinds of bosses our clients (some of them highly successful and effective executives) have been to their employees. As we've listened to them talk about their approaches to management, we've often smiled to ourselves when we've contrasted what they've said with what their employees told us about them. To use a military analogy, the war looks a lot different to generals than to troops. And troops say things *about* generals they never say *to* them. We've had the good fortune to talk to both groups.

All this thinking, listening, and observing has convinced us beyond any doubt that bosses are a major problem in the work place. We believe there are millions of employees out there who, as you do, know what it's like to:

- bust your butt to do a good job and have your boss take all the credit
- work for a boss who's so moody you never know who you're going to be dealing with in the morning, Dr. Jekyll or Mr. Hyde
- work extremely hard to achieve your career goals and end up working for a boss who's much more interested in your body than your knowledge or your ideas
- work for a boss who's so self-centered and concerned about her career goals that she couldn't give a hoot about who you are and what you want to do with your life
- work in a family-owned business where an incompetent and obnoxious person becomes your boss (and stays your boss) simply because he's the son (or other relative) of the founder of the company
- have a boss who's so authoritarian, tyrannical, or despotic that you're actually afraid of him; a boss who's destroyed

the hopes, aspirations, and careers of people whose only real mistake was to have him as a boss
- feel like you may be fired or pushed out of your job by a boss who's so threatened by your competence that she's doing everything she can to get rid of you

Unfortunately, the business and management books that've been so popular the last several years seem to have ignored the problem of the problem boss. The bosses these books describe (they usually call them managers, not bosses) don't look much like the bosses we've seen. They look like ideal bosses we'd like to work for, if only we could find them.

But we've done some digging beyond these best-selling business books. We've found that we're not the only ones who see bosses as a big problem. Not at all.

THE WORLD OF PROBLEM BOSSES

Most of the business books and articles we've read don't paint a realistic or accurate picture of bosses. But some people have explored the relatively virgin territory of problem bosses, and they've constructed a variety of different "maps" of the land. Some have emphasized certain parts of all the terrain and completely overlooked other areas. But, taken all together, they've begun to form a picture of what this fascinating world looks like.

Incompetent Bosses

No discussion of problem bosses would be complete without mentioning Dr. Laurence J. Peters and Raymond Hull's 1969 book that turned into a major cultural phenomenon, *The Peter Principle*. The principle is this: "In a hierarchy every employee tends to rise to his level of incompetence." Applying this principle to bosses, Peters and Hull say, "nothing fails like success," which is what happens when a competent employee becomes the boss: "competent followers show high promotion potential in the lower ranks, but eventually reveal their incompetence as leaders. . . . A recent survey of business failures showed that 53 percent were due to plain managerial incompetence."

Slipping Bosses

In his 1974 book, *Help Yourself and Help Your Boss*, Nathaniel Stewart argues that employees should help bosses who are "slipping." He profiles a number of bosses, some who can be helped and some who can't. Among those who can:

- *The "nice guy, but" manager*. These bosses are overly agreeable, afraid of conflict, unassertive, and can't say No. They also can't find it in their hearts to fire deadwood employees. A lot of people would call them patsies.
- *The panic-button boss*. These bosses are frantic, excitable, and live from crisis to crisis. They drive employees nuts because they're completely disorganized, can't (or won't) plan or set priorities, and always act like they're under the gun.
- *The commandant*. Commandants are easy to spot. They're autocratic, authoritarian, and tyrannical. These are the bullies of the work place. They use their power and biting tongues to get their way with employees.

These are a couple of bosses Stewart says can't be helped:

- *The petty bureaucrat*. These bosses worship the organization and its policies. They love detail and paper work. They're rigid and cautious and don't do anything that's not "by the book."
- *The POPO (Passed Over, Put On the shelf) boss*. These bosses are preoccupied with the unfair hand the powers that be have dealt them. They know they're not going anywhere. Their employees know it, too. They end up having a deadening influence on everybody who reports to them.

Deviant Bosses

Psychologist Andrew DuBrin's 1976 book, *Managerial Deviance: How to Deal with Problem People in Key Jobs*, is for executives who have deviant managers working for them. DuBrin estimates that "5 to 15 percent of managers and top-level staff people exhibit deviant behavior during working hours." And when he says deviant, he means deviant. His estimate, for example, does *not* include ineffective or incompetent managers; unintelligent bosses; managers who behave badly because of severe situational stress, like a divorce or family tragedy; and bosses whose "normal" behavior is a major annoyance or irritant to employees. These are a few of the deviant managers he describes:

- *Alcoholics and drug abusers*. DuBrin estimates that as many as one in twelve managers has a drinking problem bad enough to hurt his job performance. And that 10 to 20% of drug abusers are managers, business owners, and professionals.
- *Sexual exploiters*. These are male bosses who use their power and authority to cajole or intimidate female employees (often very young and vulnerable) into coming across with sexual favors.
- *AWOL executives*. These bosses are frequently away from the office doing personal business on company time. They often compound their irresponsible behavior by putting employees into the uncomfortable position of covering for them.
- *Pathological liars*. These are bosses who wantonly lie to achieve their goals and to escape problems and conflict. Unfortunately, they catch their employees as well as themselves in the "tangled webs" they "weave" when they "practice to deceive."

High Tech Bosses

In 1976, Michael Moccoby wrote a popular book called *The Gamesman: Winning and Losing the Career Game*. Maccoby identified four types of problem bosses who head up high technology companies in America. They are:

- *The craftsman*. Craftsmen are hard working, independent, and perfectionistic. While some are democratic and open to new ideas, others are intolerant and authoritarian. Still others are "narcissistic prima donnas."
- *The jungle fighter*. These are power-hungry predators who like to instill fear. They see people as either accomplices or enemies. There seem to be two types: "Lions," who conquer and build empires, and "Foxes," who make nests and get ahead by stealth and politicking.
- *The company man*. Company men are functionaries whose identities stem from being part of a powerful, protective company. Some are concerned and capable of commitment, but others are "fearful, submissive, and security-oriented."
- *The gamesman*. These are fast-moving, competitive, risk takers who love "the game." Some are enthusiastic, inspirational leaders, but others are pushy and overwhelming. Gamesmen tend to be impatient with (and intolerant of) anybody who's different from them.

Intolerable Bosses

In a January, 1984, *Psychology Today* cover story called "The Intolerable Boss," psychologist Michael Lombardo and Morgan McCall reported on their in-depth survey of seventy-three "highly successful executives" in three large industrial corporations. Almost *three-quarters* of these executives said they had suffered under at least one impossible boss.

Here are some of the intolerable bosses they described:

- *Heel grinders*. It's very unusual for a heel grinder to go more than a few days without belittling, demeaning, or humiliating at least one employee. These types almost seem to *enjoy* inflicting pain on people.
- *Egotists*. You could just as easily call these bosses know-it-

alls, blowhards, or pompous asses. They're easy to spot. If you've got a good idea, they've got a better one. If you've got a good story to tell, they can top it. If you just heard some important news, they knew about it a week ago. And on and on.

- *Incompetents*. These bosses don't know what's going on, but act like they know exactly what they're doing. Employees resent them for posturing and for all the extra work their ineffectiveness creates.
- *Slobs*. Slobs have personal habits that border on the disgusting. Their offices reek of cigarette smoke (or worse). Their clothes seem permanently wrinkled, mussed, or soiled. Their shoes look like they haven't been polished since they left the factory. The more time you can spend away from a slob boss, the better.

In an interesting footnote to their study, Lombardo and McCall asked each executive, "Who was your best adult teacher?" In almost every case, they named a boss. And frequently, "the best boss had one or more of the same flaws named in the intolerable ones."

Neurotic Bosses

In still another *Psychology Today* cover story ("Unstable at the Top," October 1984), Manfred Kets de Vries and Danny Miller identified five types of neurotic organizations: (1) Dramatic, (2) Depressive, (3) Paranoid, (4) Compulsive, and (5) Schizoid.

In our view, the article (as well as their book, *The Neurotic Organization*) is not so much about neurotic organizations as it is about neurotic bosses. In their words, "neurotic companies . . . often reflect the neurotic styles and fantasies of the top echelon of managers."

Here's a closer look at their five types:

- *The dramatic boss*. These bosses seem always to be "on stage." They like being the focus of attention, and if they aren't, they're likely to get moody—or even pout—until they're back in the spotlight. Employees quickly tire of indulging their temperamental natures.

- *The depressive boss.* These bosses walk around with a little cloud of gloom hovering over their heads. They don't think much of themselves, and their outlook on just about everything is pessimistic and negative. They're thoroughly uninspiring to work for.

- *The paranoid boss.* When these bosses go to a football game, they're convinced the players in the huddle are talking about them. They quickly misconstrue the most innocent remark from an employee as an unfair criticism or a sign of potential disloyalty. No amount of reassuring seems to assuage their constant suspicion of other people's motives.

- *The compulsive boss.* Working for this kind of boss is like working for Felix Unger, but worse. They're perfectionistic, preoccupied with trivial details, unspontaneous, and rigid.

- *The schizoid boss.* These bosses are emotional ice cubes. They're aloof, distant, and detached. They keep employees at arm's length. They never warm up to employees and employees never warm up to them.

Tough Bosses

In June 1981 and August 1984, *Fortune* magazine ran articles on the "Toughest Bosses in America." Here's a sampling of the twenty bosses they "honored," and some of the reasons why:

- John Welch, Jr., Chairman, General Electric.

    "[He] conducts meetings so aggressively that people tremble. He attacks [subordinates] almost physically—criticizing, demeaning, ridiculing, humiliating." Welch's pet nickname among GE employees is "Neutron Jack," because after he visits a GE facility the building is left standing but the people are gone.

- Richard Snyder, President, Simon & Schuster.

"Snyder is renowned for a quick, flaring temper that has driven talented employees from the company, their self-respect in shreds."

- Robert Malott, Chairman, FMC Corporation.

"Employees say he can grill subordinates mercilessly when there's no good reason." Malott was once quoted as saying, "Leadership is demonstrated when the ability to inflict pain is confirmed."

- Fred Ackman, Chairman, Superior Oil Co.

"He couldn't stand it when somebody disagreed with him, even in private. He'd eat you up alive, calling you a dumb S.O.B. or asking you if you had your head up your ass."

- John Smilow, Chairman, International Playtex Division, Esmark Corporation.

"He is uncannily effective at demoralizing employees [and] gives the impression he thinks of employees as throwaways." [Smilow's subordinates] have overheard him using his favorite phrase, 'Stupid is forever,' behind an employee's back; some suspect they are getting the same treatment."

- John Johnson,
  President,
  Johnson Publishing.

"He can be brutally hostile when displeased with someone [and] he has wild temper tantrums. He threatens to fire his top people every other week. It's like a crescendo. . . . First he puts you down with words. Then when you're down, he flattens you out. Then he walks on your face."

Bosses in the News

Having spent the last several years focusing on the problem of problem bosses, we now see evidence of them *everywhere*. We can't pick up a book, newspaper, or magazine these days without seeing some reference to problem bosses.

For example, while browsing through a copy of *Sports Illustrated*, we noticed an article on the St. Louis Cardinals football team. In a fascinating sidebar called "The Man Who Holds the Cards," writer John Sondereffer reported on a fairly typical kind of problem boss—team owner Billy Bidwell. Sondereffer says, "It has never been an easy task to get along with Billy Bidwell." He adds:

> Often, after a Cardinals loss, Bidwell will march directly into the locker room for a long and solemn chat with his coaches. He demands absolute loyalty and secrecy from his employees. His employees, in turn, have learned never to cross the boss. Bidwell once forced a public relations man to resign because a reporter had sneaked a look at the unreleased season schedule which was lying loosely on the fellow's desk.

Here's another example. In Harold Geneen's book *Managing*, the 74-year-old former CEO of ITT has a chapter called "Not Alcoholism—Egotism." In it he asserts that alcoholism's $33 billion cost to corporate America pales when compared to the cost of egotistic bosses. "Unbridled egotism," he argues, "blindsides a man to the realities around him; because he sincerely believes he can do no wrong, he becomes a menace to the men and women who have to work under his direction."

Ironically, Geneen probably deserves to be called a problem boss himself. In a *Boston Globe* article that appeared shortly after Geneen's book was published, staff writer Charles Stein said, "Geneen is remembered for a number of things, many of them unflattering. There is Harold Geneen the autocrat, who embarrassed underlings in front of their colleagues [and] Harold Geneen, the political operator, who allegedly used ITT's influence to manipulate governments in the United States and Chile . . ." We also heard that some former associates and employees were thunderstruck when they learned Geneen had written a chapter attacking egotistic bosses. As one said, "I've heard of the pot calling the kettle black, but this is ridiculous!"

One final example. While promoting his book at the American Bookseller's Association convention a couple of summers ago, Lee Iacocca had some pretty negative things to say about his old boss Henry Ford, II:

> I should have paid more attention to the warnings and I could have saved myself and my family a lot of anguish. I remember the time Henry said, "If a guy works for you, don't let him get too cozy. Always do the opposite of what he expects—keep him off balance." He once ordered me to fire a guy because his pants were too tight.

Iacocca neglected to tell the booksellers whether or not he carried out the order.

What does all this information tell us about the world of

problem bosses? We're reminded of what the great Russian novelist Leo Tolstoy said at the beginning of his novel *Anna Karenina*: "Happy families are all alike; every unhappy family is unhappy in its own way." We think something very similar holds true for bosses. Perhaps, "Good bosses are all alike; every problem boss is a problem in his or her own way."

You see, good bosses are very much alike. They're:

• strong, but not overpowering
• organized, but not compulsive
• courageous, but not foolhardy
• sensitive and caring, but not wimpy
• hardworking, but not workaholic
• serious when appropriate; humorous when appropriate
• ambitious, but not selfish
• careful, but not cautious
• trusting, but not foolish
• strong-willed, but not rigid
• principled, but tolerant

Problem bosses, on the other hand, differ enormously. It seems like there's a zillion ways they can drive employees nuts. For example, for every:

• tyrant or bully, there's a Casper Milquetoast
• compulsive neatnik, there's a disorganized slob
• cold, distant boss, there's an overly personal or too emotional one
• overcontrolling boss, there's one who couldn't care less what you do
• overly ambitious boss, there's a lazy one
• rigid or stubborn boss, there's a pussycat who caves in easily
• suspicious boss, there's a gullible one who trusts everybody
• boss who's always looking over your shoulder, there's one you can never find

- boss who never delegates, there's one who lets you do all the work
- moralistic boss, there's an unethical one
- arrogant know-it-all, there's a modest and self-effacing one
- hyper boss, there's a lethargic one

In fact, we've concluded that *all bosses are problem bosses* in *some* way to their employees.

But for all those millions of problem bosses out there, almost all the books on management have been written to help those bosses deal with *employees*. Only a meager few have been written to help employees cope with *bosses*. And that's why we wrote this one—to help you cope more effectively with your boss.

ON TO THE REST OF THE BOOK

In the next chapter we'll talk about something we call "the myth of the effective boss." After that we'll spend some time talking about *why* bosses are such a problem to their employees.

Following that we've put together two chapters that are designed to help you take a good look at your boss, yourself, and the quality of the relationship between the two of you.

Then it's on to the rest of the book: the strategies. We've come up with what we think are a dozen excellent strategies for dealing with problem bosses. Some you'll love. Some you'll be lukewarm about. And to some you'll say, "There's *no way* I'd even *consider* doing that." But whether or not you like them all or not isn't important. At least one or two should help you deal more effectively with your boss. The rest? Maybe they won't help *you*, but they just might help *somebody else* you know who's also struggling with a problem boss.

At the end of the book we'll help you stand back from the strategies and decided which one or ones make the most sense for you.

Enjoy!

1

•••••••••••••••••••••

THE MYTH OF THE
EFFECTIVE BOSS
OR WHY ISN'T
THE PROBLEM BOSS
PROBLEM MORE WIDELY
RECOGNIZED?

Well, this is sort of interesting, isn't it? Here we are saying that there's a big problem in this country called problem bosses. In fact, we're saying the problem is so vast that employees who don't work for problem bosses are as scarce as hen's teeth. But if we're right, why haven't lots of others raised a hue and cry? Why isn't the problem of problem bosses more widely recognized? We'll try to answer that question in this chapter.

Do you remember the famous story by Hans Christian Anderson called "The Emperor's New Clothes?" If you're a little rusty on it, here's how it goes.

> Once upon a time there was am emperor who was so vain that he spent almost all his money on expensive clothing. One day two swindlers came to the emperor posing as tailors. They told the emperor they were capable of making him the most fantastically beautiful clothes, and that these clothes would have a very special quality: They would appear invisible

to anyone in the empire who was an incompetent or nitwit.

The emperor liked the idea. Not only would he be getting a fabulous outfit, but he'd also be getting a foolproof way of uncovering the misfits and dolts in his empire. The emperor fronted the two swindlers a handsome sum and commissioned them to weave him a beautiful wardrobe.

The swindlers started to weave in earnest on their looms. But when the emperor looked in on their work, he could see only their activity. He saw no cloth, no jewels, no beautiful wardrobe. Not wanting to appear dumb, the emperor agreed with the swindlers when they said, "Your majesty, look at how gorgeous your new wardrobe is starting to look."

To hedge the bet, the emperor asked each of his top officials to look in on the "tailors" to see what they thought of the progress being made. Also not wanting to look stupid, each of the officials came back with glowing reports of how majestic and stunning the emperor's clothes looked.

Finally, the day arrived when the clothes were finished, and it was time for the emperor to display them in public to all his subjects. After putting on his "clothes," with accompanying oooh's and aah's from the swindlers and his attendants, the emperor walked out, stark naked, into the street, and began parading around. Not wanting to appear dumb, all the subjects cried out, "Oh, your majesty, you have such beautiful clothes!"

This massive delusion continued until a small child cried out, "But he has no clothes!" Soon the emperor's subject's chimed in, "But he has no clothes!" And even though the emperor knew inside that they were right, he stolidly continued his procession to keep up appearances.

HOW THE MYTH IS PERPETUATED

This simple story describes an age-old tendency. Leaders want to be seen as effective, even when they aren't, and the rest of us go along with their wishful thinking. When leaders and followers cooperate with each other like this, they create a myth. The people who lead are no longer seen as real people like the rest of us. Standing up there on their pedestals, they seem smart, wise, and effective—almost infallible.

A similar process occurs with bosses, who (like emperors) are in positions of power and authority over other people. They want to be seen as effective, even when they aren't, so they don the cloak of effectiveness. They look at the success they've achieved and say, "I must be effective to have done what I've done." Not wanting to appear stupid, the people hanging around the boss chime in, "You are effective, you are effective!" Thus a myth is born. A myth that bosses know what they're doing when it comes to managing people. That fellow we met on a plane a few years ago (see preface) called this "The Great American Management Myth." We call it the myth of the effective boss. But whatever you call it, it's a major reason why the problem of problem bosses isn't more widely recognized.

Why does this myth continue to exist? Why do so many of us mistakenly believe that bosses know how to manage people when so much evidence points in the other direction? We think it's because three influential groups help perpetuate the myth:

- people who write books on management
- the media
- bosses and employees

We'll talk about each group and how they perpetuate the myth and *why*.

People Who Write Books on Management

Go to the business section of any good public library or bookstore and you'll find a large and impressive body of literature on the field of management. If you begin to read through the books in this area, you'll quickly see the massive amount of advice that management "experts" offer to neophyte as well as seasoned bosses.

These books make it easy to conclude that bosses actually *follow* all this advice experts have laid down for them. The people who write books on management don't mention the fact that most bosses *don't* follow their advice. The most respected management theorist in America, Peter Drucker, doesn't mention this. The authors of books like *The One-Minute Manager, In Search of Excellence*, and *Re-inventing the Corporation* don't tell you this. Even Robert Townsend, in his iconoclastic *Up the Organization*, doesn't come right out and tell you this (although he implies it). The only author who's said it (and he said it tongue-in-cheek) is Dr. Laurence Peter in *The Peter Principle*.

By telling us only what bosses should do and not what bosses do do, management experts have helped perpetuate the myth of the effective boss. They've helped form the impression that, because there's a huge body of knowledge available on how to be a good boss, bosses *use* that knowledge. Unfortunately, they don't. We find that most bosses have never read a book on managing people, much less heeded the advice in these books.

We've struggled with the question of why business writers haven't pointed out this discrepancy between what bosses should do and what they actually do. We think the answer may lie in the fact that people who write about management look suspiciously like bosses themselves. Most management books are written by well-educated, upper-middle-class people for well-educated, upper-middle-class people.

If you think about it, it would be pretty tough for these

writers to step back and take a hard, realistic, critical look at people cut from the same cloth. (It'd be like asking a former president of one of the big three U.S. automakers to write an objective, balanced account of how the American auto industry ran into trouble with foreign competition. No matter how hard he'd try, he couldn't do it. In all likelihood he'd end up blaming everyone but himself.) It's natural for these writers to take on the perspective of bosses and minimize or even ignore the perspective of employees. Experts on management don't have a foot in the camp of the average employee. They really can't appreciate Johnny Paycheck's song, "Take this Job and Shove It." They don't know what it's like to work for an obnoxious, overbearing boss at the check-out counter of a busy supermarket or department store. They don't know what it's like for an attractive young woman to have a repulsive boss who's always making lewd remarks and suggestive comments. They don't know what it's like to work on the assembly line in a factory where the owner doesn't really care if you suffocate in the summer or get chilled to the bone in winter.

But, unfortunately, people who work at check-out counters and on assembly lines don't write books on management. If they did, maybe we'd have a more accurate picture of what bosses are like.

The Media

The media (TV, radio, newspapers, and magazine) are a powerful force in shaping our images of American organizations and their bosses. Two common forms are news stories and advertising. Let's look at both.

NEWS STORIES

The vast majority of news stories about business give the public a neutral-to-favorable picture of our organizations and the bosses in them. Clearly, there are exceptions to this.

There is the occasional "60 Minutes" expose of some sleazy company ripping off unsuspecting elderly customers, or a three-part series in a major daily about some multinational wantonly dumping toxic waste. But even these negative news stories make it sound like "the company" was responsible, not the bosses who actually run these organizations.

But, by and large, news stories are success stories. They show the positive, upbeat side of American organizations. Especially when it's a success story, the focus is usually on a boss-type person, not the corporation. Lee Iacocca and Chrysler is an excellent example. Look at the tremendous amount of positive press he's gotten in the past few years. Contrast this positive press with the negative press Chrysler and pre-Iacocca bosses could have (or maybe should have) gotten for the lousy management that got the company in the soup in the first place.

In many ways, it's understandable. After all, what sells magazines and newspapers? Certainly not stories about average guys who screw up a lot. No, newspapers and magazine editors know that readers want stories about movers-and-shakers, up-and-comers, on-the-movers. Thus the articles they print often read more like an authorized biography than a journalistic piece. The good stuff is accentuated; the bad stuff is downplayed, explained away, or (most often) not mentioned at all.

What's the typical reader reaction? Not hearing about the bad stuff, they think it doesn't exist. They don't realize that the people featured in this month's cover story may have terrible relationships with employees who work for them. Because it's not mentioned, they don't learn that these great American success stories may be hated (or feared or humored or resented or ignored) by their employees. A public relations consultant we know once remarked, "Hey, cover stories are about empire builders, not relationship builders." So goes the myth of the effective boss.

ADVERTISING

If organizations and bosses get portrayed positively in news stories, they *really* get portrayed positively in business advertising. In television commercials and magazine ads, these organizations look and sound as if their only mission is to provide you, the potential customer, with the very best products and services. The bosses in these ads (all actors, of course) look exactly the way we want our bosses to look: attractive, articulate, likeable, sincere, and competent.

What we don't see in these ads, of course, are the products and services that occasionally aren't worth a plug nickel after we buy them. And we certainly don't see the average-looking bosses (not to mention the unattractive, inarticulate, bumbling ones) that we'd find if we were to wander into these organizations and take a look around.

When you stop to think about the tremendous exposure the average person gets to news stories and advertising like this, it's no wonder we don't see the problem boss problem for what it is.

Bosses and Employees

The myth of the effective boss—just like the emperor's new clothes—depends on the active cooperation of bosses and employees. You might even say it requires their collusion. The conspiracy seems to have its origins in two tendencies:

1. The tendency for bosses to *deceive* themselves about their effectiveness as leaders.
2. The tendency for employees to *insulate* bosses from the truth about their lack of effectiveness as leaders.

We'll talk about this in more detail in our next chapter, "Why Are Bosses Such a Problem?" For now, though, we'll just assert that all of us have the capacity for self-deception. We tend to see ourselves in a more positive light than the one that's actually shining on us. This capacity is certainly evident in bosses. Most of them see themselves as good managers of people, even when they are not.

Here's where employee collusion comes in. The bosses believe they're good people managers and their employees think they aren't. But the employees are like the emperor's attendants. They don't straighten their bosses out. They don't give them honest, candid feedback that will counter their tendency toward self-deception.

"Hold it!" you say, "There are some damn good reasons why employees don't give their bosses honest feedback. First, bosses rarely ask for feedback. Second, even if they do and you tell them what you really think, you can get yourself in trouble. Maybe even fired." You're right. Very few bosses ever solicit honest feedback from their employees. When they do, rather than risk getting canned or transferred to the Arctic Circle, employees generally tell bosses what they think they want to hear. So the myth continues.

THE NEED FOR LEADERSHIP

Perhaps the most important reason why the myth of the effective boss is created and perpetuated is because of a basic need people have for leadership. This has been true for citizens of every country in every age. It's certainly true for the employees in organizations. We all want—no, we *need*—our leaders to be effective.

The trouble is that this need for leadership has affected the way we see our leaders. This need has caused us to invest our leaders (who are just ordinary human beings like the rest of us) with qualities they simply don't have. When we see these very human frailties in our leaders, we tend to turn our eyes away, to pretend that what we see really isn't there.

As consultants, we see this tendency when we talk to employees who are dissatisfied with their bosses and thinking about changing jobs. Emotionally, they feel as if they're the only employees in the world with a problem boss. Believing the grass really is greener on the other side, they envy the lucky employees out there who're blessed with effective bosses. In spite of their past history of problem bosses, they steadfastly believe their next bosses will be good ones. They're sure the next company will have "professional" managers who "know what they're doing." Every now and then one of them does find a company where there's a more enlightened approach to management, where their new boss is easier and more enjoyable to work with. By and large, though, theirs is a futile quest. But their hope helps keep the myth alive.

TOWARD RECOGNIZING THE PROBLEM OF PROBLEM BOSSES

We don't want to end this chapter on a sour note. We just want to say that most of the bosses in the world—including your current boss and most likely your next one—aren't all that skillful or effective when it comes to managing people. But there is a big myth going around to the contrary.

We'd like to see this myth die. In fact, we wrote this book largely to help hasten it to its grave. But if it's going to die, it'll die slowly. That's the way with myths. However, the benefits that will derive from its demise should far outweigh any value that would come from keeping it alive.

Imagine what would happen if we as a society looked squarely at the problem of problem bosses; if we could admit that millions of bosses don't really know what they're doing when it comes to effectively managing people. Imagine what would happen if we as a society decided to attack this problem in a major way. Imagine how much more strong and productive our economy would be—more profits, better services, fewer strikes, better products. Imagine how much happier and healthier our organizations would be—less turmoil, more job satisfaction, less turnover, more opportunity for personal growth, less stress.

Just imagine.

2

·····················

WHY ARE BOSSES SUCH
A PROBLEM?

If the problem boss problem we underlined in the last two chapters is so vast, then why does it persist? Why, in a civilization that has made such huge leaps forward in technology in the last hundred years, are we saddled with so many problem bosses in our organizations? If we've been able to send human beings to the moon and back, why haven't we been able to create good, competent bosses for employees to work for? In short, why *are* bosses such a problem?

We see eight basic reasons why bosses are problems to their employees, and we'll talk about each of them in this chapter. Here they are, in brief:

1. Bosses are ordinary people.
2. Being a boss is a tough job.
3. Bosses have poor role models.
4. Bosses don't become bosses because of their ability to manage people.

5. Bosses don't get good training.
6. Bosses aren't good at handling power and authority.
7. Bosses aren't always held accountable by their bosses.
8. Bosses don't get the feedback they need from employees.

Let's take a closer look at each reason.

BOSSES ARE ORDINARY PEOPLE

Magazines like *Forbes* and *Fortune* would have us believe that most bosses are like the captains of industry so frequently portrayed on their covers. But it simply isn't so. The vast majority of bosses are ordinary human beings like your uncle Fred or cousin Wanda. They're people with personality quirks and life problems just like the rest of us.

The trouble is, bosses don't leave their personality quirks and life problems at home when they come to work. They bring them into the job where they get in the way.

Oddly enough, perhaps the best example of how bosses bring their personalities into the job comes from the *Fortune* magazine article on the toughest bosses in America that we mentioned in the introduction. These bosses (almost all of them presidents and C.E.O.s of major American corporations) treat their employees like dirt, humiliate them in public, heap abuse on them in the midst of wild temper tantrums, and dismiss them arbitrarily for mistakes they themselves made.

In spite of the bottom-line success these bosses achieve, we've often wondered how much more successful they would have been had they learned to curb the darker, more negative sides of their personalities.

As we mentioned earlier, bosses bring their life problems with them to work right along with their personalities. Sharon Neely is a good example.

Sharon's the 37-year-old head librarian in one of the afflu-ent communities outside of Philadelphia. A reference librar-ian for years, she has an extremely sharp mind and an extraordinary memory. A university professor once said of her, "She's an encyclopedia on legs. If you ever want to get humbled, challenge Sharon to a game of 'Trivial Pursuit.' "

Since replacing her aging and not-very-competent prede-cessor, Sharon has brought the sleepy library back to life. She's instituted a host of new programs that have won awards from her State Library Association. She's fought hard with the town council to improve salaries and working conditions for library staff. She's computerized the collection of the entire library.

But Sharon's no pinnacle of perfection. She's an impatient person and has always been critical of people who are differ-ent from her. As she says, "I set high standards for myself and other people." She's also had a weight problem most of her life, and in the past year has been fighting a losing battle. At 160 pounds, she's heavier now than ever before. She's also unmarried, despite a lifelong dream to be a wife and mother. As the biological time clock ticks on, with no marital prospects in sight, Sharon's concern mounts. She often seems distracted and preoccupied. Over the past few months she's been much more critical and short with library staff.

As her children's librarian, a working mother of two grade schoolers, told us:

> In some ways we all feel a lot of sympathy for Sharon. She's basically a good person and deserves to get what she wants. But when she's as irritable and critical as she's been lately, your sympathy wears thin pretty quickly. I'm tired of her being on my case all the time, especially when it's not me that's the prob-lem. It's her own unhappiness.

BEING A BOSS IS A TOUGH JOB

Being a boss is a tough job:

- You have to manage a group of people with very different personalities and needs.
- You have to make important decisions quickly that you may not be well equipped to make.
- Like your employees, you have your own problem boss to contend with.

Most of us have our hands full just trying to manage a bunch of other people—each with a different personality, different needs, and different demands. One boss summed it up this way, "With all the different people and different situations I have to deal with, I play more roles than a Shakespearean actor. And I often don't know my lines!"

Gerald Weingarten, who'd been promoted to his managerial job in an office furniture chain seven months earlier, described the situation this way:

When I was an employee, all I had to think about was how well I did my job and how well I got along with my boss. Now things are completely different. I still have a job and a boss, but I have so much more to think about. I'm constantly worrying about the fourteen people who report to me—how well they're doing their jobs, how well they're getting along with each other, and how well they're getting along with me. I was talking about it with my wife a couple of weeks ago and she said, half-kidding and half-seriously, that I was like the little old woman who lived in the shoe and had so many children she didn't know what to do! Maybe I was being naive, but I thought it was gonna be great to be a boss. I never dreamed it was gonna be this complicated!

In addition to worrying about keeping a group of very different employees satisfied and productive, bosses are burdened with making lots of difficult decisions—often without the necessary knowledge, skill, and background information.

Sometimes these decisions involve problems that have never cropped up before, like burst pipes, or an expensive new phone that won't function, or some other emergency. The buck stops at the boss's desk. The boss is the one who has to decide what to do *right now*, even if it's wrong.

Sometimes these decisions simply hinge on whether or not to trust the judgment of an employee. Yes, Charlie really seems to know what he's talking about when he says this is definitely the system you should buy, but . . .

And sometimes—lots of times—these decisions involve people and their feelings. For example, does Clarise really deserve the raise she's asking for, and how do I handle her if she doesn't get it? Is it really fair for me to give Jack six more personal days than everybody else because of all his family problems? Getting rid of Andy is probably good for the company in the long run, but how do I live with the guilt of firing such a loyal old friend and employee?

Not only do bosses have to cope with lots of different employees and lots of different decisions, they also have to put up with their own problem bosses, just like their employees do. Leigh Dunston is a good example of a boss with a problem boss.

A talented interior designer, Leigh quickly moved up to a supervisory position in a well-regarded architectural firm. Leigh's what we call a Nice Boss. She hates conflict, so she's always avoiding talking about touchy subjects with her employees, like their performance, for instance. Their biggest complaint about her? Because she always accentuates the positive, they think she never gives them good feedback on how they're doing. Their other major complaint is that, as one employee put it, "She seems so insecure. She seems to lack confidence in herself as a manager."

Leigh's biggest problem now, and the main reason she feels so insecure, is her boss, Albert Framwell. Framwell's a highly talented architect and principal owner of Leigh's design firm. He's Leigh's mirror opposite. While she shuns conflict, he thrives on it. He's volatile, bombastic, super-critical, and aggressive in his dealings with people. He has a habit of second-guessing the decisions of people who report to him. Framwell's manner of giving feedback is confrontative, critical, and often abusive. More than once, in a closed-door session with one of his managers, employees have heard him bellow, "That's the stupidest thing I've ever heard! Are you out of your mind?!" As Leigh told us, "I feel paranoid. No matter how trivial the decision I make, I always feel like I'm looking over my shoulder to see what Albert's reaction is going to be. He's destroying my confidence in myself. I know my employees sense my indecisiveness. But they don't know what it's like to experience the wrath of Albert!"

Leigh has struggled mightily with her boss and there's no way she'd ever emulate his methods. But many people who become problem bosses do so in part because they pick up bad bossing habits along the way, which leads to our next reason why bosses are ineffective.

BOSSES HAVE POOR ROLE MODELS

A time-honored way for people to learn is from the example of others. It's the heart of the master-apprentice model, and it applies to bosses as much as to anyone else. For people who aspire to bosshood, however, there are precious few good examples to learn from. Often the examples that aspiring bosses get are worse than no example at all.

The analogy of parenthood is helpful. Most of us learned how to become parents on the basis of what our parents did.

Even though we vowed we'd never raise our children the way our parents raised us, what happened when we had our own kids and they started growing up? We thought, "Maybe our parents weren't so stupid after all." So we found ourselves doing what our parents did. But just because we began to behave like our parents didn't mean we were behaving effectively. Given the personal problems and hangups of many of our parents, we just continued to repeat mistakes from the past. John Wakefield is a perfect example.

While growing up in an affluent suburb of San Francisco, John never saw much of his father—a hard-driving, very successful entrepreneur. But even when the two of them spent time together it wasn't "quality" time, because John's dad was a cold and emotionally unresponsive person. His wife and several business associates told us John's father was one of the most uncaring and calculating people they'd ever met.

When we heard John's story we were reminded of Harry Chapin's "Cat's in the Cradle" song that was popular about ten years ago. It was about a boy whose father was so preoccupied with his work that he never had time to play with his son. Years later, when the son grew up and the dad retired, the situation reversed itself, and the son didn't have time for his emotionally needy father. Chapin might have been writing the song about John. His father, now retired and living comfortably in Florida, has no relationship with his son or his grandchildren. John hasn't seen him more than a couple of times in the past three years, and most of those visits have been brief and perfunctory. It's a sad story and an all-too-common one.

Now a highly successful businessman, John has picked up his father's workaholic style and coldheartedness. Rarely home, he buries himself in his work. If anything, he neglects his children more than his father did him. At work there's no comparison with his father; he's much worse. After getting his M.B.A., John inherited a mentor who was a devious and ruthless businessman who made his fortune as a corporate raider. It's a brutal business, but John took to it. After learning the business, John and his mentor had a falling out, but John quickly landed on his feet. He's now on his own, in the same business, and manages a small staff. His former secretary filled us in on his behavior as a boss:

A couple of months ago a newspaper article said that John had ice water in his veins. I thought he'd be upset, but he took it as a great compliment. I've never in my life met a man who cared as little about other people as he did. All he cared about were the "deals" he was working on. He had the compassion and sensitivity of a stone. He'd have me buy his wife and children birthday presents, without giving a damn what I'd choose for them. He also didn't have a lot of regard for the truth and wouldn't hesitate lying to people if he thought it'd gain him an advantage. He thought of people, me included, as pawns to be manipulated in some grand game. I began to see him as a poisonous, almost evil person. Finally, I had to leave.

John Wakefield had two powerful role models that shaped his behavior. Unfortunately, much of what he learned from his problem boss father and his problem boss mentor helped make him an enormous problem boss (as well as a major problem person to his wife and kids). His case may be a bit dramatic, but it illustrates the point that most bosses pick up bad traits and habits from problem boss role models they had during their pre-boss working lives. John also illustrates another fact about bosses: They can be notoriously bad at managing people and still be bosses.

BOSSES DON'T BECOME BOSSES
BECAUSE OF THEIR ABILITY
TO MANAGE PEOPLE

In many fields, there's a strong relationship between ability and the capacity to handle the demands of the job. People who become professional basketball players are gifted with height and outstanding athletic ability. Short, fat, uncoordinated folks—no matter how well-motivated—don't make it to the N.B.A. People who go on to become physicians are excellent in math and science. Those of us who barely passed high school biology aren't allowed anywhere near a medical school. In these fields (and many others) ability is the critical factor.

But, as far as we can tell, people become bosses for reasons other than a demonstrated talent to manage people. They become bosses because:

- They're good followers (remember the "Peter Principle?")
- They're loyal employees who have "good attitudes."
- They work harder than their peers.
- They have outstanding technical skills.
- They know how to play politics with company higher-ups.
- They have advanced degrees.
- They form their own companies.
- They're related in some way (son, daughter, spouse, in-law, friend, lover) to the Big Boss.

What do these factors, the main reasons people become bosses, have to do with the ability to manage people? Sadly, nothing. What happens is that the very difficult job of being a boss gets filled by people who aren't qualified for it. Millions of employees suffer because of that fact.

Howie Hadlock is an excellent example of a good worker who should never have been promoted to a supervisory job.

Howie's not a very nice person. Both his ex-wives and his children will testify to that. Even his friends (few in number) will tell you he's crude, self-centered and, frankly, a bit of a bully. More than once (usually while drinking), he's taken out his anger on his wife or his kids by hitting them. To be fair, though, that's happened rarely. Usually, he just yelled and screamed. Divorced twice, he now lives alone. He's unhappy and he spends most of his evenings watching TV programs and boozing until he falls into bed.

On the plus side, Howie's blessed with mechanical ability. If something's broken, he can fix it. After an undistinguished high school career, Howie became a tool-and-dye apprentice and took a job in a fairly large metal-working company in his hometown. Despite his personal problems, he was a hard-working, conscientious employee. This, combined with his talented hands, eventually won him a front-line supervisory job. That's when the trouble began. Working by himself, Howie was fine. But now that he has people working under him, Howie's personal problems and personality are major handicaps. He's so uncomfortable sitting down and talking with his employees (which he does as little as possible) that he calls it "baby-sitting" and "hand-holding." If Howie had his way, he'd never have to talk to his employees.

Howie's employees feel much the same way about him. One of them told us:

> If you mention this to Howie, I'll deny it, but he's the pits! You can't ask him a question without getting some smart-ass remark in response. He delights in asking you set-up questions, just to prove he knows more than you do. Howie was no Mr. Nice Guy when he was one of the troops, but now that he's a supervisor, he's impossible. Right after he was promoted, they sent him to a one-week supervisor's training course. We all knew it wouldn't do any good. Sure enough, when he came back to work he told everyone that he could have taught the course!

Howie at least got some training. Most bosses get no special training, which is another reason why they can be such a problem to employees.

BOSSES DON'T GET GOOD TRAINING

Think for a moment about the bosses you've had, or the ones you've known. Ask yourself, "How much training as bosses have they had?" If you're like most people, you'll answer "none" or "not much." Sadly, most bosses get no special training. There are no schools of bossing to send prospective bosses to, as we do with, say, nurses, engineers, or accountants. In fact, most beauticians and barbers get more training than bosses do. Most bosses become bosses and then have to fend for themselves, without any help. They're thrown into the water and expected to sink or swim.

In spite of this general lack of training, however, there are many bosses (especially ones who work for larger corporations) who do get some formal training for their roles as supervisors and managers. Then there's a small, elite group of bosses that actually gets quite a bit of training. In this section we'll offer some frank opinions on the quality of training we think both these groups of bosses get.

Let's start with the seminars and workshops that are offered either by trade and professional associations or by management-consulting firms. They have two major drawbacks. First, while these seminars often expose people to some very helpful concepts and principles, they generally don't provide the in-depth training bosses need. We don't expect beginning golf or tennis players to become experts after a few lessons. Why should we expect more of bosses?

The second drawback is that these programs don't teach bosses the most important lesson of all. Yes, they *do* expose bosses to some important managerial concepts and principles, like span of control, delegation of authority, corrective feedback, and so forth. Some of the better ones even teach bosses important interpersonal skills, like how to be a better listener. But almost all leave out the number one point bosses need to remember: the employees who work for them are human beings who deserve to be treated with dignity and respect.

Some larger companies have their own departments of training (or human resource development) to help equip bosses to do their jobs. While these programs often provide practical training in areas like time management or goal setting, we've never seen one that offered a comprehensive program for teaching the broad scope of skills necessary for managing people.

Perhaps the biggest problem with these in-house training programs is that first-line supervisors and middle managers have to take them, but not company higher-ups. Thus the common refrain heard in these courses is often, "How come our bosses aren't taking this course? They're the ones who really need it!"

Sadly, the bosses who need training the most are usually the least interested in getting it. The worst problem bosses often think they already know it all or are just too busy to attend.

But what about bosses who do get intensive preparation for their future roles as executives? What about the schools of business administration who turn out "professional managers" with M.B.A.s?

In our view, when it comes to solving the problem of problem bosses, M.B.A. programs don't help much. First, 99.9 percent of the bosses of the world never set foot inside them, so whatever gets taught in these schools is inaccessible to most bosses.

Second, while business schools often provide excellent training in areas like accounting or finance, they're weak in the area of managing people. We've examined the curricula of some of the best business schools in the country. What little they offer in this area is so theoretical and abstract that it's almost useless. Although courses on "Human Resources Management" may have some sensitizing value, they don't train prospective bosses how to deal with employees.

Another problem with M.B.A. programs is their tendency to produce graduates who see themselves as special and more deserving of respect and rewards than other employees. A *Time* cover story a couple of years ago decried M.B.A.s for what was called "short-term optimizing," their tendency to put their own career interests ahead of the long-range interests of the company and employees.

But perhaps the biggest problem with M.B.A. bosses was noticed several years ago by the famous management theorist, Peter Drucker, when he said, "The problem with a Harvard-type [business school] program is the arrogance it breeds. Students do not learn how difficult it is to accomplish anything."

We saw an ideal example of this problem a few months ago when we were hired by Gerald Bergstrom, the president of a small but fairly successful high technology firm in the Boston area.

Gerald was a talented engineer with strong entrepreneurial tendencies. Less than five years after graduating from college, he'd built a strong company with lots of promise. About a year before we were brought in, Gerald decided it was time to hire a talented professional manager to, as he put it, "start running this company the way a company should be run." So he hired Ronald Dunbar, a Harvard M.B.A., who had been working as a senior manager for a Fortune 500 firm. Gerald told us, "Ron looked perfect for us. He was fairly young, extremely bright, and seemed to have just the right managerial experience. The search firm recommended him highly."

But hiring Ron turned out to be an almost-disastrous decision for Gerald and his promising young company. As he put it:

> Ronald was smart all right, but he turned out to be "book smart" and not intelligent in a practical way. He had a tendency to pontificate on subjects in an academic-like way that turned a lot of people off. But that wasn't the worst of it. He had three problems that nearly did us in. First, he was a terrible listener. He interrupted people, talked nonstop until people began to tune him out, and almost never looked people in the eye when they were talking. People began to resent him. They felt he was a self-absorbed bore who didn't give a damn about them. Second, he was one of the most indecisive people I'd ever met and I soon began to lose confidence in him. The first time I met him we had lunch and he had trouble deciding what to eat. I should've paid attention to that at the time! Third, he was a very formal, stiff, cold kind of person who just didn't fit in here. His attempts to formalize things almost choked the life out of this place. We struggled with him for nearly a year, thinking maybe it was us and not him that was the problem. I finally had to make a choice between him and some of my most talented people, who were ready to walk! Within a month of his leaving we started moving forward again.

Unfortunately, even when bosses are highly trained, it's not as if they've learned a "science" of management. Compared to the advanced technology of the physical sciences, we live in the horse and buggy era when it comes to the "technology" of relationships, especially relationships where one person has more power than another. In a world of computers and space shuttles, we're still pretty dense when it comes to the subject of how people get along with each other. Even if all bosses were exposed to comprehensive, in-depth training before becoming bosses, a lot of what they'd be taught would still fall far short of preparing them for their tough jobs.

BOSSES AREN'T GOOD AT HANDLING POWER AND AUTHORITY

Like anyone else, bosses are imperfect and fallible. They have weaknesses and they make mistakes. Peter Drucker once said, "Strong men have strong weaknesses." We agree. And we'd add, "All men—and women—have strong weaknesses."

What do you get when you put these fallible people in positions of power and authority over other people? Too often you get t-r-o-u-b-l-e. It's an age-old problem people have been talking about for centuries. Lord Acton's dictum probably says it the best: "Power tends to corrupt and absolute power corrupts absolutely." Over 250 years ago, the philosopher Leibnitz said, "Those who have power are likely to sin more; no theorem in geometry is more certain."

Henry Kissinger, a man particularly interested in the topic, once said, "Power is the great aphrodisiac." It doesn't take a genius to figure out that being a boss puts you in a very powerful position over people who report to you. Michael Korda, in his book *Power*, said that "managing people" is simply a business euphemism for having what most people want, power over others. He also said, "the average corporation functions as a kind of broker, providing those who want power with a certain number of people over whom they can exert it. This costs nothing; every organization always has plenty of people so unimportant or easily replaceable . . . that it is simple enough to satisfy the power cravings of even the most incompetent executive by giving them someone to tryannize. For years this has been the real function of secretaries in the minds of many men."

In our research we've learned about so many abuses of

power and authority by bosses that it's hard to choose an example. Here are just two to illustrate our point.

Garth Darnell is the manager of a fast food operation that employs many high school and college students as part-time workers. Garth is also a reprobate. Married and the father of two young children, he thinks nothing of chasing after young girls. He's tall, handsome, flirtatious, and quite charming. He sees his female employees as a kind of harem. His favorite technique is to begin by "prospecting." He sends out flirtatious messages and gauges the response he gets. Young women who become serious prospects are invited to his office and, when they arrive, are asked to lock the door behind them. If the young woman objects or appears frightened, Garth quickly breaks into a hearty laugh and says, "Hey-y-y, just teasing," putting the young woman at ease. However, some lock the door. Those that do, Garth looks straight in the eye and says seductively, "I'd like to make love to you," or "I'd really like to get to know you better." Once again, if he gets a negative reaction, he quickly backs off. But some of the young women, out of a combination of attraction to him, inexperience at dealing with male advances, and fear of the consequences if they don't cooperate, go along with him. Many of these girls are only fifteen or sixteen years old, and it's a tribute to Garth's slickness that he's never been brought up on statutory rape charges.

Helen Donaldson is the executive director of a social service agency in a Midwestern city. In the words of her secretary Anna Marino, Helen is "hell on wheels." Given to periodic temper tantrums and wild outbursts, Helen thinks nothing of berating and criticizing Anna within earshot of other people. Helen doesn't focus just on Anna; all of her department managers have fallen victim to her sharp-tongued diatribes. Turnover among managers has been very high, but Anna keeps hanging in there, even though her self-esteem gets battered almost daily by her bullying boss. How does

Helen manage to keep her job? Despite her atrocious behavior, Helen is a highly intelligent innovative administrator. She keeps the board of directors happy with her enormous success at fund-raising and grantsmanship. Like a lot of boards, they ignore her bad behavior with employees because they focus most of their attention on what everyone now calls "the bottom line."

This lack of accountability for bad (sometimes abominable) boss behavior is characteristic of too many organizations and another reason why bosses are so ineffective.

BOSSES AREN'T ALWAYS HELD ACCOUNTABLE BY THEIR BOSSES

Another major reason bosses are such a problem to employees is that their own bosses often let them get away with awful behavior. We've seen some really bad managers (tyrants, sexual predators, psychopaths, back stabbers) whose bosses never confronted them or held them accountable. As in the example of Helen Donaldson, their superiors simply ignored the lousy things they did.

But why? Why do so many big bosses in so many organizations permit this kind of employee abuse to go on? Why don't they hold the problem bosses under them more accountable? There seem to be several reasons.

One is that the offending bosses are considered so valuable to the organization that the big bosses pretend not to see what's going on. They're afraid that confronting these valuable problem bosses will cause them to quit. We've heard many big bosses justify their inaction by saying, "Hey, I don't approve of his behavior, but we'd be up the creek without him. I'm willing to overlook a few of his excesses because I can't risk his leaving."

Sometimes the big bosses in an organization are guilty of

the same (or worse) offenses than the bosses they're responsible for. This makes it almost impossible for them to say, "Don't do something I'm also guilty of." We interviewed one woman who was being sexually pursued by her boss. A very attractive woman, she had many times before fended off unwanted sexual advances from professors in college and several former bosses. When she couldn't get her current boss to back off, she cranked up her courage and went over her boss's head to his boss. What she didn't know was that her boss's boss had been having an affair with his secretary for the past several years. Not surprisingly, she didn't get much support. In fact, the guy said that, given her attractiveness, her boss's interest was understandable. He even suggested that she was leading her boss on by dressing provocatively and playing hard to get. Within a month, her job performance ratings went down dramatically, especially in the areas of "work attitude" and "ability to get along with others." Even though she needed the job badly, she quit in disgust and put up with four months of unemployment before finding another position, this time for a female boss.

Another reason why big bosses tolerate bad bosses is that the big bosses are so afraid of conflict that they keep their heads in the sand rather than confront the problem bosses under them. Many of them are what we call "nicists," people who want everything to be pleasant and harmonious. Because they abhor conflict, the idea of sitting down with the problem boss makes them feel nervous. So they do what lots of people do when they get nervous: Nothing. They know they *should* sit down and have a talk with the problem boss, but they keep finding good excuses for putting it off. In the meantime, the problem boss continues to get free rein.

Finally, many problem bosses are owners or presidents of their companies and, for all practical purposes, aren't accountable to anybody. There's an old common law tradition that holds that "a man's home is his castle." Something very similar applies to business owners. Society grants them tremendous latitude in the way they run their businesses and treat their employees. Although there are laws that proscribe certain kinds of gross abuse, in general, business owners can treat employees any way they want to and get away with it.

So, for a number of reasons, problem bosses aren't held accountable. And they don't tend to curtail their abusive behavior on their own. If anything, they interpret the nonaction of *their* bosses as approval, and carry on with impunity.

We've been focusing here on the bosses of problem bosses, but the employees of problem bosses are also partially culpable, which brings us to our final reason why problem bosses are such a problem.

BOSSES DON'T GET THE FEEDBACK THEY NEED FROM EMPLOYEES

The poet Robert Burns could have had problem bosses in mind when, almost 200 years ago, he wrote:

> "O wad some Power the giftie gie us
> To see ourselves as other see us!
> It wad frae mony a blunder free us,
> And foolish notion."

Oh, how many blunders and foolish notions bosses would be freed from if they could only see themselves as their employees see them! But they don't. Very few of the bosses we've run into have an accurate view of how their employees see them. As the management textbooks say, they're "insulated from feedback." Even though bosses need it, they don't get straightforward, candid feedback from the people who work for them.

It's really a shame that bosses live in such a feedback vacuum. We see employees as "experts" on their boss's behavior, much in the way children are experts on their parents' behavior. Employees know their bosses very well. They've seen them during good times and bad. They know their patterns, habits, and idiosyncrasies. They often know their bosses intimately and yet rarely share this valuable knowledge with them. So bosses operate "in the dark," deprived of important knowledge that might help them correct their management mistakes and learn to function more effectively, if only they knew about it. The experience of Diana and Jack Whitestone is a good example.

Diana and Jack are married and own a small printing company that specializes in printing business forms. A dynamic couple, they're responsible for the rapid success of the firm, which has grown from just a dream three years ago to a fifteen-employees-and-growing shop today. They are both supersalespeople. Not only are they naturally gifted in this area, but they're constantly reading books and listening to cassettes on how to improve their sales ability. If their strong suit is sales and meeting the needs of their customers, their weak suit is sensitivity to the needs of employees. But this was not a problem they were aware of.

We met Diana and Jack at an annual convention of their trade association. They complained and complained to us about Bert Rand, their print shop supervisor, and the graphics and printing staff he had working for him. Briefly, Diana and Jack felt that they were busting their butts to bring business in while Bert and his printers were pretty lackadaisical about getting it out. This made them resentful, since they were paying Bert and his printers much more than they could make in any of the other printing companies in the area. To make matters worse, they had been hearing rumors that some employees were beginning to talk to union organizers. The situation was so bad they asked us if we could do anything to help.

We suspected the nature of the problem right away, but didn't want to say much until we talked to Bert. With ink all over his hands and face, Bert looked like a pretty tough guy, but he was one of the sweetest and most gentle people we'd ever met. For over an hour he talked about how much he admired and respected Diana and Jack. He had been fired from a previous job several years ago as a result of a drinking problem and, even though he had joined AA and straightened things out, he had struggled to find a new job. Diana and Jack gave him a shot and he said he'd be forever grateful to them. We listened patiently. Finally, when it was apparent that he wasn't going to spill the beans, we confronted Bert. "Look!" we said, "We wouldn't be here if there weren't some problems. So if you really care about Diana and Jack as much as you say you do, you've got to tell us what's really going on here."

Bert finally opened up and our suspicions were confirmed. It seems that a couple of years ago Diana and Jack had instituted a method called "red ticketing" to identify top priority orders that had to be shipped out to customers immediately. Essentially, a red ticket was placed on the order form and this signaled to Bert and his staff that the order was to be jumped ahead of nonticketed orders and rushed out right away. According to Bert, Diana and Jack tried so hard to please customers that they just couldn't say no to any of them. So, now, even though it sounded incredible to us when we heard it, almost three-fourths of the orders that came through had red tickets on them. What had started out as a good idea had become a nightmare for Bert and his printers. But, being such a nice guy, and feeling so indebted to Diana and Jack, Bert had never confronted them with his view of how awful the situation had become. In fact, Bert often stayed late, after the printers went home, without telling Diana and Jack, to print up a few extra orders.

To make a long story short, we finally got the three of them together (and also a few printers we brought in) and got them to talk out the problem. A new scheduling procedure was instituted in which Diana and Jack had to talk with Bert in order to place a new order in front of previously scheduled ones. Both Diana and Jack said to Bert, "We were so close to the situation we couldn't see the forest for the trees. So we began a policy that sounded great in theory, but became absurd in practice. We're sorry for that. But if you had only told us about it earlier, we might have seen the error of our ways months ago."

Finally, in a ceremony that brought applause from all the staff, Diana poured charcoal lighter fluid on a big bin of red tickets and burned up their entire supply at the company's first annual picnic (an idea that one of the printers suggested when we got people together to talk about the scheduling problem).

Samuel Goldwyn, the movie mogul, put his humorous finger on the problem when he once said, "I don't want any yes men around me. I want people who tell me the truth even if it costs them their jobs." That's the problem in a nutshell. Instead of actively asking their employees for feedback, most bosses actively (or unwittingly) discourage it. So, with good reason, employees are extremely reluctant to give their bosses the straight scoop. In most organizations, only the most courageous (some would say foolhardy) employees tell their bosses what they really think about how they're doing things, even when it's solicited.

We've heard lots of sad and unjust stories about employees who were booted out, forced out, or just plain made miserable after giving feedback to unreceptive bosses. Sadly, these stories are reminiscent of the ancient Greek rulers who killed the messengers who brought them bad news.

A couple of years ago, the executive director of a trade association heard us speak about this topic at his annual convention. Despite being a socially clumsy person (and a real clod when it came to dealing with people's feelings), he was very interested in what we had to say. After the convention he went back to work, designed a confidential feedback form, sent it out to all his office staff, and instructed them to return the form in unmarked envelopes through interoffice mail. The forms began to trickle in over the next couple of weeks, all of them giving the guy some awfully low ratings. Enraged by what he considered undeserved and totally inaccurate ratings, he had a new batch of forms printed up and sent them to his staff with an accompanying note that said: "I'd like you to fill out these forms again and this time rate me accurately!"

In this chapter we've tried to come up with a number of answers to the question, "Why *are* bosses such a problem to the employees they supervise?" We said that bosses are just ordinary people doing a hard job. We also said that most people become bosses for reasons *other* than their ability to manage employees. We pointed out that bosses don't have good role models to learn from, and that they don't get very good training for their difficult jobs. We mentioned that it's very tempting, and always has been, for bosses to abuse their positions of power and authority. We noted that problem bosses are often not confronted by their bosses, making it easier for them to behave ineffectively and irresponsibly. And, finally, we said that many problem bosses are insulated from feedback. They don't hear from employees what they really need to hear in order to improve the way they function.

In the next chapter we'll get you to focus on your own boss and why he or she may be a problem to you.

3

....

TAKING A LOOK
AT YOUR BOSS

In the preceding pages we've taken a look at the phenomenon of problem bosses from a broad perspective. We
started off by introducing you to the concept of problem
bosses because, frankly, it needed some introduction. Even
though it's a common problem, it's not commonly expressed. Then we talked about why the problem of problem
bosses isn't more widely recognized, laying much of the
blame on the myth of the effective boss. In the previous
chapter we offered some reasons why bosses are so ineffective when it comes to managing people.

In this chapter we want to take the focus off the general
problem of problem bosses and put it on you and the problems you're having with your own boss. The purpose of this
chapter is to help you get a clearer view of your boss and
how you feel about him or her. Doing this is going to help
you later in the book when you're looking at the strategies
for dealing with your boss.

In this chapter and the next (where you'll be taking a look

at *you*) we'll be getting you a lot more actively involved in the concepts we present. We'll be throwing a lot of thought-provoking questions at you. We'll be asking you to complete some exercises—to write some things down, to do some ratings, and to do some reflecting on the past, the present, and the future. All this, of course, will take some energy and effort on your part, but we think you'll find it stimulating and worthwhile.

In this chapter we ask you to do five things:

1. Compose your boss history.
2. Give an ideal boss analysis.
3. Examine the quality of your relationship with your boss.
4. Identify your boss's ineffective tendencies.
5. Perform a "chemistry" analysis.

YOUR BOSS HISTORY

Remember your first physical examination? There's a good chance it began with a medical history. The doctor probably asked you all kinds of questions, starting off with your parents' age and general health and going on to childhood diseases like measels, mumps, chicken pox, up to your present state of health and whatever might be bothering you right now. The doctor was trying to get some basic information about your health that would put your current problem into perspective.

That's what we'd like you to do here. But instead of taking your medical history, we'd like to take your "boss history"—to do a brief survey of all the bosses you've had over the years. This should help you get a perspective on the kinds of bosses you've worked for through the years and how your current boss fits into that overall pattern.

The best way to start is simply to list all the bosses you can remember, beginning with the most recent and working backward. For example, Sarah Murray is a 38-year-old merchandising manager for a large retail chain headquartered in St. Louis. Here's how she listed the bosses she's had since graduating from college about 15 years ago:

1982–Present:	Arnold Bronstein
1978–1982:	Jake Harris
1974–1978:	Audrey Kelly
1971–1974:	Sally Aurilio
1969–1971:	Harvey Lichter

When we met with Sarah, we suggested that she answer these three questions for each boss she listed:

1. What did you like *most* about this boss?
2. What did you like *least* about this boss?
3. Given who you were at the time, how good a boss was this person for you, and why?

Here's a portion of Sarah's boss history and how she answered these questions for the first two bosses she worked for after college:

1969–1971: Harvey Lichter

Harvey was my first real boss after college. As soon as I graduated I entered a management-training program in merchandising for a rather large retail chain. For about eighteen months until I finally quit, Harvey was my supervisor.

What did I like most about Harvey? It's hard to answer that question because, even now, I have an intense dislike for that man. I think I really hate him. I guess the thing I liked best about Harvey was that he was only in the office two days a week at most. The rest of the time he was out on the road where he couldn't bother me and the rest of the girls in our training program.

What I liked least about Harvey is also a hard question to

answer because there were so many things about him I couldn't stand. Maybe the thing I hated the most about him was his arrogance. Here was this sleazy, overweight, married man in his mid-forties who acted like we girls were his private sexual property. Harvey made it very clear to all of us that he thought he had the right to come into these tiny cubicles where we worked right on top of one another and grope us and kiss us and fondle us. He also made it clear that anyone who reported him for this kind of behavior would be out of the program the next day. And he convinced us that he had enough clout in the store to do it.

In terms of the third question all I can say is that it's hard to imagine a boss who would have been worse for me at the time. Here I was, this young, bright-eyed, bushy-tailed kid out of college looking forward to becoming a professional in what seemed like a very glamorous field. And who do I get for a leader, a mentor, for my journey into this new world? Slime-Ball Harvey. He had a devastating effect on me. I stood him for about a year and a half and finally quit the program in disgust to go to work for a woman who owned several small dress shops in upper New York State.

1971–1974: Sally Aurilio

I took the job with Sally for a couple of reasons. One, she was a woman. At the time I was so turned off by Harvey's sexual oppression I wasn't sure I'd ever be able to work for a man again. Two, I really liked Sally when I met her. She had a small but quite successful dress business, and she offered a refreshing change from the New York City hustle-bustle I had just left.

What I liked most about Sally? Hmmm . . . I guess I'd have to say it was her warmth and her creativity and her genuine concern for me as a person. I was very open with Sally about what had happened to me with Harvey, and she was extremely understanding. She was almost like a second mom to me, and I can't tell you how much I appreciated that. We're still good friends to this day and we talk long distance at least once a month.

Sally was also very creative—she was a natural at designing clothes and I really think that, if she'd been a more ambitious person, she would have become a nationally recognized designer.

But even though Sally was a great boss, she wasn't a perfect boss. For example, during the entire time I worked for her, she was having an affair with a married man. Now, it's her business what she does with her personal life, but her affair definitely affected her performance as a boss and it sometimes involved me too. That is, I'd have to cover for Sally when her husband called and that sort of thing.

One other thing I didn't like about Sally was that she just wasn't in a position to help me grow and advance professionally. I managed one of her shops outside of Syracuse for about two years, but the job wasn't very challenging. I kept encouraging Sally to open up a larger chain of stores that could operate as a distribution system for some excellent lines that we carried as well as some of her own creations. But she wasn't interested in doing that. It didn't take me long to see that there wasn't a whole lot of future for me there. So after my "recuperation" from Harvey I decided to move on.

In terms of the third question—how good a boss was she for me at the time—all I can say is that she really was a lifesaver. No, she couldn't give me the opportunities for professional growth and development that I wanted, but she was able to give me something much more important—caring and understanding at a time when I desperately needed it. She was terrific.

Now you take a shot at doing your own boss history. Take each of the bosses you've worked for and try to answer the three questions we posed to Sarah. After you finish, try to stand back from the experience to figure out what it means for you. We'd recommend that you put the history aside for a day or so just to give it some incubation time. Then sit down and try to answer these additional questions:

1. What kind of bosses have you had over the years? How did they differ? How were they the same?
2. How does your current boss stack up to your former bosses? What are some of the attributes of your former bosses that you'd like to see in your current boss?
3. How has doing your boss history clarified your perspective on your current boss? For example, do you now see your boss as better or worse than you did before?
4. Is your boss the right kind of boss for you at this stage in your career? What kind of boss do you need now, and how have your needs changed over the years?

A couple of other thoughts before moving on to the next section: Some people (maybe you're one of them) will want to write out their boss histories in the sort of detail that Sarah did above. Others will just want to jot down a few notes. And others, who don't like or can't stand writing, will want to review mentally the bosses they've had over the years, or possibly even tell a trusted friend about them. The particular method you use doesn't really matter. What's important is that you take some time to stand back and take a good, hard look at the bosses you've had.

YOUR IDEAL BOSS ANALYSIS

Years ago we conducted a seminar for business owners on how to find good employees. As an experiment, we invited the audience (almost all were married) to imagine that they were once again single and in search of a spouse. Then we asked them to do an "ideal spouse analysis"—to think of the desirable personality traits they'd like in their prospective mates. Before we could offer the rest of our instructions, the room erupted in such a furor that it took a good five minutes to quiet everybody down. Clearly we'd struck an emotional chord.

That experience convinced us of an important fact. When it comes to choosing the kinds of people we want to get involved with in important relationships, most of us don't really think about it. When it comes to getting married, we don't *think* about the qualities we want in a spouse. When it comes to hiring people, we don't *think* about the qualities we want in an employee. When we look for a job, we're so focused on how good a *job* it will be—or how good a *career move* it will be—that we don't *think* about the qualities we'd like to have in a boss.

We know firsthand that the cost of not doing this kind of careful prior thinking can be steep. Both of us have been through painful divorces. We've hired people we never should have and then faced the unpleasantness of having to fire them. We've both taken jobs with little thought about who our new bosses would be.

Now, doing an ideal boss analysis at this point is *not* going to erase a serious mistake you might have made in going to work for your current boss. But doing the analysis *will* reap some benefits. It will:

• allow you to compare how well your current boss measures up to your image of an ideal boss
• help you clarify what you like and don't like about your current boss
• help you get a better understanding of what important needs your boss is—and isn't—meeting
• give you some good ideas for what to look for in your next boss

Okay, let's get you started. There are four basic steps to an Ideal Boss Analysis:

- Brainstorm a list of traits you'd like an ideal boss to have.
- Go through this list and pick ten traits you feel would be especially important for your ideal boss to have.
- On a scale from zero to ten (where zero is low and ten is high) rate your current boss on each of these traits.
- Try to offer some specific *reasons* why you gave your boss the ratings you did.

To help you, we'll give an example. Clyde Jameson is a young physician who has recently gone to work for a medical research laboratory in the midwest. Clyde is thirty-two. His boss, Bill Gruskins, is fifty-seven, and also a physician. Clyde started his job with great expectations. But now that he's been there for three months, he's frustrated and disappointed. We got him to do an ideal boss analysis as one means of helping him find out what was bothering him.

Clyde brainstormed the following list of traits he'd want an ideal boss to have:

> fairness
> integrity
> interest in employees
> good manager
> decisiveness
> firmness
> kindness
> willingness to stick up for employees
> caring
> flexibility
> strength
> understanding
> warmth
> helpfulness
> sense of humor
> smarts
> thoughtfulness
> creativity
> inspiration
> honesty

We asked Clyde to go through this list and pick ten traits that he felt would be especially important for his ideal boss to have. After he'd made his selection, we asked him to rate his boss on each of these ten traits on a scale from zero to ten. These are the ratings Clyde came up with:

Trait	Rating
fairness	8
helpfulness	4
sense of humor	8
inspiration	3
honesty	9
interest in employees	3
decisiveness	8
kindness	4
willingncss to stick up for employees	5
flexibility	3

After Clyde finished making these ratings, we asked him to talk about why he rated his boss the way he did on each trait. These are the reasons Clyde offered for three of the traits.

"3" on Inspiration

Why did I give Bill a "3" on inspiration? Hmmm, well, I think the main reason is that Bill is just not an inspirational boss. In fact, I'd have to say he's pretty much the opposite of that. One of the women I work with refers to Bill as a "wet blanket" because that's what he throws on any new idea that somebody comes up with. He's forever giving us reasons why we *can't* do something. It's frustrating and demoralizing to work for a guy like that if you see yourself as a creative person.

"9" on Honesty

Bill's got a lot of negative traits, but dishonesty isn't one of them. He's always straightforward with me. He tells me what's on his mind. Now, I don't always *like* what he's got to say, but I do appreciate his candor. Everybody always says you know right where you stand with Bill, and I think that's true.

"4" on Kindness

I think I would have given Bill a higher rating on kindness if it hadn't been for something he did just a few weeks ago. It was the day before Christmas, and Sandy, one of our technicians, couldn't get a babysitter for her four-year-old. She asked Bill if she could bring him into the office for the afternoon. Well, I couldn't believe it, but he said no. He said the lab was no place for kids. He just kind of read her the policy manual. I wanted to read him the riot act! None of us were really working that day, with all the office parties going on, and any one of us could have looked after the kid. I don't know, I just don't see Bill as a very kind person after that incident.

By doing his ideal boss analysis Clyde discovered that a lot of his "job" dissatisfaction was really more a case of "boss" dissatisfaction.

THE QUALITY OF YOUR RELATIONSHIP WITH YOUR BOSS

Several years ago one of us came up with the notion that, in some respects, a relationship is like a human body: Both have vital signs we can monitor to tell how they're functioning. For the body these signs are temperature, pulse, blood pressure, and respiration. For a relationship it's not so clear, but four that seemed to make pretty good sense to us were: trust, respect, affection, and confidence.

For the body, of course, vital signs are extremely important. If they fall below certain levels, you may die. The same holds true for relationships. When levels of trust, respect, affection, and confidence fall below certain levels, the relationship between two people is in poor health, if not already dead.

To help people remember them, we gave our vital signs the acronym TRAC. Since then we've tried out the concept on hundreds of people in two-person relationships (spouses, business partners, friends, and so on). We ask them on a scale from zero to ten:

1. How much do you *trust* the other person?
2. How much do you *respect* the other person?
3. How much *affection* do you have for the other person?
4. How much overall *confidence* do you have in the other person?

What we've learned is what you'd expect. People in unsatisfying, unhappy, or unproductive relationships give each other low TRAC readings. Conversely, people in happy and productive relationships give each other relatively high ratings. For us, TRAC has become a simple but useful tool for helping people in any relationship step back and take a look at the quality of that relationship.

In this section, of course, we'd like you to look at the quality of the relationship you have with your boss. Specifically, we'd like you to do three things:

1. Rate (on a scale from zero to ten) how much you *trust* your boss; how much you *respect* your boss; how much *affection* you have for your boss; and how much overall *confidence* you have in your boss.

2. Offer some specific reasons why you gave your boss the ratings you did.
3. Describe what your boss would have to do on each of the four dimensions to get higher ratings.

What follows is an example of how Jim Faulkner TRAC-rated his boss, Charlie Chubb. Jim and Charlie are about the same age—mid-thirties. Charlie started the company—a rapidly growing software house—over ten years ago when he was in his early twenties. About five years later he hired Jim as a salesman, and, seeing his obvious talent, promptly promoted him to his current position of sales manager.

Here's how Jim rated Charlie on TRAC:

- trust   = 6
- respect   = 5
- affection   = 4
- confidence   = 9

These are the reasons Jim gave for rating Charlie the way he did on two of the vital signs, trust and affection:

Trust

I guess I *trust* Charlie on most things, but he's got some tendencies that are puzzling and . . . well, they just cause me to wonder about him. It's hard to be really specific here, but I can remember several times when Charlie said he was definitely going to do something for me, and then for one reason or another he didn't do it. So I would go to him and bug him about it, and then he would *deny* ever having made the commitment. Once, on a raise he was supposed to give me that got delayed for months and months, I called him on it. I even pulled out my calendar and showed him the date he promised me the raise and everything. Well, he just went into a long-winded spiel. But he did give me my raise.

Affection

As you can see, I gave Charlie a fairly low rating on affection. And Charlie's a guy who really is pretty likeable a lot of the time. He's funny . . . I mean the guy is talented enough to be a stand-up comic. But he has a nasty streak in him. It seems to come out when he's nervous or tense about something, and the way it comes out—and this is what I *don't* like about Charlie—is that he starts yelling and screaming at people. And he's just as likely to do it in a group setting as he is in private. I can't stand that about him and I've even told him that several times. That's why I gave him a "4."

After Jim told us why he had rated Charlie the way he did, we asked him to think about what Charlie would have to do differently to earn higher ratings from Jim on each of the four dimensions. This is what he told us:

When it comes to *trust*, I guess the major thing I'd like from Charlie is a little more honesty when it comes to keeping his word and admitting when he's wrong. I think I'm really good about 'fessing up to my mistakes and apologizing for them. But getting Charlie to admit he's wrong and say he's sorry is like pulling teeth. If he would, my *trust* level would go up a lot.

As far as my *respect* for Charlie goes, I think if he'd admit when he's wrong more and learn to control his temper, I could rate him a lot higher on this one.

I did give Charlie a low rating on *affection*. I'm not exactly sure what he'd have to do to get a higher rating here, but he'd certainly have to work on getting rid of his nasty streak. He'd have to stop yelling and screaming at people, especially in public, when he's upset about something. I know he tries to control that a little every now and then, but he forgets and backslides. I think that'll be a hard area for him to change in.

My *confidence* in Charlie as C.E.O. of this place is

really high. He's built the company from the ground up, and the growth picture for us looks great. I guess the only reason I didn't give him a "10" on *confidence* is because of some of the personality things I've already mentioned.

When we've talked to bosses about TRAC, many of them have said (somewhat smugly, we'd add), "I know my employees pretty well and I think I could estimate quite accurately how they'd rate me on TRAC." Before moving on to the next section, you might want to think about this question: Does your boss have *any* idea how you just rated him or her on TRAC?

YOUR BOSS'S INEFFECTIVE TENDENCIES

In our *Problem Employees* book we talked about five common ineffective tendencies that bosses engage in when they deal with employees:

1. avoiding
2. overreaction
3. complaining
4. lecturing
5. externalizing

Identifying the ineffective tendencies that are characteristic of your boss is another useful method for getting a better perspective on your boss.

The rest of this section is a description of each of these tendencies.

Avoiding

Some people hate conflict. They'd do almost anything to avoid an unpleasant confrontation with another person. On the basis of our research, we'd conservatively estimate that 50 percent of all bosses are like this. That is, they're very reluctant to sit down with an employee and talk about performance problems. The thought of doing that makes them so nervous and uncomfortable that they just don't do it.

There are lots of reasons why avoiding is a bad tendency. But from your perspective, it's bad for at least two reasons. One, if your boss is a conflict avoider, you're not going to get the kind of feedback you need in order to improve your work performance. (With an avoiding boss, you're in the same kind of feedback vacuum most bosses find themselves in because their employees won't be straight with them.) Two, you're going to be frustrated with your boss for not talking to some of the people you work with who need talking to. Over the years we've interviewed hundreds of employees whose respect for their bosses has dropped almost to zero. Why? Because their bosses simply will not confront employees who are slacking off and leaving their fellow employees with that much extra work and stress to deal with.

Overreacting

Some people have volatile temperaments. With very little provocation, their temper builds up like the pressure in a volcano until they blow their tops. These are the overreactors of the world. We'd estimate that about 15 to 20 percent of all bosses are overreactors. All of a sudden they're yelling and screaming their heads off about something and you don't exactly know why. All you know is that you've got this loose cannon rolling around your deck and you better watch out.

For some employees, overreacting bosses aren't that much of a problem. They just walk away until the raging storm dies down and come back when things are calmer. But some employees—most of them, in fact—find overreacting bosses very offensive. They get scared and intimidated and, sometimes, emotionally scarred. They're the adult version of kids who are psychologically battered by their parents.

Complaining

All of us complain about something from time to time. But some people are chronic complainers, especially about people they're not getting along with. Many bosses are chronic complainers when it comes to their employees. Here's what happens. The boss is dissatisfied with the performance of an employee but *won't* sit down and confront that employee. Rather, these bosses go to somebody *else*—a spouse, another boss, a sympathetic friend—and complain and complain and complain about the employee.

Oftentimes, employees don't know their bosses are complainers because the bosses are discreet enough to complain to somebody outside the office. But sometimes (more often than we'd like to believe), bosses will complain about one employee to a fellow employee. This is bad. First, it puts the employee who's being complained to in an awkward position. Second, when employees who're being complained about get wind of what the boss is doing, they get upset. Finally, it lowers the morale of other employees who know it's going on. Your boss, like quite a few bosses, may be guilty of it.

Lecturing

Lots of bosses lecture to their employees. What happens is that an employee does something that upsets the boss—like filling out a form incorrectly, keeping a messy office, or being rude to a customer. But rather than *tell* the employee he feels upset, the boss delivers a lecture: "Now, John, I want you to understand that that's not the way we do things around here. If you're going to advance in this company, you'll have to learn to . . .''

The lecturing that bosses do to employees sounds like the lecturing parents do to their kids. It's got a condescending, ''I-know-better-than-you'' tone to it. It's a real turn-off. Employees, like kids with their parents, want their bosses to talk to them on a person-to-person level, not on a superior-to-subordinate level.

Externalizing

Externalizing is the tendency we have when something goes wrong to put the blame and responsibility for what happened on the *other* person. It's the tendency for bosses to put the white hat on themselves and the black hat on their employees; in effect, to say, ''Hey, you're the problem here, not me!''

Bosses are as guilty of externalizing as anyone else. But some are superexternalizers. They blame everything that goes wrong on employees. They rarely, if ever, look at how they're contributing to the problems.

Employees resent bosses who externalize for two major reasons. First, as one employee once told us, ''It's bull!'' We agree. Most problems that occur at work are at least as much the boss's fault as the employee's. Second, bosses get paid to take responsiblity for mistakes. In our view, it's part of their job description.

Think for a moment how well each one of these ineffective tendencies fits your boss. Some won't apply at all. Some will fit like a glove. Set up your answers on a chart similar to this one below:

	Like a Glove	Pretty Often	Now and Then	Not Too often	Not at All
Avoiding					
Overreacting					

	Like a Glove	Pretty Often	Now and Then	Not Too often	Not at All
Complaining					
Lecturing					
Externalizing					

You might also want to spend a few moments thinking about which of these five ineffective tendencies is most (and least) characteristic of *you*. When some employees have done this, they've been surprised to find that they have more in common with their bosses than they had previously thought. For example, many employees have learned that both they and their bosses are avoiders. It's helped other employees figure out why their bosses "get" to them as much as they do: for example, the employee who is an avoider often has an overreacting boss. We think you'll find it an enlightening comparison.

A "CHEMISTRY" ANALYSIS

Every now and then we hear somebody talking about the good (or bad) "chemistry" that exists between two people. For a while now we've been intrigued by this concept. (We've even claimed that the chemistry between the two of us is good.) But, until recently, we hadn't thought a great deal about what chemistry between two people actually means.

Whenever we've asked people to offer their definitions of chemistry, they've had a tough time being precise:

- "It's a special quality that two people have when they really 'click' together."
- "It sort of means that two people are in 'synch' with each other—that they fit together like a hand and a glove."

• "I don't know, I think it's just something you have when you're good friends with somebody."
• "Good chemistry is two people who are on the same 'wave length'—two people who are really 'tuned in' to each other."

We've also had trouble defining chemistry precisely, but we think there are some common elements to the concept:

1. *Shared humor.* People who have good chemistry with each other usually have similar senses of humor. They laugh at the same kind of jokes and incidents, and can often get each other to "crack up" pretty easily. Their relationship is usually characterized by a lot of good-natured teasing and bantering. They just seem to have fun with each other a good bit of the time.
2. *Comfort.* People who share good chemistry feel comfortable and relaxed around each other. They rarely embarrass or upset each other, and, if they do, they're able to patch things up quickly. When around each other, they feel like they're wearing an old, comfortable slipper—not an ill-fitting new shoe.
3. *Mutual enjoyment.* Good chemistry between two people almost invariably means that they enjoy one another's company. They have fun together. Spending two hours in a car with some people would seem like an eternity. But two hours riding with someone with whom the chemistry is good seems like just a few minutes.
4. *Emotional trust.* We've already touched on trust when we discussed the "vital signs" of a relationship earlier. But one special kind of trust might be called "emotional trust"—that is, the willingness to share intimate thoughts and feelings with another person. People who have good chemistry open up to each other in ways that they never would do to other people.
5. *Good teamwork.* Another characteristic of two people who have good chemistry is their ability to work smoothly and efficiently together. People who have poor chemistry often

just get in each other's way, but folks with good chemistry seem to almost sail through a job. Not only do they turn out quality work fairly rapidly, but they also have a good time doing it.

6. Similar thought patterns. It's a little uncanny, but people who have good chemistry almost seem to be able to read each other's minds. At any rate, their thoughts, ideas, and reactions often run along similar lines. You can frequently hear them say things like, "Yeah, I was just thinking the exact same thing." People with good chemistry really *are* on the same wave length.

Now we'd like you to do a quick assessment of the chemistry you have with your boss. To help you, we've listed the six elements of chemistry below. For each one we'd like you to rate, on a scale from zero to ten, how good you think the chemistry is between you and your boss. After you finish all six, add up your ratings to get an overall rating.

Element	*Rating*
Shared humor	
Comfort	
Mutual enjoyment	
Emotional trust	
Good teamwork	
Similar thought patterns	
Total rating	_____

It's a good idea not to attach too much significance to any of the numbers you put down on this form. Just let the entire exercise *stimulate your thinking* about the chemistry between you and your boss. Here are some guidelines to help you interpret the overall rating you came up with:

Overall Rating	What It Probably Means
6–14	Lousy chemistry
15–23	Pretty bad chemistry
24–41	So-so chemistry
42–50	Pretty good chemistry
51–60	Unusually good chemistry

When we began this chapter we said that our purpose was to help you get a clearer perspective on your boss. This is a good point to decide how much we've been able to help you achieve that goal.

We'd like you to sit back now and think over what you've learned about your relationship with your boss. As you ponder the questions we'll be asking, you may want to jot down your ideas, discuss them with a friend, or just mull them over on your own. It doesn't matter what method you use. What's important is your thinking:

- What have you learned about your boss that you weren't so aware of before reading this chapter?
- How has your view of your boss changed, if at all?
- Having thought about all this, do you feel more optimistic or more pessimistic about your relationship with your boss?
- You've spent a lot of time thinking about areas where you'd like to see your boss change. How confident are you that your boss would be willing or even able to make these kinds of changes?
- Even though the focus of this chapter has been mostly on your boss, what have you learned about yourself here?

In the next chapter, we'll give you an opportunity to think about and answer this last question in more depth.

4

···············

TAKING A LOOK
AT YOURSELF

I n the last chapter you took a look at your boss. In this chapter we'll help you take a good, hard look at what's on the other side of the boss-employee coin: you. We'll help you think, for instance, about who you are as a person, how you look from your boss's point of view, and how you might be contributing to problems with your boss. But before talking about *how* to do this kind of candid self-assessment, let's talk briefly about *why* it's a good thing to do.

WHY IT'S IMPORTANT TO TAKE
A LOOK AT YOURSELF

When employees struggle with their bosses, they generally focus most of their attention on their bosses. They spend a lot of time and energy thinking about what their bosses do and why they behave the way they do. However, we think it's a good idea for employees to occasionally turn the spotlight away from their bosses and put it on themselves. This makes sense for several reasons.

It Takes Two to Tango

Whenever two people struggle with each other, both are likely to blame the other for the problem. This is the tendency to externalize that we mentioned in the last chapter. We're as guilty of this tendency as most people and often find ourselves doing it with each other when we run into problems. Being completely honest with yourself, you may conclude that you're doing something like this with your boss.

The problem with externalizing is that it is rarely accurate. That is, in most problem relationships, there's rarely a completely "good" or "bad" guy. Usually, both people are contributing to the problem in the same way, even if one person is contributing more than the other.

How does this apply to you? Let's say that we were to come into your organization and talk to you about how things are going. If you're like most people, very soon you'd start talking about your boss. You'd probably describe some things your boss does that drive you up the wall. Given your pain and frustration, there'd be an understandable tendency for you to portray your boss as *the* problem. But what would happen if we were to leave the meeting with you and sit down to interview your boss? Would your boss agree with your assessment and say, "Yes, it's true, I am a problem boss." We doubt it. More likely, your boss would tell us *you're* the problem!

From our point of view as outsiders, we see the true picture in between these opposing views. Of course, sometimes the "truth" lies a whole lot closer to one person's view than to the other's. But even if you think your contribution is minor compared to your boss's, it'd still be good for you to know how you're contributing to the problem.

It's Hard to See Ourselves as Others Do

If you're like most employees, you've gotten to know your bosses *very* well. You've spent mega-hours with them, under all kinds of conditions, and in all kinds of circumstances. You've seen the good-looking side and you've also seen the warts and pimples. A person we interviewed once said, "Having a boss is a lot like having a spouse; you have to take the bad with the good. With my boss, I've seen it all!" That's why we often say that employees are "experts" on their bosses.

We could even make a case that employees know their bosses better than their bosses know themselves. As you'll recall from the chapter on "Why Are Bosses Such a Problem?" many bosses have an inflated and distorted view of their effectiveness. Over the years we've heard many bosses pompously describe themselves as highly competent managers. Then a few minutes later we'll hear *employees* of these bosses describe them as extremely difficult people. If bosses could only see themselves as clearly and accurately as their employees see them, they'd be a lot more humble.

Well, if you're an expert on your boss, your boss can also be seen as an expert on you. As bitter a pill as this is for employees to swallow, bosses often know as much about their employees as vice versa. And, in addition to your boss, your co-workers get to know you well also. If you could see yourself as clearly and accurately as these people do, you'd probably be a whole lot more self-aware.

If Your Boss Can Be in the Wrong Job, So Can You

As we mentioned in chapter 2, many people with poor "bossing" skills become managers and supervisors. Not well-suited for their jobs, they become problem bosses to the people who report to them. But employees can be in the wrong job, too. For example, we routinely see shy, introverted, or socially clumsy people in jobs demanding good interpersonal skills. We see creative, high-energy, ''hyper'' people in boring, repetitive, mundane jobs. We find careless, easily distracted, or even sloppy people in jobs that call for precision and attention to detail.

Both of us have worked in jobs we weren't particularly well-suited for, and it was no fun. Dissatisfied with our jobs, we easily became dissatisfied with our bosses. Not surprisingly, our bosses also became dissatisfied with us. It's a common phenomenon; much of the dissatisfaction employees feel for their bosses (and vice versa) comes from the fact that employees are simply working in jobs they're not well-suited for. If this is true for you, just realizing it will be helpful.

HOW TO LOOK AT YOURSELF

There are several techniques we've found helpful in getting employees to do a thoughtful self-analysis. They are:

1. doing an employee history
2. walking in your boss's shoes
3. interviewing an ''expert'' on you and your boss

   Let's take a look at each one.

An Employee History

In the last chapter we asked you to do a boss history. We asked you to think of all the bosses you could remember and answer some thought-provoking questions about each one. Here we'd like you to do something similar. We'd like you to think about all the jobs you've had and answer questions that will shed light on what kind of employee you've been over the years.

When we asked Lisa Carpenter, a thirty-three-year-old executive secretary for the executive vice-president of an electronics firm, to do her "employee history," here's how she listed her jobs since graduating from high school in 1970:

1981–1985:	Executive Secretary, Alpha Electronics, Inc.
1978–1981:	Secretary, Harrisonville Automotive (car dealership)
1975–1978:	Switchboard/Receptionist, Hearndon Medical Clinic
1972–1975:	Clerk-Typist, Elite Typing Service
1970–1972:	Secretary/"Go-Fer," Carpenter Machining (family business)
1966–1970:	During high school I worked at a number of part-time jobs, including cashier work and waitressing at a couple of restaurants, general office work in my family's business, and I typed term papers for students at a local college.

We'd like you to do the same. List all the jobs you can remember, starting with your current one and working backwards. Go ahead and do that now.

After you finish your jobs, we'd like you to think about what your job history says about you. Here are a few questions to help stimulate your thinking:

1. All in all, what kind of employee have you been over the years? Have you generally been a hard worker or a goof-off? Have you been easygoing or somewhat difficult to get along with? Conscientious or uncaring? Even though you've had different jobs and different bosses, what's your common style or pattern as an employee?
2. In what jobs have you been most satisfied and most dissatisfied? Most and least effective? Most challenged and most bored? What does all this say about your characteristics as an employee?

3. How have you changed over the years—especially in terms of what you like or need from a boss, what you don't like but are willing to put up with, and what you definitely cannot live with in a boss?

4. What do you need in a job to make you feel happy and satisfied? In what kind of work environment do you function best and worst? Have different kinds of jobs or bosses brought out different kinds of things from you? What does all of this say about the kind of person you are?

5. What does your job history say about how you generally respond to people in positions of power? Do you tend to kowtow to authority figures, try to get around them, or fight them? Do you tend to be obsequious, manipulative, or rebellious?

Here are some samples from Lisa Carpenter's employee history. The samples were taken pretty much verbatim from a tape recording she made for us while she was doing it:

I've always been a hardworking person. I think I got that from my mom and dad, who started me working in the family business when I was in junior high school. I'm also a very organized person. Some people would call me compulsive, but I don't think I'm *that* fussy. I just like to have things neat and clean and organized at work and at home. I hate clutter and disorganization. That's a pet peeve of mine.

I like to work hard, but I like to play hard, too. One thing I like most about my job now is that the company sponsors a lot of "extracurricular" activities, like soft ball in the summer and volleyball in the winter. I'm definitely a social person, maybe even too social sometimes. I think Herb, my boss, might say that I spend too much of my work time thinking about what I'm going to do during my playtime.

I've been happiest with my last two jobs, but I'm still not completely satisfied yet. I hope that doesn't make me sound too fussy! Anyway, when I worked at

the switchboard and at the typing service, I was almost —
chained to my desk. If that wasn't bad enough, I didn't
have any co-workers around to talk to or socialize with.
I was just starting out then and, to be honest, I was
pretty miserable. When I started working at the car
dealership, it seemed like a dream come true. It was a
freewheeling kind of work environment, and I enjoyed
the banter and camaraderie with all the salespeople.
Well, not *all* of them, but most of them. But that place
had problems, too. It was one of the most disorganized
places I've ever worked in. There was clutter all over
the place. I don't know how they were as successful
as they were. We used to call my boss's office, "the
compost heap." I mean, he was a nice person and all
that, but what a slob! I eventually left because I couldn't
stand the mess, even though I liked what I was doing
and I really got along well with the people I was working with.

Even though I like to work hard, I *do* need my playtime! I get four weeks vacation in this job, which is
twice as much as any of my previous jobs. I like that.
If I don't get to a warm, sunny beach for at least a
week every winter, I'm miserable all year long! If you
haven't guessed it already, I also need a clean, organized work environment, which I definitely have in this
job. I guess I'd also say that I have a lot of social needs
that must be met at work. My boss, Herb Reed, is a
nice person, but he's a bit shy. He's also very analytical and intellectual, and sort of on the emotionally
cold side. I guess you could say he's a typical high
tech engineer turned manager. Anyway, there are two
things about him that bug me. One is that he thinks I
spend too much time socializing. Maybe I do, but I
think I do a lot of good public relations for him. And
let me tell you, he needs it! Not because he's a bad
guy, mind you. He's just somewhat of a nerd when it
comes to dealing with people. So I feel like I have to
do a lot of explaining about Herb to other people in the
firm. Second, even though it's not essential, I like to

have a boss I can clown around with. And Herb is not exactly what you'd call the get-down-and-get-funky type. He's a classic "stiff" and I feel sort of uncomfortable around him. He tells me I should act "more professional." But I feel like telling him he should "loosen up." I'd like a boss who was warmer and more of a social person. I guess I'd say Herb was a problem boss in some ways; but he's a wonderful boss in other ways.

I need to feel like I'm growing and developing in a job. When I worked at the typing service, I was a production typist. Type! Type! Type! All day long! Then I vegetated for a few years at the clinic, pretty much chained to that damned switchboard! The car dealership job was a welcome relief in many ways, but I wasn't learning anything new there. This is the first job I've had where I feel like I'm learning new skills and developing myself as a person. Despite my complaints about Herb, he's primarily responsible for my growth. For example, he's getting me involved in some of the marketing presentations and he's made me completely responsible for the logistics of the long-range planning session we'll be having this winter in Florida. I may even get to attend the session!

I guess I'm a bit of a coward when it comes to people in positions of power. My father wore the pants in our family and I learned pretty early not to challenge the guy in charge. I don't think I've ever stood up to my bosses, even when I thought they were making mistakes. I know I should, but I haven't. I *could* give Herb valuable feedback on how people in the firm see him, if only I had a little more courage. Even though I seem like a very self-assured person, I don't think I've ever spoken frankly to a boss.

Go ahead now and do your own employee history. Since it'll take some time and energy on your part, you may be thinking, "Maybe I'll just bag this and keep on reading." It's an understandable reaction, but we'd strongly recommend you give it a try anyway. At the very least, sit down and think about the questions we posed earlier. We think you'll discover that it's helpful. Whatever you do, though, don't make it a cumbersome, unpleasant exercise. It'll be a lot more fun and profitable if you do it with someone you like and feel comfortable with. If you do do it with someone else, list the jobs you've both had and ask each other the questions.

As with the boss history, you may want to put your employee history aside for a day or so. This incubation period may lead you to new insights or a fresh perspective.

Walking in Your Boss's Shoes

There's an old Indian saying that goes something like, "You can't fully understand another man until you've walked a mile in his moccasins." What this means, of course, is that it's important to try to see things from another person's perspective. That's our purpose here—to get you to try to see how you look from your boss's point of view.

TRAC IN REVERSE

In the last chapter we introduced you to the concept of TRAC, which we called the vital signs of a relationship. To refresh your memory, the four vital signs are *trust, respect, affection,* and *confidence.* In our view, how people rate each other on TRAC is a good shorthand way to assess the quality of their relationship.

In the last chapter you rated your boss on TRAC, as did Lisa Carpenter, the person we introduced earlier in this chapter. When Lisa rated her boss, Herb Reed, she gave him the following ratings:

- trust   = 8
- respect   = 7
- affection   = 5
- confidence   = 9

After explaining her ratings to us (a task which took her nearly an hour and a half to do), we said to Lisa, "That was a reasonably complete analysis of how you feel about Herb. Now how about turning the coin over and thinking about the other side. What kind of ratings do you think Herb would give you on TRAC?" Lisa's reaction was interesting and fairly typical of people we've asked to do TRAC in reverse. She said:

> Whoaaa! That's a *good* question! I was so focused on how I'd rate Herb that I never thought for a second he'd also be rating me. But, now that I think about it, it makes sense that he would. Let me see . . .

Like a lot of people, Lisa had a hard time estimating how her boss would rate her. But even though it was difficult, she found the experience stimulating and helpful. Here's how she thought Herb would rate her (unfortunately we never met Herb and don't know if her figures are an accurate reflection of his views or not. However, when people do TRAC in reverse, they generally overestimate how other people rate them by at least a point or two on each dimension.):

- trust   = 6
- respect   = 7
- affection   = 8
- confidence   = 5

Here's how Lisa explained her thinking on two of the vital signs, *trust* and *confidence*:

> In some way he *Trusts* me a lot and in other ways he doesn't seem to trust me at all. For example, sometimes he tells me the most sensitive and confidential things. You know, like stuff about the financial condition of the company or sleazy stuff about some of the other executives. When he does, I say to myself, "He

must trust me a lot to be telling me all of this.'' And, believe me, Herb's not exactly the type who goes around blabbing things to people either. In some other ways, though, I'm not sure he trusts me all that much. For example, sometimes when I go into his office he'll quickly close the folder he's looking into and put it into his desk drawer. For a moment he'll seem a little startled or distracted. Obviously, he's working on something he doesn't trust me enough to tell me about. Here's another example. He has a tendency to interrogate me about some things. I remember coming back from a company trip about a year ago and he "grilled" me about my travel expense voucher. It almost seemed like he thought I was trying to cheat the company or something. I mean, I'd never falsify *anything*! But I can remember thinking two things to myself at the time. One was that he doesn't know me very well. And the other was that he must not trust me that much.

In terms of his *Confidence* in me, I'd say that in some things he'd give me high ratings and in others low ratings. So I'll compromise on a rating of "5." Professionally, he seems to have a lot of confidence in my abilities. He delegates a lot of important things to me—like the logistical arrangements for the long-range planning conference—and doesn't keep checking up on me. I think he feels like he can depend on me most of the time. But not all of the time. I've had a few problems in my personal life the past few years and to be honest, it's spilled over into my professional life. I don't think Herb has a lot of confidence in my judgment when it comes to men. I've also noticed that when I'm going through a tough period, Herb doesn't delegate as much important stuff to me. It's almost like during the hard times he doesn't have as much confidence in me to handle things as he does when things are going well. I think his confidence ratings of me fluctuate a lot. He's never said anything like that directly to me, but I'm sure it's true.

Now that you've seen how Lisa did TRAC in reverse with her boss, we'd like you to try it out with your boss. Simply ask yourself the question: On a scale from zero to ten, how much *trust, respect, affection,* and *confidence* do you think your boss has in you? Think about it for a moment (don't take too long, though) and record your estimates below:

- trust   = ____
- respect   = ____
- affection   = ____
- confidence   = ____

When you finish recording your estimates, take some time to think about the question, Why? That is, why do you think your boss would give you these ratings? What is it that you do (or don't do) that would lead your boss to give you ratings like these? To come up with a thoughtful answer, you'll have to "walk in your boss's shoes" for a while. Put your view of yourself on hold. Try to see how you look from your boss's perspective. This is an easy thing to talk about, but it's hard to do. Just try it and see.

After speculating on why your boss would give you these ratings, it might be useful to try to answer one more question: What do you think you'd have to do for your boss to give you higher ratings on each of the four dimensions of TRAC? This will give you some additional practice in trying to see things from your boss's point of view.

Ideal Employee Analysis

In the last chapter we invited you to do an ideal boss analysis. As you recall, that was designed to help you think more clearly about what you really want in a boss. Here we'd like you to imagine that your boss has done an ideal employee analysis. That is, we'll ask you to write down the traits you think your boss would list for an ideal employee. Then we'll ask you to estimate how your boss would rate you on each of these traits.

As an example, we've chosen Clyde Jameson, the young physician who did an ideal boss analysis on his boss, Bill Gruskins, in the last chapter (pp. 54–56). We asked Clyde to list what he thought were Bill's top ten traits in an ideal employee. We then asked Clyde to estimate how Bill would rate him on each of the ten traits. Here's what Clyde came up with:

Trait	Rating
Dependability	7
Hardworking	6
Conscientious	7
Loyalty	4
Honesty	9
Creative	7
Organized	7
Ambitious	7
Cooperative	5
Ability to get along with others	6

After he finished his estimates, we asked Clyde why he thought Bill would rate him this way on each trait. Here's what Clyde told us about two of the traits, *hardworking* and *loyalty*:

Hardworking

I think Bill would give me a "6" on *hardworking*. Why? Well, Bill's what you'd call a "workaholic" physician. He puts in more hours than anyone I know, and he expects the people who work for him to follow suit. In my view, Bill's also a one-dimensional person.

He doesn't have much of a family life and he doesn't seem to have any interests outside of work. On the other hand, I have a lot of outside-of-work interests: bicycling, wind surfing, rock climbing, that sort of thing. I see these as part of a balanced life. But I think Bill sees them as distractions that take my mind off what I'm supposed to be doing, which is work, work, work. Given where he's coming from, I don't think a rating of "6" or so is out of line. There's no question that, because I don't put in the hours he does, I don't stay as up-to-date on current research and new developments as he does. I think this bugs him.

Loyalty

I think Bill would give me lower ratings on *loyalty* than most of the other traits. He's kind of an old-school boss. You know, more like a military officer than a manager. Come to think of it, he was an army medical officer and still is a big muckety-muck in the reserves. Anyway, I think there are a bunch of things about me that bug him. First, he's a "by-the-books" kind of guy. He's always referring to the policy manual like it was the Bible or something. Hell, I've been trying to get around rules since I was a kid, and he knows I think the policy manual is a big joke. Second, when he wants something done, he wants it done *right now*, preferably without a lot of questions. But I tend to be a questioning person, maybe even to the point of being difficult at times. I've even been called "contrary" by some of my close friends. Third, Bill's kind of an "organization man" type. He's been working here since he got out of medical school and has a lot of loyalty to the organization. However, I feel my loyalty is to my profession, not to the place where I work. It's not that I don't do a good job for them. After all, they're paying my salary. But I know this is just another area where Bill wouldn't see me as an ideal-type employee.

Clyde told us that the ideal employee analysis helped him to see things from Bill's perspective and crystallized some of the key differences between them. His analysis also helped point the way towards ways of dealing with Bill that Clyde hadn't thought of before. But that's getting ahead of ourselves. For now, we'd like you to think about your boss's ideal employee. In the space below, write down what you think your boss would say are the ten traits of an ideal employee. After you've listed them, estimate how you think your boss would rate you (on a scale from zero to ten) on each of them.

	Ideal Employee Traits	*Your Rating*
1.		
2.		
3.		
4.		
5.		
6.		
7.		
8.		
9.		
10.		

When you finish your estimates, take some time to think about why your boss would give you these ratings. Once again, try to see things from your boss's perspective. Put *your* perspective on the shelf, if you can. Try to see yourself as your boss sees you.

INTERVIEWING AN "EXPERT" ON YOU AND YOUR BOSS

From time to time we've mentioned that it might be helpful if you completed the exercises with the help of another person. With the exercise we're about to describe, you'll need a friend or co-worker to do it with (preferably, someone who knows you and your boss well).

As we said earlier, it's just plain hard to see ourselves objectively and clearly. We usually tend to see ourselves more positively than we actually appear to other people. However, if our goal is to learn what's really going on in our relationships with others, we need to do something to counteract this tendency. One good way is to go to somebody who knows the situation fairly well, but who's not involved in it; someone who has a more objective perspective than those caught up in the struggle.

Think about someone who knows you, your boss, and your job situation reasonably well. If your could get this person to talk to you openly and candidly about how *you're* contributing to some of the problems with your boss, it could be extremely helpful. But this happens rarely. Usually, either because people are afraid to hurt your feelings, or because we're not very good listeners, we get cheated out of their valuable perspective.

When we asked Clyde Jameson, the physician we talked about earlier, to think of somebody he might interview, he had no difficulty coming up with several names. He thought first of Laura Jacobson, the chief medical technologist, a person who knew both Clyde and Bill well. He also thought of Charlene Masters, the executive secretary to the company's C.E.O. and the one person in the firm who knew *everything* that went one. He selected Charlene because he trusted her judgment and discretion.

These are the instructions we gave Clyde:

1. When you invite Charlene to talk with you, begin by telling her the purpose of the meeting, that is, why you want to talk with her. For example, you might say:

    Charlene, I'm not 100 percent pleased with how Bill and I are working together and I want to do something about it. I've been doing quite a bit of thinking about it, but I'm afraid I'm too close to the situation to see it as objectively as I can. I also think I might be ignoring how I'm contributing to some of the problems we're having. I'm hoping that talking to you might help me see things more clearly. So what I'd like to do is ask you to talk about your view of our relationship, what you see as some of the major problem areas, how both of us—especially me—are contributing to the problems, and what I could do to resolve some of the problems and maybe improve the way we're working with each other.

2. When you do sit down and talk with Charlene (preferably in a private, quiet place) here are a number of questions it would be helpful to get her thinking on:

- "You know Bill and me pretty well, Charlene. What's your view of our personal and professional relationship? In what ways do you see us working well together and in what ways do we seem to struggle with each other?"
- "What are some of Bill's characteristics as a boss that make him good to work for? Bad to work for?"
- "How about me? How do you see me contributing to the problems we're having? What am I doing to make things worse rather than better? What am I doing in particular that maybe rubs Bill the wrong way?"
- "What suggestions do you have about what I could do to improve the quality of my personal and professional relationship with Bill?"

3. When Charlene starts to talk, give her the floor completely and give her your undivided attention. Look her straight in the eye and listen to what she has to say. Don't interrupt to straighten her out when she seems off base. Don't shake your head or roll your eyes to the ceiling when she says something you disagree with. Don't counter or become defensive when she says something

critical of you. Just *listen*. After she talks for awhile she'll begin to wind down. When she stops, don't start talking. Encourage her to talk more. Look her squarely in the eye and say, "Charlene, this is good stuff! What would you add?" She'll add more, which is what you want; but she'll eventually stop, saying something like, "Well, that's about it." When she does, think to yourself, "That's not the half of it; she's just talked about the tip of the iceberg. There's a lot more good stuff if only I can get her to talk about it." The best way to get her into the really good stuff is to do something we call "reading back." So when she stops talking, instead of offering your view or asking her more questions, simply try to summarize the essence of what you've heard her say. Begin your "read back" like this: "Well, Charlene, I heard you say a lot of things. First, you said . . ." Then try to capture what she said in your own words. As you're reading her back, she'll probably interrupt you to build upon what she said earlier. That's great! Hearing you read her back is proof positive to her that you were listening and will almost invariably get her to talk more. Keep reading her back until you've exhausted her thinking. During the meeting Charlene should talk about 90 percent of the time and you 10 percent of the time. If you're talking more than this, you're talking too much!

We met with Clyde the day after he met with Charlene. The meeting had obviously affected him:

You know, I always felt like I was a perceptive person who was really on top of things. But meeting with Charlene has opened my eyes to some things I've never seen clearly before.

A couple of times I felt an overwhelming need to talk. But I remembered what you guys said and bit my tongue. I put my thoughts and reactions on hold and tried to read her back as best as I could.

I thought that reading her back was going to seem

artificial and contrived, but she didn't even notice what I was doing. She just kept talking. She started off pretty tentatively, not saying a whole lot. But after I read her back a few times she got pretty wound up. She ended up telling me things I never would've heard—things I never even would've thought of—if I hadn't been a good listener. This was one of those eye-opening experiences you hear people talk about but think will never happen to you.

We won't go in to all the details, but here's a sample of what Clyde learned:

• Charlene told Clyde that most people get along very well with Bill, but some people have trouble working for him. Those who do get along with him are willing to let Bill "be the boss" and those who don't are people who "buck his authority." She talked some about Bill's unhappy (she called it "tragic") home life—a wife who's been an active alcoholic for decades, and a teen-age daughter who ran away from home several years ago. She said she understood why he's escaped into his work. She also suggested that some of his negativism toward employees was simply an expression of his general life unhappiness. She painted a picture of Bill as a good, but somewhat pathetic, man.

• Charlene told Clyde that he had a reputation in the lab as being highly talented, but arrogant. She suspected that his manner had turned off quite a few people, and possibly had alienated Bill. She said that a number of people had referred to Clyde as a "know-it-all" who felt nobody could teach him anything. She speculated that his arrogant manner was a bit of a defense, possibly masking some insecurities he had about how bright or competent he really was. Charlene said that Bill had always seen himself as an intellectual mentor for younger physicians, but that Clyde had never allowed Bill to assume that role with him. She also told Clyde that she saw him as the kind of person who didn't take feedback and criticism well. She offered a couple of examples where Clyde had either explained away a mistake or blamed it on others. She suspected that Bill, because he valued honesty so much, was bothered by Clyde's tendency to become defensive and avoid responsibility.

• Charlene told Clyde that she had never heard him say anything really nice about Bill to others or to Bill directly, even though she knew that Clyde did have a great deal of professional respect for him. She told Clyde that "the first step" in warming things up with Bill was for Clyde to approach him and ask his opinion about some medical questions or laboratory procedures. She predicted that if he was willing to let Bill be more of a mentor and a teacher, there would be a dramatic improvement in the relationship. However, she also said she didn't hold out a lot of hope that Clyde would do this because, in her view, he wasn't personally secure enough to go to anybody to ask for help or guidance. However, she said that Clyde's coming to her to ask her opinion (and the fact that he didn't "get offensive even once") was a very good sign that maybe something positive would happen.

Go ahead and find an "expert" you can interview. Follow the same instructions we gave to Clyde earlier. You may or may not have the eye-opening experience he did. It'll depend on the person you select. But it'll mainly depend on whether or not you can be the kind of listener who can get someone else to tell you the stuff you really need to hear. Good luck!

ON TO THE REST OF THE BOOK

You've now finished the first part of the book, but before moving on, it'll be helpful to review briefly what we've covered so far.

First, we introduced you to the concept of problem bosses and tried to make a case that all bosses are problem bosses *in some way* and *to some degree*. Then we offered reasons why the problem of problem bosses isn't more widely recognized. From there we talked about a slew of reasons why bosses are such problems to their employees. In the previous chapter we shifted gears and got you to do some in-depth thinking about your current boss as well as some past ones. And in this chapter we suggested ways to take a close look at yourself.

Now it's on to finding some solutions to the problems you're having with your boss. Some of the strategies may not seem terribly appealing or appropriate to your situation, but we hope they'll all be interesting and enjoyable to read about.

5

....

GATEWAY TO THE STRATEGIES

I n chapters one through four, you've done a lot of "background" thinking. Now you're probably eager to get to the strategies. You're probably thinking: "Okay, I've got a problem boss. I know that. My concern is what to *do* about my boss."

In the upcoming chapters, we'll be laying out a dozen different strategies for dealing with problem bosses. Some of them you'll love. Some of them you'll be lukewarm about. And to some you'll say, "There ain't no way I'd even consider doing something like that." That's fine. Our purpose here is to *stimulate your thinking* about the many *alternatives* you have.

In a moment we'll preview each strategy so you'll have a better idea about what's coming your way. Before we do that, though, we'd like to offer a few thoughts about the choices employees have when it comes to dealing with problem bosses.

WHAT ARE YOUR OPTIONS?

Over the years we've talked in-depth to hundreds and hundreds of unhappy and disgruntled employees. Most of them felt as if they had very few choices when it came to dealing with their problem bosses. These folks were so caught up in their situations that they weren't thinking creatively or resourcefully about what they *could* do about them. Most thought they had one or two choices at best. They tended to engage in black-and-white, either-or thinking: "Either I stay here and suffer or I quit and find another job." What they didn't see was the huge gray area between these extremes. It's that area we'll be exploring in the remainder of this book.

When we'd talk with these people, we'd usually hear them out for a while and then, respectfully, say something like: "We disagree." We'd go on to say:

> You have many more options than you think. Just stand back from your situation and think creatively and resourcefully. You've got a lot more power and choices than you think you do. Your alternatives are limited only by yourself and your imagination.

Unfortunately, simply exhorting people to be creative and resourceful didn't always work very well. Like a water pump that needs priming before it flows, these people needed their thinking stimulated before they could get their intellectual motors off and running by themselves.

That's what we'll be doing when we present our strategies—trying to stimulate your thinking. After you finish reading them, we don't think you'll ever see your boss or your work situation the same way again. Some of the seeds we'll be planting may take root immediately. Some may take weeks (even months) to germinate. But we're sure that reading the strategies will open up your thinking. It'll help you to take off your blinders and see some alternatives you wouldn't have considered on your own.

So, do you have options? Absolutely! You've got more options than you think. Some you may feel are right on the money. Some may seem pretty farfetched. Some may make you feel uncomfortable or nervous. But you *do* have options. That's why we call this chapter a "gateway" to the strategies. We see you about to embark on an adventure of sorts, a thought-provoking, vista-opening, personally rewarding adventure that will help you achieve a goal we think all employees want: To be able to deal more effectively with a problem boss.

A PREVIEW OF THE STRATEGIES

At this point you might be thinking, "You've been talking a lot about alternatives. What *are* all these options that are available to me?" Here's a brief summary of the strategies we'll be presenting in detail in the remainder of the book.

Doing Nothing

Most employees with a problem boss do nothing, primarily because the thought of *doing something* makes them feel nervous. It's usually not a very good strategy, but we'll talk about a couple of situations where it makes good sense. We'll also talk about what employees *do* when they do nothing—things like complaining, commiserating, internalizing, and slacking off—and get you to identify how *you've* been "doing nothing."

Accepting Your Boss

Some employees think they have a problem boss when all they have is a boss with a personality or operating style that's different from their own. We'll examine the problem of employee intolerance in this chapter, get you thinking about some of the "good" and "bad" differences between you and your boss, and talk about when to be more accepting of bosses who aren't really problem bosses.

Changing Yourself

Sometimes the best way to deal with problem bosses is not to expect them to change, but to change yourself. We'll talk about why this can be an excellent approach and lay out a four-step strategy:

1. thinking about how you might change
2. deciding whether or not to change
3. changing
4. looking at the results of change

Changing Your Thoughts and Feeling

While some employees are almost oblivious to their problem bosses, others get upset, frustrated, unsettled, and driven crazy by them. This chapter will be especially helpful to those of you who don't want to be so bothered by your bosses. We'll introduce you to a number of tried-and-true psychological methods for changing your thoughts and feelings and we hope, for helping you to get a new perspective on you, your boss, and the relationship between the two of you.

"Managing" Your Boss

Most people think "managing" is something bosses do to employees, not vice versa. But over the years we've run into lots of employees who "managed" difficult bosses very effectively. We'll share some of their secrets of boss management with you and teach you a two-step strategy that can dramatically improve the way you're "managing" your boss.

Talking To Your Boss One-On-One

We frequently advise people who are struggling with each other to sit down face-to-face and talk things out. It's not always a good idea, however, especially with bosses. We'll begin by helping you determine how good a candidate your boss is for this approach. Our main goal in this chapter is to show you how to conduct a problem-solving, relationship-building meeting with your boss. In the process, we'll also give you a short course in how to be a better listener, since that's probably an area where you (like most people) could use some help. We'll walk you though a detailed example of an employee conducting a face-to-face meeting like this with his boss. Because it's such an important strategy, we'll devote many more pages to this strategy than any of the others. In fact, this lengthy chapter is almost a "minibook" about how to sit down with another person and talk problems out. (What we have to say in this chapter should also help you with other people you might be struggling with, like spouses, children, lovers, and, since you also may be a boss, employees.)

Talking To Your Boss as a Group

Talking to your boss as a group (as opposed to the individual approach mentioned above) is another direct strategy for sitting down with problem bosses, giving them feedback, and trying to get them to change. Many employees prefer the group approach because it's less risky than the one on one strategy and it's based on the "strength-in-numbers" principle. Many of the one-on-one techniques apply, but there are a number of differences we'll talk about in this chapter.

Talking To Your Boss Indirectly

Employees would like to give their bosses *direct* feedback (either one-on-one or as a group), but most don't. Many are afraid of the consequences (whether real or imagined) if they told their bosses what they *really* thought. Sometimes an indirect approach is more appropriate. In this chapter we'll talk about how to confront your boss indirectly—and anonymously. We'll talk about a wide variety of techniques for giving indirect feedback, and how to do this so your boss won't be able to identify and get back at you. It's an often controversial, sometimes humorous, and usually low-risk way of sending a message to bosses *and* getting their attention.

Going Around Your Boss: Getting a Transfer to a New Boss

Many employees work for organizations they like but bosses they dislike. They've put ten, twenty, or more years into a company that has treated them well, and they don't want to leave. But they're working for a boss who's become so much of a problem that they're seriously considering quitting just to get away from the boss. This chapter will describe a strategy—getting a transfer—that allows employees to stay with the organization but get out from under their problem bosses. We'll talk in detail about what you need to do to stay in the organization and get a new and, we hope, better boss. (We think of a transfer as something like trading in your old heap for a new car, or at least a better one. But if you're not careful, your new one can be a lot worse than the one you traded in.)

Going Over Your Boss's Head

In this chapter, we'll talk about going to your boss's boss (or some other powerful boss in the organization) to express your dissatisfaction with your boss and ask for help in resolving your situation. It's a high-risk strategy, but sometimes the risk pays off and the matter is handled in a way that's satisfactory to the employee. But often the boss's boss will either ignore the complaint or side with the problem boss *against* the complaining employee. It's not fair, but using this strategy often makes things worse, not better, for the employee who tries it. In spite of its low probability of success, we'd like to offer it because it *can* work if it's done skillfully and under the right circumstances.

Taking a Stand Against Your Boss

Like it or not, far too many bosses wantonly abuse their power and authority, either through some illegal activity or arrant mistreatment of employees. What's worse, though, is that most of these bosses *get away* with their transgressions— nobody, including their bosses and employees, holds them accountable. But, while there's some risk, employees *can* (and sometimes should) take these kinds of bosses to task. In this chapter we'll talk about why it's so important to hold these bosses accountable as well as the types of bosses who should be held accountable. Most important, though, we'll talk about the wide variety of methods (e.g., grievances, formal complaints to government agencies or ethics committees, whistle blowing to the press or law enforcement agencies, and even lawsuits) that are available to you if you want to take effective action against a bad boss.

"Firing" Your Boss

Millions of employees work for bosses they detest, but they continue working for these bosses in spite of their unhappiness. Very often, these same employees have highly marketable skills and experience. Without a great deal of effort they could find new jobs with better bosses, better pay, and better working conditions. We could have called this final strategy "quitting" or "resigning," but we don't like the negative connotation of these words. Then we thought, if bosses can fire employees, why can't employees fire bosses? In this chapter, we'll explain why we think "firing" a boss can be an excellent strategy, talk about why people who *should* use this strategy don't, and tell you how to "can" a problem boss.

THE STRATEGIES AND HOW TO APPROACH THEM

Before you dig into these strategies in detail, we'd like to share a few thoughts on how to get the most out of them.

There's Nothing Sacrosanct or Exhaustive about the Strategies

Nothing we'll be saying is carved in stone. It's just the thinking of two guys who've tried to come up with a bunch of ideas for helping employees deal with their problem bosses. Other people might have emphasized different things, or even offered very different advice. You may find we've completely overlooked something that seems important for you, or you may creatively combine elements of several different strategies into something new that works for you.

Each Strategy Is an Entity unto Itself

Even though there's some overlap among the strategies, each one is largely independent of the others. So you don't have to read them in order. If you want to immediately go to one that captures your interest, fine. However, there is a rough "order" to them: We start off with ones that are less risky and require less commitment. But even that's not a hard-and-fast rule.

Read the Strategies with an Open Mind and a Creative Eye

Even though a particular strategy might not appeal to you at first, try it on for size and see how it feels. If it doesn't feel comfortable, don't reject it out of hand. After reading each strategy, you might ask yourself, ''What are my attractions and reservations to this strategy?'' Try not to reject a strategy prematurely just because it makes you feel nervous or it doesn't seem to be your style. And don't fall into the trap of throwing the baby out with the bath water. That is, don't reject an entire strategy just because there's a portion of it you don't like. Simply modify the strategy to make it more acceptable to you.

Think about How Much *Risk* and *Commitment* Each Strategy Entails

The strategies vary enormously in terms of how much risk and commitment is involved in carrying them out. By *risk* we mean the severity of the consequences to you if a strategy doesn't work. For example, a high-risk strategy might cause you to get fired or have more problems with your boss than you started out with. On the other hand, a low-risk strategy, even if it doesn't work, probably wouldn't make things any worse. By *commitment* we mean the amount of time and effort you'd be willing to put into implementing a strategy. A high-commitment strategy would mean a big investment of time and effort; a low-commitment strategy a small one.

You won't be able to assess levels of risk and commitment in the abstract. You'll have to think carefully about a number of important factors, like:

- who you are (e.g., How much of a risk-taker are you?)
- who your boss is (e.g., How receptive is he or she to feedback?)
- the kind of relationship you'd *like* to have with your boss
- the prospects of change (on your part and your boss's part)
- important situational variables (e.g., How important is it for you to stay with the company you're in?)

Get Involved and Involve Others

Psychologists and educators agree that the more actively people get involved in the learning process, the more they learn. So jump into the water with both feet. When we ask you to jot down your thoughts, complete an exercise, or answer questions, don't just skip on to the next section. Try it out. Involve others. You'll learn even more. Have a friend read the book with you. Compare notes on your problem bosses and what the two of you are thinking about doing about them. Become consultants to each other. You can each recommend strategies you think the other should use, and talk about why. It'll be a great deal more effective than simply commiserating with each other about your problem bosses.

Don't Make Any Immediate Decisions

The first time you read the strategies, do it thoughtfully and reflectively and tentatively. It's also a good idea to read through all of them before deciding exactly what you'll do. After you finish reading them, let them incubate for a while. Take some time to make up your mind about which you'll use and which you won't.

Make This an Enjoyable Experience

The motto that guided our efforts as we wrote this book was, "If you've not having fun, you're not doing it right." That's the spirit we'd like you to read it with. Even though the topic is a serious one, we (and you) don't have to take it *too* seriously.

6

....

DOING NOTHING

"Doing nothing? What kind of strategy is that?" you might be asking yourself. "I could've done that without reading the book!" Well, you're right , it *is* an unusual title for a strategy, but, in some situations, it may well be the best thing for you to do with a problem boss.

To help you decide if Doing Nothing is a strategy that makes sense for you, we'll try to answer three questions in this chapter:

1. What does *Doing Nothing* mean?
2. How do most employees *Do Nothing*?
3. When is *Doing Nothing* a good strategy?

WHAT DOES DOING NOTHING MEAN?

Let's say that you've got a boss who treats you in ways you don't like. Maybe your boss does things that upset

99

you, annoy you, frustrate you, anger you, or humiliate you.

All doing nothing means is that you don't take any direct, positive action to curb the upsetting effect your boss is having on you. You just continue to put up (sometimes year after frustrating year) with the pain your boss causes you. You don't confront your boss. You don't quit. You don't go over your boss's head. None of that. You just suffer and endure your boss without doing anything effective to staunch the pain or to make the misery go away.

HOW DO MOST EMPLOYEES DO NOTHING?

If we've noticed anything in our work with organizations over the years, it's that doing nothing is exactly what most employees do when they have a problem boss. In fact, if there's one single reason we decided to write this book, that's it. We just got tired of seeing hundreds and hundreds of workers putting up with bad (sometimes abominable) treatment from their bosses without doing *anything* to make things better.

Partly to ease our frustration and partly to get the book launched, we asked ourselves: "Why *do* so many employees do nothing in the face of such bad treatment from their bosses?"

When we sat down and really tried to answer this question, we decided that nobody really does nothing when they have a problem boss. Frightened and scared by the risks of taking positive action, we saw them doing one or more of these five things:

1. complaining to somebody other than the boss
2. commiserating with fellow employees
3. internalizing their pain

4. slacking off
5. escaping

In the rest of this section, we'll introduce you to these five types of *doing nothing*. We'll describe them; we'll talk about why employees do them; and we'll talk about why they're generally ineffective. One other thing: At the end of the section, we'll invite you to try each one of these types on for size and see how well it describes you and how you deal with your boss.

Complaining

Many employees spend a lot of time complaining about their problem bosses to other people who aren't really in a position to do anything about the problem boss—like bartenders, friends, and spouses. Valerie Goodenough was a good example of this kind of employee.

Valerie was a highly intelligent, capable woman in her early thirties who worked for Courtney Whitfield, a woman in her late fifties, who was the regional manager of a nationwide job placement service. Courtney was a caustic, unhappy person who was hypercritical of Valerie and made her life miserable. In Courtney's eyes, Valerie was never quite "right." One day Valerie was too "slow." The next day she was "performing marginally." The next day she was "just about incompetent." And so on.

In all the years that Valerie worked for Courtney she never stood up to her and confronted her. Not once. But Valerie complained constantly to her husband (and us, when we were around) about how much she resented Courtney and what an awful person she was. Valerie's husband and we gave her all kinds of advice on how to deal with this woman. But we might as well have been spitting in the wind for all the good it did. Valerie rejected all our suggestions as being "unworkable.'' And Valerie would probably still be working for Courtney (and complaining about her) had the woman not been fired by a vice-president who finally got sick and tired of her destructive criticism.

Employees like Valerie complain to other people about their problem bosses for lots of reasons. But the main reason seems to go something like this: They feel tremendously frustrated with their bosses, but afraid of the consequences of sharing that frustration directly with their bosses. They seek out somebody they trust who will listen to their frustration with a sympathetic ear. That's what Valerie's husband did for her, and that's what the spouses and friends of millions of other employees do for them.

Why is complaining to others about your problem boss generally an ineffective thing to do? Actually, a certain amount of complaining is natural, understandable, and probably a good thing to do. All of us complain about something now and then simply because we need to get it off our chests. But that's not the kind of complaining we're talking about. We're talking about chronic complaining, the kind that Valerie was doing about Courtney. Complaining like that is not effective for at least two reasons:

1. It's ultimately a waste of time and energy. If all you do is complain about your boss, things aren't going to get any better. The only way things will improve is if you take some action to make them improve. Unfortunately, too many employees use complaining as a replacement for doing something to make the situation better between themselves and their bosses.

2. Chronic complaining is a turn off to people. Wives, husbands, and friends get tired of employees who complain, complain, complain but do nothing about the situation with their bosses. Valerie's husband simply got to the point where, whenever she brought up the subject, he'd say, ''Honey, I love you but I don't want to hear about it

anymore! I've told you a hundred times what I think you should do, and you've never done anything! Case closed, okay?''

Commiserating

Commiserating is a close cousin to complaining. When you complain about your problem boss, you usually do it to somebody who doesn't work for the same boss. When you commiserate, however, you do it with fellow employees— with people who endure the same kind of frustration and dissatisfaction with your boss as you do.

Commiserating about the boss is a common habit among employees whenever they get together in groups. The next time you go out to lunch at a restaurant frequented by business people, or during "happy hour" in a bar, just eavesdrop for a moment on a few conversations. It's extremely likely that you'll hear bits and pieces of conversations like this:

SHE: . . . I don't believe that. You're not serious, are you?

HE: I have never been more serious in my life. I mean, you know him. You know what he's like. Why are you so surprised?

SHE: I know but that's going a little far, even for Snidely. You're saying that he told the executive vice-president that *he* wrote the report and never mentioned word one about all the work we put in on it?

HE: You got it.

SHE: Unbelievable!

Why do employees commiserate with each other about their problem bosses? Maybe the simplest answer is the old adage, "misery loves company." People afflicted with the same problem feel better when they can vent their feelings to one another. They know that the others really understand what they're talking about. They don't have to explain anything. They can even share some fun and laughter by coming up with nicknames for the problem boss, or trading stories about the last incredible thing the boss did. When you think about it, commiserating is a rather harmless, even enjoyable way for employees to join ranks against a common foe.

Why is commiserating ineffective? Well, as we've already pointed out, it's not completely ineffective. It can make a dark situation seem a little brighter at times. But like complaining, it's ultimately ineffective because it doesn't do anything directly to make the problem go away. In terms of all the things employees *could* do as a group or team to make the situation better, commiserating is an impotent strategy. This will become clearer in chapter 12 when we talk about how employees can act as a group to deal with a problem boss.

Internalizing

When Thoreau wrote, "the mass of men who lead lives of quiet desperation," he might well have been thinking about employees who internalize the pain they experience from problem bosses.

Unlike employees who complain and commiserate about their problem bosses, people who internalize their pain don't share it with others. They hold it in; they let it eat away at them. They *accept* the unjust criticism and abusive treatment of problem bosses and begin to believe that they deserve it.

If there's any group of employees who we really worry about, it's these folks. At least employees who complain and commiserate have an outlet, a release, for their pain. Their complaining and commiserating may not lead to a better situation with their bosses, but they don't tear themselves apart with self-doubt. But employees who internalize keep their pain hidden where it can do severe damage in the form of chronic depression, ulcers, and years and years of needless unhappiness.

Slacking Off

Slacking off may be *the* most common form of *doing nothing*. We've been guilty of it ourselves. Year ago, before we went off on our own, each of us worked for several different problem bosses where the pattern became pretty predictable. We'd begin the new job under the new boss with great expectations; we really were the bright-eyed, bushytailed, young professionals. But then things would start to go sour. Our creative new ideas (at least we thought they were) would get dumped on. Or the boss would stretch the truth with us. Or chew us out in front of our peers. Or take credit for work we had done. Or in some other way prove to us that he wasn't the exciting, dynamic leader we'd expected him to be. So what would we do?

We'd start to slack off. Instead of coming in early and leaving late, we'd start to come in a little late and leave a little early. We'd stop taking initiative and begin waiting for instructions from the boss. When the boss wasn't around, we'd often goof off or commiserate with other employees about what a jerk we worked for. In short, we'd start doing the minimum necessary to hang on to our jobs. What happened to all that extra effort we started off with? Out the window.

Why do employees slack off on the job? The answer seems simple and straightforward. They simply decide (just like we did) that working hard and doing a good job isn't worth it. Consciously or unconsciously, they ask themselves:

> Why should I bust my butt to do a good job when the boss obviously doesn't appreciate it? Who wants to work hard and not only not get appreciation for it, but even worse, get abused for it? Why not just put in my eight hours, collect my pay, and avoid all that aggravation?

Why is slacking off ineffective? As understandable as it is for you to slack off when you have a problem boss, it doesn't work. In fact, it often makes things worse. Here's what typically happens. The boss notices that you're slacking off and that your performance has dipped. But, conveniently, the boss doesn't notice why you're slacking off. All the boss sees is that you've become a problem employee who used to be a hard worker. And then what happens? Your performance ratings go down. Or you get labeled as an "attitude" problem. Or you even get canned. It just doesn't work.

Escaping

Lots of bosses cause lots of employees pain and misery. And sometimes this pain and misery leads employees to try to escape from it in unhealthy ways:

Tom Clayton is a securities analyst for a large investment bank in New York. Tom is bored with his job, and he can't stand his narrow-minded, stubborn boss, Harry Lenzo. Tom told us he always smokes two joints before going back to work after lunch. "That's the only way I can make it through the afternoon with Harry," he told us.

Julie Frammer is an account executive whose supervisor, Howard Boise, is a partner in a public relations firm in Atlanta. Julie is so exhausted at the end of the day from Howard's constant nit-picking criticisms that she just goes home and plops down in front of the TV. "I know it's a total waste of time to watch all that junk," she told us. "But at least it gets rid of some of the tension I build up from working for that compulsive S.O.B."

For the last year, Al Jenks has been consuming three martinis at lunch and four scotches before going to bed. A couple of his friends have encouraged him to get into an alcoholism treatment program. But Al insists he doesn't have a drinking problem: "My only problem is that useless sales manager I work for. I was doing great until he came in here last year and completely ruined my job."

It's understandable that a lot of employees use booze or drugs or television to numb the pain their bosses cause them. But these escape routes don't work in the long run. Television may not do a lot of harm, but it cheats you out of enjoying other more interesting and fulfilling pastimes. Drugs and alcohol, if overused, lead to more misery and, all too often, an early death.

Before moving on to the next section we'd like you to do a little self-assessment. Take another look at the five kinds of *doing nothing* we've described here and, being as honest with yourself as you can, try to decide how well each one fits you. For example:

1. Are you a complainer? Do you tend to complain a lot to your husband or your wife or friends about your boss? Do you also have a tendency to reject any advice they offer on what you can do to make things better?
2. Are you a commiserater? Do you spend a great deal of time commiserating with other employees about your boss?
3. Are you an internalizer? Do you tend to internalize most of your negative feelings about your boss, or even conclude that the problem is mostly *you*, and not your boss?
4. Are you a slacker? Has your work performance slacked off because you just don't feel like putting in any extra effort because of the way your boss has been treating you?
5. Are you an escapist? Have you become a captive of television or alcohol or drugs to escape some of the pain that working for a problem boss causes you?

WHEN IS *DOING NOTHING* A GOOD STRATEGY?

So far in this chapter we've made a strong case against *doing nothing* when you've got a problem boss who's generally making things difficult for you. However, there are at least two kinds of situations we know of where some form of *doing nothing*—rather than taking direct, positive action— probably makes good sense.

The two kinds of situations we're talking about are:

1. when your boss will shortly be out of the picture
2. when you will shortly be out of the picture

Here's the first situation. Imagine that you've got a real problem boss—somebody who makes life genuinely unpleasant for you at least once or twice a week. But, let's say that your boss is about to:

- retire
- quit to take another job
- be transferred or promoted so he or she won't be your boss anymore
- be fired

Here's the second situation. Imagine that you've got the same problem boss as we just described. But this time you are about to:

- retire
- quit to take another job
- be transferred or promoted to another job where you'll no longer have to work for your present boss
- be fired

In either of these situations it doesn't make sense for you to take some direct action—like using one of the other strategies we talk about in the rest of the book—to try to improve the situation between you and your boss. Why? Because in a short time you or your boss will be gone. So why bother?

If your boss or you will shortly be out of the picture, *doing nothing* may well be your best strategy. But before moving on to the next chapter, we'd like to offer a few suggestions.

We think the most important thing for you to keep in mind if you find yourself in either of these two situations is this: Don't do anything you'll eventually regret. Unfortunately, over the years we've seen employees do things (when either they or their bosses were about to be out of the picture) that later on they wished they hadn't.

Specifically, we'd recommend that you:

BE CAREFUL WHO YOU SAY WHAT TO

If your boss has been a real problem, and now one of you is about to be out of the picture, there'll be a strong tendency for you to express feelings openly about your boss that you've been keeping inside a long time. That is, you'll be inclined to do a little "venting." That's natural and understandable. After all, you've been putting up with the jerk for a long time, right? All we're saying is, be careful who you vent these feelings to. Obviously it would be a mistake for you to walk in and tell your boss to go take a hike. But it would also be a mistake to be too honest with people who can't keep confidences. For example, when you leave a job, there are usually a bunch of people who get together to take you out to lunch and a few drinks. With your tongue loosened by a couple of beers or martinis, it's awfully easy to let a few derogatory comments about your boss slip out. Unfortunately, these comments have a way of getting back to bosses. And bosses can be pretty vindictive when it comes to handing out future job references, severance pay, or retirement benefits.

DON'T SLACK OFF TOO MUCH

Once you know that you're leaving or that your boss is leaving, you're probably going to slack off a bit. And that's fine—unless you overdo it. Don't be like a good friend of ours who, hearing that his boss would be leaving to take a new job, really started to slack off. Eventually he was fired when his boss decided not to accept the new job.

On to the next strategy.

7

....

ACCEPTING YOUR BOSS

People who work in organizations differ from each other in countless ways. Some are neat, some are sloppy. Some are analytical and logical, some are emotional and intuitive. Some are happy-go-lucky, and some never crack a smile. Given this tremendous variability, personality and style differences are a fact of organizational life. But bosses and employees are often not very good at dealing with these differences.

In our *Problem Employees* book we asked the question, "When is a problem employee *not* a problem employee?" Our answer? Many bosses consider an employee a "problem" simply because the employee has a personality or operating style that's different from theirs. These bosses don't like a whole lot of diversity when it comes to employees. They seem to operate on the principle, "Employees should be just like me." When they do make a selection error and hire someone who's not like them, they try to reform the employee. (And, of course, if the employee doesn't change, you know what happens.)

Obviously, bosses like this are a major problem in the work place. They're rigid and inflexible people who make the managerial mistake of confusing *process* with *outcome*. That is, they concentrate their attention on how employees work or how they look or act, and not on what employees actually get done. So instead of focusing on bottom line issues like quantity or quality of work, they focus on trivial or nonessential things, like the orderliness of a desk, the appropriateness of a tie, or the wisdom of a political opinion.

However, intolerance or rigidity isn't the sole province of bosses. Employees can be equally guilty of ignoring the quality of the bossing they're getting and focusing too much on nonessential personal differences. Pamela Ritenour is a good example.

Pamela Ritenour was one of the most health-oriented, exercise-conscious people we'd ever met. A marathon runner and competitive cyclist, Pam took everything she did seriously. Some people would say *too* seriously. A staunch vegetarian, Pam has lost more than one friend as a result of her lectures and disparaging comments about the dangers of eating "dead animal flesh." But Pamela's not a morbid person, either. She just thinks she's on the right track and that people who disagree with her are not.

For several years Pam worked for Gil Heller, a chain-smoking, beer-drinking, garbage food-eating sloth. Gil was fond of saying that his only exercise was weightlifting, which he did daily, one twelve-ounce can at a time. Pamela was so bothered by Gil's lifestyle that, after about two years, she decided to quit to take another job. As she put it:

I liked Gil and many people—including me—actually thought he was a pretty good boss. But how could I respect someone who lived such an unhealthy lifestyle? Every time I'd walk into his office it'd smell of cigarette smoke, and there'd be remnants of hamburgers and french fries in his waste basket. And, after work, when I was going to work out at the health club, he'd head straight to the local tavern for what he called his "attitude adjustment hour." It began to bother me so much I had to leave.

Unfortunately, Pamela's new boss turned out to be much worse than her old one. She said it directly: "Yes, he's an athlete. But he's also an idiot! He's easily the most self-centered person I've ever met." When we last talked to Pam she was in the process of looking for another job. She was also second-guessing her original decision to leave her job with Gil. She said, "Looking back on it, I think I made the mistake of jumping out of the frying pan into the fire. If I'd been able to overlook some aspects of his unhealthy life-style—maybe even accept his right to be the way he wanted to be—I might have been able to avoid the trouble I've had since leaving him."

Like bosses who think they have a problem employee when they don't, sometimes employees think they have a problem boss when all they've got is a boss who: (1) has a personality or operating style that's different from theirs, or (2) doesn't look or act the way the employee thinks a boss "should." In situations like these, we think it's a good idea to consider a strategy we call *accepting your boss*.

As with *doing nothing*, which we discussed in the previous chapter, the initial reaction to this strategy is often negative. "Accept my boss?" we've heard people say. "Why can't my boss be more accepting of me?" That's a good question, and one we'll try to answer a bit later.

For now, though, we'd just like to say that, at times, *accepting your boss* is an excellent strategy for dealing with bosses. In this chapter we'll talk about what it is, when it's a good idea (and when it isn't), and how it applies to your situation. Our goal is to help you better understand some of the differences between you and your boss. Sometimes, these differences can be healthy—they can make things much better than they'd be if you and your boss were completely alike. At the same time, some of the differences between you and your boss may not be good—they may work against a satisfying and productive relationship. The trick is being able to tell the good differences from the bad ones. But before we get into all of that, we'll talk about why people have so much trouble accepting people who are different from them.

WHY ARE PEOPLE INTOLERANT OF EACH OTHER?

When we introduced this strategy in a seminar we conducted a couple of years ago, someone in the audience interrupted us and said, "Before you go on, I have a question. Why *are* people intolerant of each other? It seems to me that if people were more accepting of each other there wouldn't be any need for this strategy." We thought it was a thought-provoking question, and we stumbled through a half-thought-out answer that didn't seem to satisfy the question asker or us. We resolved to be better prepared the next time someone asked a question like that.

So, why don't employees accept their bosses (and vice versa)? Why are people often so intolerant of others? This is a big question whose answer goes far beyond the arena of bosses and employees. But here are a few of our thoughts on the matter:

Intolerance Is Extremely Commonplace

Everyone is guilty of it to a certain extent, but some people are especially intolerant. There are a lot of words and phrases used to describe them:

- dogmatic, rigid, inflexible
- unyielding and unbending

- judgmental and evaluative
- stubborn, obstinate, pig-headed
- prejudiced, racist, and sexist
- parochial and narrow-minded
- set in their ways

Whether they're bosses or employees, intolerant people share one thing in common: They spend a lot of time sitting in judgment of other people. They're constantly evaluating— negatively, of course—other people: Who they are, what they're doing, what they're thinking, what they're saying (or how they're saying it), and in general how they're leading their lives. We've run into many people like this over the years. We're sure you have too.

People Learn to Be Intolerant

Lots of people grow up in families and cultures where it's extremely common to view people who are "different from us" as wrong, misguided, or even "bad" in some way. From their earliest years, they form a habit of judging and evaluating other people. They grow up learning to look askance at or suspicious of:

- people from different racial, ethnic, or national backgrounds
- people with different religious or political views
- people from different classes or socioeconomic groups
- people who look, act, think, or dress "differently from us"

By the time they become adults, they've learned their lessons well. They have very definite ideas about what's acceptable and—especially—what is not. Maybe it's people who talk too much or too little. Overly emotional people or overly analytical people. Or fat people, exercise nuts, showy people, sloppy people, or people with long hair.

Intolerance Is Born of Insecurity

On the surface, it looks like intolerant people feel superior to other people. But that's just the way it looks on the surface. Most intolerant people have an underlying problem psychologists call a poor self-concept. In plain English, they have a rotten view of themselves. This personal insecurity leads to intolerance in two ways. First, it's impossible to truly accept other people when you don't accept yourself. Second, because they lack the emotional maturity to deal with this problem directly, they walk around shining the negative spotlight on other people. It's an effective—unhealthy, but effective—way to avoid a more painful issue: How they feel about themselves.

Intolerance Happens at Work as Much as It Does Anyplace Else

Several years ago we wrote an article for business partners called, "Why Can't My Partner Be More Like Me?" In that article, we talked about the nearly-universal tendency to see people who are different from us as "wrong" and the desire to want them to be more like us. As partners and friends, we've fallen into that trap ourselves. (We once got into a serious row over the differences in our writing styles, both of us convinced, naturally, that the other guy's style was "wrong.") You've probably also fallen into the intolerance trap with people you've worked with, including bosses you've had.

Unrealistic Expectations Are a Key Component of Intolerance

People often have unrealistic—and sometimes downright unreasonable—expectations of other people. Two things usually happen when we have unrealistic expectations of other people. First, people don't live up to them. Second, rather than see our expectations as the problem, we almost always see the people who fall short of them as the problem.

It's especially common for youthful and overly exuberant employees to have unrealistic expectations of their bosses. We were that way in our youth, and you might have been, too. We wanted our bosses to be effective, but were disappointed to discover that they weren't. Of course, nobody could have lived up to our expectations (including ourselves, as we were to discover years later when we became bosses). But we didn't see it that way. All we saw were our problem bosses.

WHAT DOES *ACCEPTING YOUR BOSS* MEAN?

Basically, *accepting your boss* means letting your boss have the right to be different from your image of what a boss *should* be like. It means learning to believe, perhaps even convincing yourself, that it's okay for your boss to be different from you or from the way you'd like him or her to be. The goal of *accepting your boss* is for you to become less upset or unsettled over what, for all practical purposes, are stylistic and personality differences.

To see if you've got the idea, we'd like to give you a little practice deciding whether or not *accepting your boss* is a good idea. On the following pages are examples of boss behavior that employees have asked us about in our seminars. Read over each one and decide if you think it's a situation where *accepting your boss* would be an appropriate strategy.

To Accept or Not To Accept

On a separate sheet of paper, answer yes if you think *accepting your boss* would be an appropriate strategy and no if you think it would not. When you finish, compare your answers with ours:

1. "I'm a liberal Democrat and my boss is a right-wing Republican. It doesn't make any differences what the topic is, from social service programs to nuclear disarmament, the two of us are on the opposite side of the fence. He's also a pompous windbag who's always on his soapbox broadcasting his Neanderthal views. Plus, because he's the boss, he gets a lot more 'air time' than I do, which bugs me."

2. "I'm a proper type of person and my boss is, to be frank, coarse and vulgar. I get very upset when he uses profanity or speaks with vulgarity, which he does regularly in front of me and some of the other older ladies who work here, even though he knows it bothers us. I also know for a fact that his crude behavior has caused several people (very good workers, I might add) to resign from the company."

3. "I'm the type of person who believes strongly that people should work hard to get ahead. However, my new boss got her job simply because she's having an affair with the executive vice-president of the company (I think she's what you call a 'paramour of the boss' boss). She's actually reasonably competent and isn't even that bad a boss, but it just ticks me off that she got the job for the reason she did."

4. "Even though my boss is a good person, he has a bad temper. When he gets mad he storms around and says a lot of hurtful things I know he really doesn't mean. One time he got so mad he even put his fist through the wall in his office (even though I laughed about it later, for a moment I actually got scared for my own safety). After his outbursts he usually apologizes, but not always. He says he's inherited his bad temper from his father, that we shouldn't take it personally, and that we should learn to accept it."

5. "I'm an organized person and a big believer in using my time as efficiently and effectively as I can. Every day I construct a 'to do' list, where I categorize everything into high, medium, and low priorities. I don't start on a thing until I finish the list. My boss, on the other

hand, doesn't even know what a 'to do' list is. For a guy who knows nothing about time management, he gets quite a bit done. But I'm sure he could be much more effective if he'd change just a little. I gave him a book on the subject last year for Christmas, but he didn't seem too interested and I know he didn't read it.''

6. "My boss hates staff meetings, which she considers a waste of time. She insists that it's far more effective for her to meet individually with each of the employees who report to her. On the other hand, I believe very strongly in a team approach to management. To be honest, morale is pretty high and there does seem to be good communication among us. But I believe things could be much better if we had more staff meetings.''

7. "My boss has been 'coming on' to me in subtle but obvious ways since I started this job several months ago. He hasn't exactly come right out and asked me to go out with him, but he's hinted at it a bunch of times. Maybe he's just teasing in a flirtatious way, but I don't think so. So far I've just been ignoring his remarks, hoping he'll eventually back off. But he shows no signs of letting up. By the way, he's married, and when his wife comes around the office, he behaves in a proper, professional manner. But as soon as she leaves, he's back at it again.''

8. "My boss is the kind of person who goes around asking employees 'set-up' questions (questions he knows the answer to, but pretends he doesn't). I think he does this for two reasons: (a) to test employees to see if they know what they're doing, and (b) to keep them on their toes. Everybody knows he does it and we all hate it. It's had a definite impact on morale, too. I see this as a manipulative, even devious, thing to do. I know he does it consciously, too, since I once heard him talk about it as part of his overall approach to management.''

9. "My boss's father started this company more than thirty years ago and made it possible for many members of his family—including my boss—to earn a pretty decent living without having to work too hard. My boss has the

title of vice-president, but I don't think he really deserves it or earns his high salary. But what really gets to me is how he walks around quoting from books like *The One-Minute Manager* and *In Search of Excellence*. He comes across as if he got to where he is because of his executive ability.''

10. "I've worked for the same construction company for over twenty years. A few months ago, they hired a female construction engineer and put her in as project manager over me. Maybe she knows her stuff, but I'm having a hard time taking orders from a woman.''

11. "My boss looks more like Humpty Dumpty than a 'real' boss. He's short, fat, and has the physique of a billiard ball. He's so short that when he sits at his desk his feet don't touch the floor. To make matters worse, his clothes are about twenty years out of style. When my friends drop by after work, I'm actually embarrassed to introduce them to him.''

To Accept or Not To Accept: Our Thoughts

YES 1. *Boss with Different Political Beliefs*. Blowhards bug us too, but he has just as much right to his political beliefs as you do to yours. And it's a fact of organizational life that bosses get more "air time" than employees. But as long as he's not trying to jam his views down your throat, we think you should accept this aspect of your boss. After all, think how boring it would be if everyone you knew thought the same as you. However, since he's also a bit of a blowhard, you may find some welcome relief in several upcoming strategies.

NO 2. *Vulgar Boss*. We could use a few more specifics here, but on the basis of what you've said, we don't think you should accept his crude and vulgar behavior. What people believe is one thing, but what they *do* is quite another. Even though the two of us can get a little coarse at times, his behavior sounds extremely insen-

sitive and clearly unacceptable. You should find help
in several later strategies.

YES   3. *Paramour of the Boss*. Like you, we'd prefer it if
people got their jobs because they earned and deserved
them, not because of "other" factors, like *who* they
know and *how* they know them. However, if that were
true, hundreds of thousands of bosses (sons, daughters,
spouses, relatives, friends, and lovers of bosses) would
be immediately thrown out of work. Since your boss
sounds like a reasonably competent person and a fairly
good boss, we'd recommend that you forget about how
she got the job and concentrate on how she's doing it.

NO   4. *Bad-Tempered Boss*. No employee should have to
put up with verbal abuse and temper tantrums from an
emotionally immature boss, no matter how "good" he
is in other ways. Unacceptable. Period.

YES   5. *Poor Time Management Boss*. Your boss may be a
better manager of his time than you think. Maybe he just
doesn't do it the way you do it. Since he seems to be
reasonably effective on his own and doesn't seem to be
interested in your approach, we'd recommend that you
accept him the way he is. Who knows, maybe if you
back off he might come around to your way later on.

YES   6. *No Staff Meetings Boss*. Like the time management example above, this sounds a bit like a case
of, "Why can't my boss be more like me?" In general,
we think staff meetings are a pretty good idea, too. But
if things are going well and your boss doesn't seem at
all interested in staff meetings, maybe you should focus your attention on something else. What's the old
saying? "Why try to fix something that's not broke?"

NO   7. *Sexual Boss*. There are thousands of bosses like
yours and, quite frankly, we're getting more and more
disgusted hearing about them. We feel strongly that
this kind of boss behavior should not be accepted.
However, how you handle sexual bosses like this is a

delicate and tricky matter. Even though he's clearly in the wrong, you could be the one who gets burned. We'll have more to say about this later.

NO   8. *Set-up Boss*. This is not an approach to management. It's an approach to mismanagement. Not acceptable.

YES   9. *S.O.B. (Son of the Boss) Boss*. The somewhat angry tone of your note concerns us a little. Perhaps there's something else your boss does that you haven't mentioned. But all we get from what you have told us is a boss with a severe case of self-deception. Since we're big believers in intellectual honesty, it'd bug us too; but we'd try not to let it get in the way.

YES   10. *Female Boss*. Come on, get with the program! This is 1986, not 1886! You want to be accepted as a competent person. So does she.

YES   11. *Novelty Boss*. Your boss may not look like he just stepped off the pages of *Gentlemen's Quarterly*, but that doesn't mean he can't be a good boss. You don't want people to judge you solely on how you look or what you wear, do you? Neither does he.

DECIDING WHETHER OR NOT TO *ACCEPT YOUR BOSS*

Now let's take a look at some of the differences between you and your boss and see which ones it might be wise for you to accept (and, of course, which ones you'd be better off responding to with one of our upcoming strategies).

The first step is for you to list what you think are the key differences that separate the two of you—in plain English, some of the things that bug you about your boss. When we asked Lawrence Kander to do this (even before we explained the strategy), he came up with the following:

Key Differences between Me and My Boss

1. I live a healthy lifestyle: I watch what I eat and exercise daily. She smokes, has terrible eating habits, never exercises, and is about thirty pounds overweight.
2. I think it's wrong to humiliate people and treat them like dirt. She frequently berates people (including me) in the presence of others.
3. I like to live one day at a time and have sort of a "hang loose" attitude when it comes to the future. My boss is always talking about the future and how to plan for it.
4. I think it's important for young mothers to be home taking care of their youngsters. She's a mother of preschoolers, works full-time, and sends her kids to a daycare center.
5. I think it's important to have some social interaction at work. All she does is work, work, work!
6. I like to clown around and have fun at work; she's always deadly serious. (Sometimes I get the urge to sneak up behind her and tickle her, just to see if she'd laugh!)
7. I'm an intuitive, pretty creative, "right brain" type of person. To be honest, I'd have to say I'm also kind of disorganized. She's logical, analytical, organized, and (ugh!) *very* neat and orderly. (Another urge I get is to sneak into her office and mess up her desk. I bet it'd drive her crazy!)

Larry's list should give you a good idea of how we'd like you to approach this task. Sit down and think about some of the differences between you and your boss (especially some of the things that really bug you) and write them down.

After Larry came up with his list, we explained the strategy we call *accepting your boss* (much like we did for you in the first part of this chapter). After doing that, we asked him to answer these three questions:

1. What are some things about your boss you don't like but you may be able to accept because they're nonessential style or personality differences?

2. Being as honest as you can, what are some things about your boss that, even though they're different from you, you might be able to learn from or benefit from?
3. What are some things about your boss you don't like and won't be able to accept because they are:

   • violations of your person or privacy;
   • hindering your work performance;
   • getting in the way of some of your important life or career goals?

In response to the first question, Larry said:

I guess I'd have to put items one and four from my list here. Even though I may not like it, she's got a right to live an unhealthy (from my perspective) life-style if she wants. And even though I'd like my wife not to work when we have kids, I don't want to impose my value system on her. So those are two things I guess I'd say I should probably accept about her.

To our second question, Larry responded:

Looking over my list, I guess it would be possible to put items three, five, six, and seven here. Let me explain. Regarding item number three, people who know me well—including my wife and my parents—say I should be more future-oriented and more planful. Since that's about all she thinks about, I guess I could learn something from my boss there. In terms of five and six, I'd have to admit that I could be a little more serious and work oriented than I am. Maybe my boss and I could both change some and meet somewhere in the middle. She could lighten up a bit and I could get a bit more serious. In terms of item number seven, everybody agrees that I'm a disorganized slob at work. So I'd probably benefit a lot if I was just one-tenth as organized and orderly as she is.

In response to our third question, Larry said:

> Item number two definitely belongs here. I can't accept—I won't accept—my boss humiliating me and other employees by criticizing us and yelling at us in public. I'm still not sure how to deal with that aspect of her behavior, because I don't think she's going to be too receptive to feedback on it. But I definitely won't accept that kind of behavior from her.

Now that you've seen how Larry "processed" the differences he had with his boss—and decided which ones to accept, which ones to learn from, and which ones not to accept—we'd like you to go over your list in the same way. If it'd help, don't hesitate to enlist the aid of a friend or coworker. Sometimes they're able to see things more clearly simply because they're not as close to the situation as you are.

When you're ready, go on to the next strategy.

8

· · · · · · · · · · · · · · · · · · · ·

CHANGING YOURSELF

If you're like most employees, your attention is focused on how your boss should change to make things better, not on how *you* should change. If you've thought about what your boss wants of you, maybe you've even concluded you'll be damned if you'll change. But simply expecting other people to change—with you doing nothing at all—isn't a particularly effective approach. As a matter of fact, sometimes the best way to deal with a problem boss is to put the spotlight squarely on you and think about how you can change to improve things between you and your boss.

Before talking about *what* we mean by *changing yourself*, and whether or not it's an appropriate strategy for you, let's see why it's often an effective approach.

WHY IS *CHANGING YOURSELF* A GOOD THING TO CONSIDER?

People who're having problems with each other (e.g., an employee and a boss, a husband and a wife) almost always engage in a power struggle over the issue of change. Person *A* wants Person *B* to change in some way, but feels Person *B* can't or won't change. Person *B* feels the same way about Person *A*. Both frustrated, they believe, somewhat accurately, that they aren't getting what they want or need from each other. Often, they play a waiting game with each other, each one looking for some sign of movement from the other. The message they send each other is: "I'm not going to give you what you want—a change in my behavior—until I start getting what I want from you, a change in your behavior." It's a lot like the cold war between the superpowers: Each waits for the other to make the first move. The result is a frustrating and unproductive stalemate.

We've experienced this problem in our relationship with each other as well as in our relationships with family and friends. However, we've also noticed that when one of us takes the first step and begins to make some changes—or even just shows a willingness to change—good things usually begin to happen. Often, the stalemate is broken and the walls that divided us start to crumble. Differences that once seemed irreconcilable begin to look more resolvable. It all starts with one person changing just a little.

There are a number of other important reasons why you might want to consider this strategy.

Since You're Part of the Problem, Become Part of the Solution

As people are fond of saying, "It takes two to tango" when people are struggling with one another. In the case of you and your boss, this means that you're not wearing the white hat and your boss the black hat. It means you're doing something, even if you think it's minimal compared to what your boss is doing, to contribute to the problems you're having. If this is true, it's possible that a small change in your behavior could go a long way toward improving things between you and your boss.

A Simple Willingness to Change Often Has a Big Impact

Lots of people become stubborn and intransigent when others expect them to change. They almost seem to fold their arms across their chest and say, "No way! I'm not changing one bit!" To us, this attitude is shortsighted and self-defeating because often just a simple willingness to change on the part of one person can have a major impact on the other. When you say, "Okay, I'm willing to consider changing in a way you'd like me to change," you send a powerful message. You almost always see the other person soften his or her position as a result.

What Other People Want Us to Do Is Often Good for Us to Do

Even though bosses sometimes make unreasonable demands, they generally have legitimate and reasonable expectations. They want tardy employees to come in on time, shy salespeople to make more sales calls, or aggressive employees to tone down with co-workers. That is, bosses often want employees to change in ways that would be very good for employees if they did change in those ways. Employees wouldn't simply be "doing what the boss wants," they'd be doing what's best for themselves.

Effective Problem-Solving Often Requires Taking the Bull by the Horns

Employees who find out what their bosses want and begin to initiate appropriate changes are doing effective problem solving. They're not standing on the sidelines waiting for their bosses to do something. Instead of acting like passive wimps, they're trying to get things off the dime with their bosses. Of course, there are some risks. But what effective course of action is without some risk?

Changing Yourself Often Leads Others to Change Themselves

One of the best ways to get another person to make some changes for you is for you to make some changes for them. In Latin, the expression for this is *quid pro quo*, which translates as "something for something," or "one thing in return for another." What fascinates us is that the "something" you give often leads to "something plus" from the other person. We don't know how many times we've seen a modest change on the part of Person *A* lead to a big, even dramatic, change on the part of Person *B*.

WHAT DOES CHANGING YOURSELF MEAN?

We'll break down the strategy into four parts:

1. Thinking about how you *might* change.
2. Deciding whether or not to change.
3. Changing.
4. Looking at the results of change.

Let's take a look at each one.

Step One: Thinking about How You *Might* Change

The first step of the change process is figuring out how you might change to improve things between you and your boss. There're three ways to do this:

1. the armchair method
2. asking friends and co-workers
3. asking your boss directly

Let's take them one at a time.

THE ARMCHAIR METHOD

Unlike bosses, who often don't know what their employees want from them, most employees are not insulated from feedback from their bosses. Many know *very clearly* how their bosses would like them to change. Maybe you're one of them. If you're in this kind of situation, all you have to do is sit down and think about the question, "How would my boss like me to change?" Here're some additional questions to ask yourself:

- What are some things I do that bug my boss?
- What would my boss like me to do more of (or less of)?
- In performance review meetings we've had, what has my boss told me I should work on?
- What could I do differently to function more effectively at work?
- What could I do to make my boss's job more satisfying and less frustrating?

Over the years we've asked lots of people to do this. These are a few of the things we've heard them say:

Art seems threatened when I challenge his ideas in staff meetings. I could confine my challenges to times when just the two of us are alone together.

Even though I don't think getting my paper work in on time is very important, it drives Gerry crazy when I don't. I suppose I could at least try to get it in on time from now on.

George is always accusing me of beating around the bush and not giving him a straight answer when he asks me a question. I don't really see it that way, but I could try to make my answers to his questions briefer and more concise.

My boss is always saying that I'm not enough of a self-starter. I think what she means is that she'd like me to begin working on things that need doing before she asks me or reminds me to do them. I think she'd faint if I actually came to her once with a list of things I think needed to be done.

Every year I've worked here I've taken every personal day and sick day that was allowed me, even when I wasn't necessarily sick. I sort of think of them as mental health days. My boss thinks I'm using these personal and sick days almost as vacation days (which, to be honest, is fairly accurate). I guess she'd like me to use sick days only when I'm really sick.

My boss would like me to go to bed with him. If you think I'm going to change in that area, you gotta be crazy!

Obviously, bosses want employees to change in all kinds of ways, some rational and reasonable, some clearly unacceptable. But, for the moment, don't worry too much about how reasonable your boss's expectations are (we'll talk about unreasonable or unacceptable expectations in a moment). For now, just think about a few ways your boss would like you to change. You might even find it helpful to review the section, "Walking in Your Boss's Shoes," from chapter 4.

ASKING FRIENDS AND CO-WORKERS

In this section we'll be echoing some of the thoughts we shared with you in the section on interviewing an "expert" from our chapter on "Taking a Look at Yourself." If you'd like to review that portion of the book after reading what we've got to say here, it certainly wouldn't hurt.

It's difficult for us to see ourselves clearly and objectively, especially given the human tendency to ignore our weaker points and accentuate the positive ones. It's almost impossible for us to truly see ourselves as others do. This is why close friends and co-workers can be such a valuable resource. Unfortunately, however, most of us never really consult these "experts." Or when we do, we spend so much time debating or disagreeing with them when they say something we don't want to hear that it ends up being a frustrating waste of time for both. It doesn't have to be that way. Good friends and co-workers can be a big help, if only we can *listen* to what they have to say.

We'd like you to think of someone who knows you and your job situation well. Someone who could be helpful in identifying some ways you might change in order to improve things between you and your boss. Once you think of someone, ask that person to meet with you. When you meet, make the *purpose* of the meeting clear. For example, you might say:

I've been thinking about my relationship with my boss and what we can both do to have a better working relationship. It's easy for me to think about what *she* needs to do to change, but it's a lot harder for me to do that about myself. I'm hoping you might help by telling me, as frankly and candidly as you can, how *I'm* contributing to the problems we're having and what *I* could do to make things better between us. Don't worry about hurting my feelings. I need to know your opinion, even if it hurts. And don't worry about me getting defensive or disagreeing with you. All I'm going to do is *listen* to what you have to say, without offering my own opinion.

Meet in a private place and have a number of thought-provoking questions ready to ask. For example:

How do you see me contributing to the problems I'm having with my boss? What am I doing that's getting in the way of the two of us having a smooth and productive working relationship?

What could I do differently in order to improve the way we're getting along with each other? How do you think my boss would answer that question? How would you answer it?

Forget about my relationship with my boss. What are some things you think I should work on in order to be a better or more effective person? What are some things you've thought of telling me, but didn't because you were worried about how I'd react?

When the person starts to talk, your job is to listen. Here's what we'd like you to do:

- Give the person your undivided attention. Make good eye contact and periodically nod your head to signal that you're listening. Don't interrupt, shake your head, or roll your eyes when you disagree. Don't debate, counter, or get defensive. Just be quiet and listen attentively.
- When the person begins to wind down, encourage him or her to talk more. Say things like: "This is very helpful. What would you add?" "What other thoughts and ideas do you have?" "Can you think of anything else?"
- When the person finally stops talking, don't offer your thoughts and ideas. Instead, try to summarize the essence of what the person said. As you may recall from a previous chapter, we call this a "read back." It's an excellent way

to prove you're listening and the best way to get the person to talk more. Begin your read back something like this: "Well, Ted, I heard you say a number of important things there. You started off by saying . . ." Then try to "capture" each of the main points in your own words. Chances are, the person will interrupt you in the middle of your read back to build on what you've said. That's terrific! A good read back will almost always get people talking even more (it also increases the chances they'll talk about sensitive subjects that people have a tendency to hold back on). Just continue reading back until the person runs out of steam.

In chapter 4, we reported on a meeting like this between Clyde Jameson, a young pathologist in a medical laboratory, and Charlene Masters, the executive secretary to the president of the company. As you may remember, it was an eye-opening experience for Clyde. When we met with Clyde after the meeting, we asked him to think about what Charlene had said to him and list the changes he might make to improve things between him and his boss, Bill Gruskins. Here's what he came up with:

I've never given much thought to Bill's personal life, although Charlene tells me it's been filled with a lot of bad experiences. Apparently, that's one of the reasons why he escapes into his work. I could show more interest in him and his personal life.

Bill's a by-the-books kind of guy and likes to be the boss. But Charlene says I "buck his authority" and in general don't show him a lot of respect. I guess I could change by not being so difficult and contrary (that is, disagreeing with him simply for the sake of disagreement).

Bill likes to see himself as a mentor and developer of the younger physicians in the lab. I could change by going to him more (I hardly ever do it now) and asking his opinions on medical matters or laboratory procedures. Charlene says I also have a bit of a "know-it-all'' reputation (she even used the word ''arrogant'' once), so maybe I could tone that down a bit, especially when I'm talking with Bill.

Another way I could change is to not show so much public disregard for the policies and procedures of the lab. I don't think I'm talking about changing my opinion here; just not be such a loud mouth about my opinions, especially when I know they rub Bill the wrong way.

Now that you've seen how it's done, why don't you find a friend or co-worker to interview? Do the best you can, following the instructions we offered above. After you finish, sit down and think about what you've learned about how you might change to improve things between you and your boss. If you'd like, record your thoughts on a separate sheet of paper.

It's possible to construct a fairly long list of potential changes just by thinking things out on your own or asking friends and co-workers. However, you also have the option of going one step further and talking with your boss directly. That's the third, as well as the most difficult and risky, method for identifying possible ways you might change.

ASKING YOUR BOSS DIRECTLY

In our management seminars, we advise bosses to sit down with their employees and ask the question, ''What could I do as your boss to make your job more satisfying and less frustrating?'' When we suggest this, we often hear a lot of tittering and groaning in the audience, including a few ''no ways'' and comments about opening up Pandora's box. But after we explain why it's important to ask their employees, as well as their spouses and children, a question like this, quite a number of them say they'll give it a try. (It's common for managers we've trained to refer to this as *the* question. For example, one of them will come up to us several days after one of our seminars and say, "I asked one of my employees *the* question yesterday and you'll never guess what happened.") However, most bosses *never* ask their employees a question like this. None of our bosses ever did and we'd bet you haven't heard too many bosses ask a question like it either. But it's an extremely thought-provoking question that *can* lead to some very valuable information if bosses who ask it can be good listeners.

Most employers never ask their bosses a question like this, either. However, at least theoretically, asking your boss *the* question is a potentially good idea and could lead to a couple of valuable new ideas about how you might change. It's also a risky approach, so we don't think you should do it without thinking it through thoroughly. If you are interested in giving it a try, we'd suggest you do so only after reading chapter 11 (Talking to Your Boss One On One), where we talk in-depth about the various aspects of a face-to-face meeting, including which bosses to definitely *not* ask this question of.

If you decide to give it a try, remember to be clear about the *purpose* of the meeting when you ask your boss to meet with you. For example, you might say:

> I've been doing a good deal of thinking lately about how well we're working together and what I could do to improve things between us. I thought it'd be a good idea for you to tell me what I could do—as somebody who reports directly to you—to make your job as my boss more satisfying and less frustrating. I'd especially like to hear what you think I should work on, or what I should think about changing, in order to improve my work performance and the relationship we have with each other.

We don't want to say any more about the rest of the meeting here, other than our standard pitch about being the best listener you can be. In chapter 11 we'll go into detail about how to conduct a meeting like this with your boss.

Step Two: Deciding Whether or Not to Change

Once you've done some thinking about how you *might* change, it's time to make some decisions about how you *will* (or will not) change.

People who wrestle with this decision almost naturally engage in a kind of "cost/benefit" thinking. Sure, they may gain something if they change. But will it be worth the "cost" to them? For example, the employee who decides to stop challenging her boss's ideas in staff meetings may gain her boss's appreciation and approval, but may lose a little of her sense of feisty independence. The salesperson who starts getting his paper work in on time may become more organized and gain the boss's good will, but may pay the price of feeling that he's doing something trivial at the expense of something important. The employee who begins to answer the boss's questions more directly and succinctly may gain a more satisfied boss, but give up a preference to "think out loud" when posed with an important question.

You may find this kind of approach helpful as well. To try it, take the list of possible changes you made earlier and spend some time thinking about the costs and the benefits of each one. For example, under "costs" you might want to ask yourself:

- How big (or small) a change is this?
- How difficult would it be for me to make this change?
- Would I feel worse about myself if I made this change?
- What would I be giving up or losing if I made this change?

Under "benefits" you might want to ask:

- How would my boss benefit? How would it benefit me?
- How would making this change improve my effectiveness as a person?
- Would I feel better about myself if I made this change?
- What would I be gaining if I made this change?

Below is an example of how Clyde Jameson did a cost/benefit analysis on one of the possible changes he listed, the one about letting his boss be more of a mentor by going to him for professional advice or asking his opinion on medical or laboratory matters:

Costs	*Benefits*
"This would be hard for me because I'm extremely self-reliant and not used to asking for advice."	"Bill would love it. He'd feel better about himself, and me."
"I'm not sure, but it might make me feel just a little phony."	"There'd be a lot less friction and 'distance' between us."
"It's hard for me to admit I don't know what I'm doing. I'd be giving up believing that I *should* always know what to do on my own."	"He's a smart guy. I could learn some things I don't know."
	"I may play the role of a mentor someday, so I might learn some things about doing that."

Why don't you give it a try yourself? Take one item from your list of possible changes and think about the costs and benefits, like Clyde did above, and write them on a separate sheet of paper.

WHAT ABOUT UNACCEPTABLE DEMANDS?
We'd like to say one more thing about "deciding" before we move on, and this has to do with unacceptable or unreasonable demands that bosses make.

First, bosses *do* make them. Over the years we've seen or heard of hundreds of examples of bosses who've (a) asked or expected employees to engage in illegal or highly questionable behavior, or (b) pressured employees to engage in what they considered to be unethical, "bad," or "wrong" behavior.

Second, time and time again we've talked to employees who've gone along with the unreasonable or unacceptable demands of their bosses. Many felt they had no choice but to go along with their bosses, even though they knew it was wrong to do so. Some rationalized their decision by believing that going along would actually pay for them. But, almost invariably, it's a big mistake for employees to accede to unreasonable or unacceptable demands. The costs are too high!

Step Three: Changing

As everyone knows, deciding to change and actually changing are two very different things. For most of us, change doesn't come easy, even with our best intentions. For example, no matter how beneficial it might be to stop smoking or start exercising on a regular basis, it's very hard for most people to make these changes. (As a matter of fact, it's the changes we "know" we should make that seem to be the hardest.) It's also likely to be difficult for you to make some of the changes you're thinking of making with your boss.

The subject of change is an important one, and it's impossible to do justice to it in just a few pages here. But we would like to offer a few thoughts and ideas about how to increase the probability of successfully making the changes you set out to make.

THINKING ABOUT YOUR COMMITMENT TO CHANGE

As we've said, changing is hard. But change without commitment or motivation to change is almost impossible. One of the main reasons why so many attempts at change fail is because they're so halfhearted. So think about how much you want to change. If the motivation's not there, maybe you should reconsider using this strategy.

BE CLEAR ABOUT YOUR GOALS

Sometimes people set goals that sound good, but are so fuzzy, abstract, or hazy that it's not clear what they're trying to accomplish. For example, let's say you've set a goal to be more sensitive to the needs of your spouse or lover. It's a great-sounding goal, but what does it mean? In our opinion, it's too abstract to tell. With goals, it's very important to *get specific*. If you're talking about behavior change, try to identify the *behaviors* you'll be changing. Using the example above of becoming more sensitive, you'd be better off if you specified things like:

- Ask him what he's thinking or feeling when he looks distracted or preoccupied.
- At least once a week give her a token (a card, note, present, flower, etc.) that lets her know you've been thinking of her.
- Periodically ask him or her what *you* could do to improve the quality of the relationship you have with each other.

Talking about being a more sensitive person is easy, becoming one is a different story. But it's a more achievable goal when you're clear what you're aiming for. The kinds of things we've listed above are the *acts* of a sensitive person. They're the kind of things you'd have to do for the other person to say, "Yes, you've achieved your goal of becoming more sensitive." (Or, if you haven't done them, "No, you haven't even come close.")

DON'T BITE OFF MORE THAN YOU CAN CHEW

Sometimes people get carried away with themselves and set goals that are so ambitious they'll never accomplish them. They fail because they try to achieve too much. We think it's more important to set small, achievable goals—and achieve them—than it is to set big ones you can't reach.

BE PATIENT
This is related to the advice we gave you about not trying to achieve too much. Very few people make substantial changes overnight. Be patient.

BE PREPARED FOR FRUSTRATION AND FAILURE
People often begin their change efforts with the best of intentions and maybe even get off to a good start. But then, as Robert Burns said, "The best laid schemes o' mice an' men gang aft agley." And because they weren't prepared for it, this momentary setback completely throws them off and they give up completely. So, be prepared for frustration and even a failure or two. Be a little forgiving of yourself if you happen to fall off the wagon. Just get back up, say to yourself, "They warned me this might happen," and do your best to get back on track again.

BE PREPARED FOR LITTLE OR NO REACTION FROM YOUR BOSS
Be prepared for little or no reaction from your boss, even if you're tremendously successful in your attempts to change. It'll confuse you. Maybe even make you mad. But the reality is that many bosses don't even notice these kinds of changes. Who knows why? Maybe the boss is completely oblivious to such subtleties of human behavior. Maybe the boss is just not good at giving employees feedback. Or maybe the boss thinks you're beginning to do what you always should've been doing anyway. If this happens to you, celebrate your behavior change success on your own. Don't let your boss's insensitivity get you down.

BRING SOMEONE ELSE
INTO YOUR CONFIDENCE

Many people are Lone Ranger types who don't like to involve others in personal matters. But sometimes just telling other people that we're going to do something increases the chances that we'll do it. You may want to tell a close friend or co-worker what you're up to, and even ask them for a little support and encouragement. As we said earlier, sometimes you'll make some changes and your boss won't even notice. That's when it's nice to get some encouragement from another quarter.

Now let's turn to the final step in this strategy.

Step Four: Looking at the Results of Change

A lot of people look at this strategy as a kind of interpersonal experiment. As with any experiment, the question you'll eventually want to ask is, "What happened? I changed my behavior and what was the result?" To find the answer all you need do is monitor—unobtrusively, of course—your boss's reaction and subsequent behavior.

This is not an idle exercise either, for it's going to help you make important decisions about what to do and where to go in the future. Like all people, you and your boss are at a fork in the road when it comes to your relationship. One branch of the fork has a sign that says, "Work on it." The other has a sign that reads, "Dead End! Forget it!" By monitoring your boss's response to your change you'll probably gather all the evidence you'll need to decide to continue working on the relationship or, if the evidence suggests it, do something else.

Obviously, there are only three things that can happen after you change yourself:

1. Things will get worse.
2. Things won't change.
3. Things will get better.

Let's take a look at each of them.

THINGS WILL GET WORSE

Can you imagine anything worse than things getting worse? Here you are, changing yourself in a way your boss would like, and your boss's behavior actually becomes more intolerable! This is unlikely. We've scanned our experience and haven't been able to come up with a single example where things got worse *as a direct result* of an employee changing for the better. That's not to say things won't get worse. But if they do, it probably has nothing to do with you. It's much more likely to be because of something beyond your control, like a personal crisis in your boss's life, or her incompetence finally catching up with her. However, if things *do* get worse, that's important information to pay attention to. It may mean you'll want to consider one of the higher risk strategies we'll be laying out in later chapters.

THINGS WON'T CHANGE

Of the three possible outcomes, this one is the most likely. So it's a good idea to be prepared for it. Basically, it means that what you did had no discernible impact. Your boss is behaving the same as before.

However, sometimes things can *seem* worse, even when they haven't changed at all. Here's what happens: You make a good faith effort to change in order to improve things with your boss. But your boss neither acknowledges the change nor changes in any detectable manner. You think, "Hey, what's going on here? I'm working on this relationship, but my boss isn't. This is unacceptable."

Acceptable or not, this is certainly the time to ask the question "Is this the kind of relationship I want to be in?"

And, again, you may decide to move on to another strategy, like confronting your boss directly, talking to your boss's boss, getting a transfer, or even "firing" your boss.

THINGS WILL GET BETTER

Of course, this is what you want. It's the return on your investment. And it *can* happen. For example, when Clyde Jameson, the young physician we met earlier, began to treat his boss, Bill Gruskins, more like a mentor and leader, Bill responded by changing in positive ways for Clyde, even though the two of them had never sat down to talk things out face-to-face. Clyde told us:

It hasn't been dramatic, but since I've started being more deferential to Bill and periodically going to him for advice and counsel, I've sensed a number of changes in him. First, he's nicer to me and much more relaxed in my presence. The "edge" has sort of vanished from our relationship. He even asked me if I'd like to drive with him to the state medical association meeting next month. Second, I'd say his view of himself has improved. It's as if he feels more secure in himself and isn't as much of a wet blanket as he used to be. For example, he's not as likely to abruptly criticize people or dump on their ideas. That used to really bug me. He hasn't done it nearly as much as he used to. Third, he's not only been nicer to me, but I'd swear he's behaving nicer to other people around here, like some of the med techs and staffers he used to treat pretty curtly. Some of them have even made comments to me about the change in his behavior. I'm not saying it's all been because of me, but I'm sure my treating him differently has been a contributing factor.

Sometimes changing yourself can be a *very* effective way to deal with problem bosses.

9

·····················

CHANGING YOUR THOUGHTS
AND FEELINGS

While some employees are almost oblivious to the behavior of their bosses, countless others are bothered, upset, or depressed by it. The things their bosses say and do—a snub, a critical remark, a tirade—disturb them, cause them to doubt themselves, and throw them into a funk. Sometimes, employee reactions like these are appropriate, "justified" responses to a boss's behavior. But sometimes they are overreactions. One person we interviewed put it this way: "Some employees make mountains out of mountains and some make mountains out of molehills. People in the latter group cause themselves unnecessary trouble."

When a person's response *is* out of proportion to a stimulus it's helpful to ask the question, "Why? What's going on here?" A closer look often reveals that the "culprit" is the way the person is looking at or thinking about the situation. That is, an employee's strong negative reaction is "caused" as much by what he or she *thinks* or *believes* as it is by the boss's bad behavior.

144

If you're this kind of a person—someone who has a tendency to get all worked up over your boss—this chapter should help. We'll begin by getting you to think about the kind of emotional impact your boss has on you. Then we'll help you answer the question, "What's causing you to have such a strong reaction?" After thinking about it, you many conclude your reaction is quite appropriate. But you may also conclude that it's not—that somehow, in some way, you're doing some things that magnify the problem.

If you are, we'll talk about how to combat your inappropriate reactions. We believe it's possible for people to exert a fair amount of control over how they *feel* about any problem. So even though your boss does unpleasant, distasteful, ineffective, and even stupid things, we think you can exert a fair amount of control over how much (or how little) this behavior bothers you.

Now let's take a look at the relationship between thoughts and feelings, and particularly how your thoughts can dramatically affect the way you feel.

HOW THOUGHTS "CAUSE" FEELINGS

Almost everyone these days is familiar with the psychological concepts of stimulus and response. Briefly, a stimulus elicits or brings forth a response; for example, the presence of food leads a hungry animal to salivate. Or the sight of a vicious dog leads to a response of fear and flight. In situations like these, it's easy to conclude that the stimulus "causes" the response.

But the relationship between stimulus and response is not always so clear. How about when the stimulus is the presence of a baby mouse or a harmless garden snake and the response is fear and flight? Or how about when the stimulus is sitting in an airplane seat or standing inside an elevator and the response is panic and terror? In cases like these, does the stimulus *cause* the response?

Obviously, something else is going on. And that something else happens somewhere *between* the stimulus and the response. Nowadays, almost all psychologists agree that this "something else" has to do with *thoughts and mental images* that intervene between the stimulus and the response. From this point of view, it's not the vicious dog that elicits the response of fear and flight, but the thought, "I may get bitten!" and the mental image of the dog's sharp teeth tearing into the flesh. An animal trainer, skilled in the handling of animals, would probably have quite different thoughts and mental images—and because of this would respond in a very different way, perhaps even by reaching out to the dog in a friendly manner.

This helps to explain what happens when emotional reactions seem inappropriate or out of proportion to a stimulus. Take the example of a person who feels terror when flying in an airplane. Here, obviously, the person is consumed with thoughts of airplane safety, mechanical failure, and dying. The mental images filling the mind are of planes crashing and bursting into flames, people screaming in terror, and inability to escape. Even though it's easy to argue that a reaction like this is irrational—after all, airplane transportation is one of the safest ways to travel—because of these thoughts and mental images, the natural response is a *feeling* of terror. So it's not the stimulus that leads to the response as much as it is the intervening thoughts and mental images. (In our view, almost everyone experiences a certain amount of anxiety when traveling by air, especially when the aircraft is taking off and landing or is flying through air turbulence. To experience for yourself the close relationship between thoughts and feelings, try this experiment. The next time you begin to feel some anxiety while flying, *immediately* begin to visualize the most positive experience you can recall. Maybe it'll be the birth of your child, the best sexual experience you've ever had, a "glory days" moment from the past, or simply the memory of lying peacefully on a white, sandy, isolated beach. Whatever it is, picture it as vividly as you can in your mind's eye. Try to recapture and relive the moment in your imagination. If you do, we predict you'll experience very little anxiety. There may be white knuckles all around you, but you'll be feeling calm, comfortable, and relaxed.)

Although this direct relationship between thoughts and feelings has been recognized by philosophers for thousands of years, it's only recently become an accepted facet of modern-day psychology (thanks mainly to the pioneering work of Dr. Albert Ellis in the 1950s and 1960s). For decades psychologists chased after unconscious motives or hidden conflicts to "explain" irrational behavior. And all they had to do was look to the thoughts and mental images of the people they were trying, often unsuccessfully, to help.

We don't think most people need years on the couch to come to terms with the way they're reacting to their bosses. But many do need some help. And sometimes all they need is to (1) become more aware of the thoughts and images floating around in their minds, and (2) learn to recognize and restructure some of their irrational thoughts and unhealthy imagery patterns. If they can do this, many of their bad feelings will begin to change.

CHANGING YOUR THOUGHTS AND FEELINGS

This strategy has three steps, each of which requires you to answer an important question. Here's the entire process in brief:

Step	*Question to Answer*
1. Identify the stimulus.	"What does my boss do that upsets me?"
2. Identify your response.	"How do I feel when my boss does this?"
3. Identify and modify your thoughts and mental images.	"What are the thoughts, ideas, and mental images that cause me to feel this way? What can I do to modify my thoughts, ideas, and mental images so I'll feel differently when my boss behaves the same way again?"

We'll take you through each step of the process with examples from two employees, Gail Jenkins and Lew Findley. Both were able to use this strategy so successfully that their problem bosses stopped getting to them.

IDENTIFYING THE STIMULUS

The stimulus, of course, is your boss's behavior. It's what your boss *does* that upsets you or bothers you in some way. So, to get started, think for a moment about what your boss does that upsets or bothers you. Obviously, many of you will be able to construct a rather long laundry list here. That's fine. Write down as many things as you'd like, trying to describe your boss's behavior as specifically and precisely as you can. For example, instead of saying something general like, "He acts like a fool," you might say something like, "He tells off-color jokes to people who are obviously offended by them."

Gail and Lew answered the question in this way:

GAIL: He yells and screams at me when I make a mistake.

LEW: She never shows any interest or enthusiasm for my ideas.

Why don't you take a shot at it? What does *your* boss do that bothers you? Think about it for a moment and record your thoughts on a separate sheet of paper.

IDENTIFYING YOUR RESPONSE

This is easier said than done. A lot of people have a hard time talking about and identifying how they feel. The process becomes even harder because one piece of boss behavior can provoke a large number of very different feelings (e.g., frustration, sadness, self-doubt, anger). So if you experience trouble doing this, that's to be expected. You may find the whole process easier if you sit down with someone else and spend a little time thinking out loud about how you feel.

Gail and Lew did a great job of taking us up on our offer to identify *feelings* provoked by their boss's behavior. In both cases, however, we had to do some pretty good listening to get them to become aware of many of their feelings. (By the time we finished, both were surprised at the wide range of feelings stimulated by a single piece of boss behavior). Here's a summary of what they told us:

GAIL: Well, I'm not really sure how I feel. Let me think for a minute. First of all, it's a fairly total reaction, but it also has some component parts. Upset, for sure! I feel like I want to cry. Then I get mad at myself for behaving like such a baby! I also feel scared, frightened, almost like I want to run away and hide somewhere. I'd also say I feel powerless, you know, powerless to stop him from doing it. Oh yes, also very embarrassed—maybe humiliated is a better word for it—if he does it in front of others. And I guess lastly I'd say intimidated. *Really* intimidated! Oh yes, one more thing. Anger. Yeah, I feel scared and intimidated and all that. But it also makes me very angry.

LEW: Oh, I don't know. Frustrated mainly, I guess. I feel I have all these ideas percolating inside of me, just waiting to come out. But she's clamping a tight lid on top of them. I feel disappointed, too. You know, let down. Maybe deflated is also a good word to capture that feeling. It's like the wind is being taken out of my sails. I think it also causes me to doubt myself, like maybe the ideas I have aren't good enough to get enthusiastic about. Then that makes me question myself as a person. You know, do I have anything good to say, and that sort of thing. I have to admit to feeling angry, too! It really ticks me off when she shows such little interest in what I've got to say! Sometimes I feel like I just want to shake her and say, "Dammit! Pay attention to what I'm saying!"

That's how Gail and Lew explored and identified the range of feelings they were experiencing as a result of their boss's behavior. Now go ahead and give it a try yourself. Just think about the question "How do you *feel* when your boss behaves the way you described above?" If you wrote down more than one item that bothers you about your boss, just focus on one of them here. Record your feelings on the same sheet of paper.

IDENTIFYING AND MODIFYING YOUR THOUGHTS AND MENTAL IMAGES

We said earlier that how people respond is not so much a function of the original stimulus as it is the result of intervening thoughts and mental images. If this is true, the implication is obvious: If you want to change how you feel, you've got to do something to modify these thought processes. In this section we'll offer a number of suggestions about identifying *and* modifying thoughts and mental images.

Get in Touch with What You're Saying to Yourself

A lot of what happens between a stimulus and response is what Albert Ellis called "self-talk." Self-talk is like an internal dialogue or conversation we carry on with ourselves about what's going on and what's happening to us. It's an activity that goes on almost constantly during our waking hours, but we only tend to notice it when we're alone or not concentrating on some other task or activity. We think it also goes on while we're asleep.

However, people are usually unaware of the tremendous amount of mental activity that's going on inside their brains. And, as a result, they're not very clear or conscious about this self-talk, even though these thoughts and images have a dramatic effect on their behavior. In our view, a major step toward personal growth is simply *becoming more aware* of the things we're saying to ourselves on a daily basis. A good way to start is, every now and then, stop what you're doing and say to yourself, "What am I thinking? What thoughts, ideas, and images are floating around in my head?"

Some of Our Self-talk Is Rational, Some Irrational

When people begin to pay closer attention to this fascinating inner world, they discover an area filled with ideas, values, beliefs, attitudes, and opinions. A lot of them have to do with how things are *supposed* to be. Sometimes these thoughts are quite rational and reasonable, sometimes they're not. For example:

- "Since I'm a neat and organized person, my boss *should* be that way, too!"
- "If I don't get what I want, I'll never be able to live with myself again."
- "The only way to get anywhere in this world is to play politics."

This is also an area where people might encounter what Karen Horney once called "the tyranny of the should." Albert Ellis called the same thing "musterbation." Both were simply pointing out that our self-talk is filled with many irrational ideas and unrealistic expectations we impose on ourselves and others. We've had our fair share of *shoulds, musts,* and *have to's*. We'll bet you've had yours too.

Irrational Ideas Often Have to Do with Self-worth

A lot of the irrational ideas people carry around with them have to do with what psychologists call self-concept and feelings of self-worth. They're irrational thoughts—often barely conscious ones—about how "good" a person you basically are. This is why so many people hit the dumps when other people criticize them or put them down. They start off with a shaky self-concept and, partly because of this, completely "buy" the opinion of the person who's putting them down. The result is predictable: They end up feeling bad about themselves. The process goes something like this:

STIMULUS: Your boss criticizes you for something you say or do ("What is wrong with you? That's the most ridiculous thing I've ever heard! How could you be so stupid?")

YOUR THOUGHTS: What kind of person does stupid things? Obviously, a stupid person! How *could* I have been so dumb? I *should* know better. I *shouldn't* say such stupid things and make such stupid mistakes! I wonder what other dumb things I've done I'm *not* aware of. And it's not the first time I've done something stupid. Why I can remember . . .

RESPONSE: Feelings of sadness, worthlessness, and depression.

We know people who do this kind of thing all the time. It's something we called "internalizing" in our chapter "Doing Nothing." People who internalize accept their boss's view of themselves as the "truth" and, because they do, end up feeling miserable. People who do this often pick up the habit early in life, as Lew Findley did:

> I grew up in a family where my stock in trade with my parents went up or down depending on how good my grades were, how clean my room was, how I looked, the kind of friends I had, and so forth. If I did what my folks wanted, things were great! If I didn't, I fell from their good graces. In therapy I learned to see that my parents' affection for me was very conditional. Because I never felt they really cared about me as *me*, I've had a lot of trouble learning to accept myself as I really am. They've both passed away now, but their legacy lives on. Even today, when people criticize me or don't show a lot of interest in me, I have a tendency immediately to assume that *I'm* the problem and that there's something wrong with me.

Irrational Thoughts and Ideas Need to Be Challenged

While we don't have much direct control over our feelings, we do have a fair amount of control over our thoughts and ideas. When we become aware of the presence of irrational ideas, it's important to challenge them and fight them off. It's important to replace the self-denigrating thoughts with self-affirming ones, with what is called "positive self-talk."

Take the example of the person who became depressed after his boss criticized him for being stupid. Imagine how different he'd feel if he were able to challenge his irrational thoughts and replace the negative self-talk with positive self-talk, like:

> Yes, maybe what I did was stupid. But *doing* something stupid and *being* stupid aren't the same. Even very smart and effective people do stupid things from time to time. Besides, my worth as a person isn't tied to a success experience here or a failure experience there. I'm a worthwhile person either way. And what's the big deal about making mistakes anyway? Psychologists agree it's one of the best ways to learn. So maybe I made a mistake. I can get all down in the mouth about it or I can figure out what I can learn from it. That's the sign of an effective person.

If more people could challenge some of their irrational ideas and engage in positive self-talk, there'd be a tremendous reduction in the extent of unhappiness and depression in our world.

There's as Much "Imagery" as There Is "Self-talk" Going On in Our Minds

In addition to the self-talk that goes on in our minds, there's an awful lot of nonverbal stuff happening there too. This nonverbal dimension goes under the name of "mental imagery" or "visualization." A good way to understand what it's like is to think of pictures or scenes that form in your mind's eye.

We see two basic types of imagery—positive and negative.

In terms of impact on our feelings, positive imagery has positive effects and negative imagery has negative effects. We offered an example of negative imagery and its effects when we talked earlier about the anxiety people experience while flying in an airplane. Simply *visualizing* or *imagining* things like crashing planes, people screaming, and raging fires leads inescapably to anxious feelings (and replacing it with positive imagery is usually all it takes to take the anxiety away).

Positive Imagery Can Be Fun as Well as Helpful

Many positive imagery techniques have a fanciful or fantastical quality to them that many employees really like. For example, a couple of years ago we worked with Sheila Isaacs, an executive whose boss—a highly intelligent but emotionally immature woman—was a bullying sort who'd erupt at the slightest provocation. The recipient of many of these volcanic explosions, Sheila would often go home at night shaken and scared.

When we helped Sheila explore the thoughts and images behind her feelings, she recalled how volcanic and verbally abusive her own mother and father had been to her. She also confided to us that she'd been physically abused by both parents as well. Even though seeing this connection between her present and past was helpful, it didn't keep her from becoming extremely upset when her boss exploded. She needed extra assistance.

We offered help in the form of positive imagery. Since Sheila's boss was grossly overweight, we suggested that, every time her boss launched into a harangue, she *visualize* her boss doing it with no clothes on. We suggested that she vividly *imagine* all that flab—the expression Sheila used was "oceans of cellulite"—rippling over her boss's stark naked and not-very-attractive body as she stood there ranting and raving. It worked like a charm. "Now my problem isn't getting upset,'' Sheila confided to us a short time later. "Now I have to bite my lip to keep from cracking up."

Positive Imagery Can Also Be a Prelude to Action

There's a close relationship between imagery and action. It seems like every major sports team these days has a consultant helping athletes with imagery and visualization techniques. Locker rooms around the country have all these 265-pound defensive linemen sitting on tiny little benches with their eyes closed *visualizing* how they're deftly eluding pass blockers and successfully sacking opposing quarterbacks. Does it really work? Who knows for sure? But who's to argue with a guy as big as a refrigerator who says it does?

Positive imagery works with little people as well, often helping them do things they probably wouldn't have done if they hadn't "rehearsed" it so many times in their minds. This happened a couple of years ago when we were trying to help an S.O.B. ("Son of the Boss") who was having a lot of trouble with his father, the founder and sole owner of a family business.

The dad was a tyrant who frequently chewed out his son, as well as other employees, for minor mistakes and transgressions. He ruled his little fiefdom with an iron hand and had everybody in the small company totally intimidated. We laid out a variety of options for the son, including some of the riskier ones we'll be describing a little later in the book. However, the son was a quiet, passive sort and didn't want anything to do with strategies that had risk attached to them. But he did like our imagery suggestion, which went like this: The next time his father started ranting and raving, we asked him to vividly *imagine* himself slowly standing up, looking down at his father, pointing his finger straight in his father's nose, and saying in a loud, firm voice,

Stop! Just sit down and shut up because I'm going to tell you a few things you need to hear. After I do, I'm going to walk into my office, pack up my things, and find a job working for someone who doesn't treat people like dirt. I'm sick and tired of you treating me and everyone else around here like a doormat. You think just because you own this place you can do and say anything and not be held accountable. Well, you can't. The judgment day is at hand and you lose a son as well as an employee!

We then suggested he imagine himself turning on his heels, packing up his things, walking out into a new world he was going to create for himself, and eventually going to work for a boss who trusted, valued, and respected him.

The son really liked our suggestion and visualized the scene almost every day. He told us it made his situation much more tolerable. About a month later the father launched into an attack on the son in the small hallway between the front office and the factory area, in clear view of the clerical staff and about a half-dozen employees who were working at their machines. To his amazement—not to mention that of his father and the employees—the son acted out what he'd been visualizing for the past month. The father was in such a state of shock at seeing his Casper Milquetoast of a son behave so assertively, he was speechless. When the son turned on his heels and walked out, the entire group of employees stopped what they were doing and gave him a standing ovation.

The father left work immediately and went home to tell his wife what had happened. Taken by the story and the courage her son had shown, the wife told her husband some things she had been keeping to herself for years—the biggest message being that he was also in danger of losing *her* unless he cleaned up his act. To make a long story short, they got Dad's attention that day, and the entire family got involved in a counseling effort to work things out.

We're not suggesting here that you engage in visualization techniques as a form of behavior rehearsal, only that visualizing what you *might* say to someone increases the chances you'll eventually say it to them, and say it well. The purpose of this chapter (unlike some later ones) is not to spur you to action, but merely to help you bring some of your thoughts and feelings under control. If it also leads you to do something different, that'll be a bonus.

We explained self-talk and imagery to Gail Jenkins and Lew Findley and then invited them to think about the following questions:

1. "Why do you think you feel the way you do when your boss behaves the way you described earlier? What are the thoughts, ideas, beliefs, and mental images that are causing you to feel the way you do?"
2. "What are some things you can do differently—like modifying irrational beliefs, engaging in more positive self-talk, or using visualization techniques—to help you change your feelings so you won't be so bothered or upset by your boss's behavior?"

It took quite a bit of time for us to get Gail's and Lew's reactions to some of the suggestions we offered. Here's a brief summary of what they came up with in response to these questions and some of our suggestions:

GAIL: My father would yell and scream at us kids whenever one of us made a mistake. I can still remember it vividly! It's possible that every time my boss yells at me I see my father and not my boss. Well, he's not my father, so maybe I can stop "seeing" my father when he rants and raves. That's not going to make me like it any more, but seeing it from this perspective may stop me from becoming so upset. One of the images I have of myself when he yells at me is of a small, weak, powerless person who's defenseless against this powerful, scary person. It's like I can't do anything to defend myself or protect myself. I can think of two imagery techniques that would help me. One is Sheila's technique of imagining him yelling at me without any clothes on. I think he'd actually look pretty funny, even if he were in the middle of a tantrum. Last year I saw him in a swimsuit at the company picnic, and I can still remember chuckling to myself over how funny he looked there. Another is to come up with an image that could give me some power, like having a 'trapdoor' button I could push every time he goes into one of this tirades. I could just imagine myself pushing the button and 'seeing' him disappear into the floor. I don't want him to get hurt or anything. Maybe I could imagine that the floor below is completely filled with marshmallows that he'll land in!

Another thought has to do with feeling embarrassment or humiliation when he yells at me in public. I don't think he has the right to do that. I don't think he *should* do that. And I don't think this is a case of me laying my value system on him. I think my thoughts on this subject are rational and my feelings justified. So, the more I think about that, the more appropriate those feelings seem to me. I'm not so sure I want to change those feelings. Or even the feeling of anger I experience for his acting like a bully and picking on people who have less power and who won't fight back for fear of losing their jobs. I think I'll hold onto those feelings. Who knows, maybe it'll be those feelings that'll motivate me to do something else to deal with my boss.

LEW: I took this job right out of graduate school, where the environment was filled with intellectually curious people who really *valued* ideas. This is a *very* different kind of place. Most of the people here, my boss included, have a *practical* rather than a theoretical orientation. Maybe I've been expecting my boss to be more like my former professors. I guess she has a "right" to be unenthusiastic. I think maybe I've been laying an unrealistic expectation on her.

But I've also been letting her lack of enthusiasm get to me more than it has to. I've doubted the quality of my ideas, and even myself, when she hasn't responded enthusiastically. However, she rarely shows *any* enthusiasm, for my ideas or anyone else's. So it seems more accurate to say that it's not the quality of my ideas that's at issue here as much as it is her capacity—or lack of capacity—to respond enthusiastically to other people. I've been seeing it as a deficit on my part when it's probably more accurate to see it as a deficit on her part. Seen that way, I kind of wonder where that all comes from and I almost feel a little sorry for her. You know, it's kind of sad that she doesn't experience the joy and exhilaration that comes from getting excited with other people.

Some of my other thoughts, of course, have to do with my family background. As you know, I tend to doubt myself when people criticize me—or, worse, ignore me or my ideas. But my self-worth doesn't *have* to go down just because my boss or my parents or anybody else doesn't like my ideas. I see now how irrational it is for me to doubt myself like that. What's important is what I think. There's all kinds of evidence that I'm an intelligent person and a first-rate thinker. Not to brag or anything, but I've come up with some damn good ideas over the years. Now I've come up with some stinkers, too! But whether I come up with good ones or bad ones,

I'm still a worthwhile person. Nobody—except me and my screwed-up thinking—can take that away from me.

That's a brief summary of how Gail and Lew tried to identify the thinking behind their feelings and, more important, began to modify their thoughts and mental images in order to be less bothered by the behavior of their bosses. Why don't you give it a try. Just sit down and ask yourself the questions:

1. "Why do I feel the way I do when my boss behaves the way I described earlier? What are the thoughts, ideas, beliefs, and mental images that cause me to feel this way?"
2. "What are some things I can do differently—like modifying irrational beliefs, engaging in more positive self-talk, or using positive visualization techniques—to help change my feelings so I won't be so bothered by my boss's behavior?"

You can certainly do this alone, but this is one of those exercises it'd probably be better to do with a close friend or co-worker. Just give them the book and ask them to read this chapter. Tell them it's a strategy you think has some implications for you and your situation. Then, after you've both read it, sit down in a quiet, comfortable place and discuss the chapter, the two questions above, and anything else that seems relevant to the topic of changing your thoughts and feelings. Who knows? Maybe you'll end up being much less bothered by the behavior of your boss. Wouldn't that be nice?

10

•••••••••••••••••••••

"MANAGING" YOUR BOSS

In the past few years we've seen a raft of books, magazine articles, audio cassette tapes, and seminars offered on the subject of employees "managing" their bosses. When this subject is discussed, it's often called "upward management," apparently to distinguish it from the "downward" management that bosses do. When we first heard the concept, it sounded like a novel and attractive idea, and a good strategy to include in this book.

To learn as much as we could about this topic, we decided to concentrate our attention on the *real* experts on this subject— employees who are especially adept at "managing" their bosses. We figured if we could learn what they were doing, we could combine their ideas with ours and pass on some good advice to you. The first order of business was to find some "experts." As it turned out, we didn't have to go far.

At the time, we were doing consulting work for a company that was founded and headed by Joe Bartofsky, a fascinating

man, but a very difficult one to work with. He was undoubtedly a genius. Not only had he invented an extraordinarily
clever product, but he also came up with a novel way to
manufacture and market it. But he was also moody, self-
centered, a nonstop talker, and unable to accept criticism. In
five years he had gone through a succession of vice-presidents who reported directly to him. At a roast held in his
honor one of his friends commented, "Turnover among vice-
presidents is so high over at Joe's place they're installing
revolving doors in the executive suite."

However, in the midst of all this turmoil was an anchor of
stability. Joe's executive secretary for the past twelve years,
Stella Dalworthy. While everyone else struggled with Joe,
Stella worked extremely well with him. One day one of us
said to the other, "Stella is definitely doing something right.
We've got to learn her secret. While Joe intimidates the hell
out of everybody else, she's got him eating out of her hand."
We decided to take her to lunch.

We didn't tell her what we were up to when we invited
her, figuring we'd surprise her when we got to the restaurant.
So, as soon as we sat down in the quietest corner, we said:

"Okay, Stella, what's your secret? Everybody who
works for Joe struggles with him. He's chewed up more
vice-presidents than you can shake a stick at. Yet, the two
of you seem to get along like Bonnie and Clyde. In fact,
one employee we talked to said you play Joe like a fiddle.
Now, in our opinion, this is no accident. We think you're
doing something to make it happen. And we'd like to know
what it is."

The waiter came, we ordered our food, and she began,
"Well, it's really not all that complicated."

"That's fine. We'd like to hear it anyway."

"Well," she started, "there are lots and lots of employees who aren't very good at handling their bosses. And
because they aren't, it causes them a lot of needless frustration and gets them into a lot of unnecessary trouble. Just look

at all the people who've been in and out of here in the past five years. I mean, we brought in some pretty impressive people, right? But I'll tell you something—for a bunch of smart people, it seems to me they were dumb when it came to handling Joe. You know what I mean?''

We said we weren't quite sure and asked her to go on.

''Well,'' she continued, ''Joe's not a very complicated person and it doesn't take a genius to figure him out. But, in my opinion, none of these hotshots that've come and gone even tried to understand Joe the Person. They were so preoccupied with themselves or trying to impress Joe the Big Boss that they didn't know what he was like as a human being. They didn't know what he needed, what he wanted, where he needed help, what he believed in—that sort of thing. I mean, how could they have a decent relationship with him if they didn't really know him?''

''Makes a lot of sense to us,'' we said. ''Go on.''

''So, anyway, I think the reason I have such a good relationship with Joe is because I know him so well. With the possible exception of Dorothea—you know, his wife—I know him better than anyone in the world. Actually, because I see him in such a different setting, in some ways I know him even better than she does. I know his strong and weak points. I know what bugs him. I know what gets his juices flowing. I know his doubts and insecurities. I know his values and his goals. I know him *very* well. So that's my secret. Pretty complicated stuff, huh?'' she said with an engaging smile.

One of us decided to read back what she said: ''Stella, the way you're talking here Joe is almost like a big area of land that you've surveyed and mapped out in detail. Because other people—like these vice-presidents you're talking about—don't have a very good 'map' of the area, they're always getting lost or running into unforeseen problems. But because you know the territory so well, you know how to get around.''

''Exactly!'' she interjected. ''Because I know him so well, I know what to do—and I guess also what not to do—to make things work smoothly. I guess you could say I give him what he *wants*. But I also think I give him what he *needs*, and that's much more important.''

She paused to collect her thoughts and one of us said, "So you're saying that your 'secret' to handling Joe is understanding who he is as a person, knowing in detail what he wants and needs, and basically giving it to him. Is that it?''

"Yeah, exactly," she said, and then paused for a moment. "Well, not *exactly*. I mean, I'm not a doormat or a slave or anything like that. I won't let him abuse me or mistreat me in any way. And he doesn't. Do you know why?''

"We could venture a guess or two, but no, not really," we said, waiting for what she was about to say.

"Because he needs me," she said. "Because I meet some of his basic *needs*. I've become very important to him to have around. And I'm not just talking about being a confidante or a supportive person either, although I do those things as well. But, in addition, I also happen to do some things very well—like writing, time management, and handling organizational detail—that he's not so hot at.'' She leaned over as if to tell us a secret, "Now if you mention this to anyone I'll scratch your eyes out, but do you *really* think Joe's been responsible for writing all those letters and articles that've come out of his office the past few years? No way! Joe is so self-conscious about his writing it takes him two hours just to write the alphabet. All I do is shore him up in some areas where he's weak. It makes him function far more effectively than he could on his own. If I were to leave tomorrow, Joe'd be up the creek without a paddle. I know that and he knows that. And because he knows that, he treats me well.''

"So what you're saying is that you've become indispensable to him. And because he knows that and doesn't want to lose you, he treats you well," one of us said.

"You got it!" she smiled. "But it's not like I have him over the barrel or anything. You see, I need Joe too. When I started working for him years ago, I said to myself, 'Joe's got a lot of potential. If he goes places, I go places.' And since I don't have his inventive mind and his total devotion to work, I'm not going to head up a company like this. But because I've helped Joe accomplish what he's set out to do, it's paid off very well for me. I make at least five thousand dollars more a year than any executive secretary in this town—and that includes some of my friends who work for presidents of companies that are a lot bigger than this one. I also have equity in this company. Whenever I need to take a personal day, I can do it. All I have to do is make sure I get a 'temp.' Plus, Hal and I have become personal friends with Joe and Dorothea. Last year they took us to the Caribbean for our twenty-fifth anniversary. So, yeah, you could say I've been very good for Joe. But you could also say Joe's been very good for me!''

We decided to challenge her just a bit. "Stella, what you've said makes an awful lot of sense. But is it really true that something so simple can work so well? I mean, all we've heard for the last couple of months is how difficult a person Joe is to work for. What do you have to say to that?''

"Look," she said, "Joe is a hard guy to live with. I'm not going to deny that. But who isn't? I'm no piece of cake. Just ask Hal. I'll bet you two wouldn't exactly be beds of roses either.''

"Well, actually," we said, "we're both extremely easy people to live with.''

"Sure!" she countered.

We were all guffawing when the waiter came with the check. After a couple of unsuccessful attempts to get Stella to pick up the tab, we paid and drove her back to work.

After our talk with Stella, we interviewed a number of other employees who were also good at handling their bosses (by the way, they were mostly women with male bosses). What they told us, with a few variations here and there, was very similar to what Stella had to say. Compared to some of the theoretical stuff we'd read in some books and articles on the subject, those interviews really drove home the point that, simply by paying attention to a few concepts and principles, it's very possible to learn how to manage your boss.

WHAT "MANAGING" YOUR BOSS MEANS

"Managing" your boss seems to break down into two major components:

1. Figuring out what bosses want and need.
2. Giving bosses some of what they want and need, without compromising yourself or your integrity.

Let's take a closer look at both.

Figuring Out What Bosses Want and Need

Most employees don't know nearly as much about their bosses as they think. When employees take a new job, their attention is so focused on *what* they'll be doing (or some other aspect of the *job*) that they don't pay much attention to *who* they'll be working for. Even after taking a job, though, most employees don't really get to know their bosses. And employees who think they know their bosses well often know only the tip of the iceberg. But it doesn't have to be that way.

The first step is getting to know your boss much better than you currently do. Basically, it means doing some analytical thinking about your boss, and it means listening to your boss in a way you haven't done before. This won't be virgin territory because we talked about some of it in our chapter, "Taking a Look at Your Boss." (You may even want to briefly review that chapter as you're working your way through this one.)

To figure out what your boss wants and needs, we think it's useful to look at your boss from a number of different perspectives. For example, your boss's:

- overall operating style
- strengths and weaknesses
- life and career goals
- needs
- interests
- values

We'll talk briefly about each area below and offer a few suggestions to stimulate your thinking.

OVERALL OPERATING STYLE

In our view, everybody has an overall operating style that's a composite of all their individual characteristics. So step back and take a big picture look at your boss. For example, is your boss:

- outgoing and personable or shy and reserved?
- hardnosed and feisty or a "softy" who's afraid of conflict?
- unflappable and cool under fire or easily upset and crisis-prone?
- ambitious and goal-oriented or a sort of lazy pleasure seeker?
- authentic and genuine or artificial and phony?
- showy and a little arrogant or self-effacing and humble?
- fast-and-loose and a little sleazy or trustworthy?
- sophisticated and refined or socially clumsy and rough around the edges?
- a giver or a taker?
- evaluative and intolerant or accepting and tolerant?
- overcontrolling or undercontrolling?
- enthusiastic and optimistic or lethargic and depressed?
- formal and stiff or casual and very informal?

STRENGTHS AND WEAKNESSES

Everybody's got some of both. You do. We do. Your boss does. To begin, just get out a sheet of paper and draw a line down the middle. On the top left side of the page write, "Strengths." On top of the right side write "Weaknesses" (or, if you'd prefer, "Areas Needing Improvement"). Then with a pen in your hand to jot down your thoughts, ask yourself these questions:

- What are his strong points? His weak points?
- What does she do well? Not very well?
- What are some of his special gifts and talents? His fatal flaws?
- What are some things I especially like, admire, and respect about her as a boss? In what ways would she have to improve to be a better boss to me?
- What does his boss see as his strengths? His weaknesses?
- What does she think are her strong points? Her weak points?

Let your mind wander freely as you think about each of these questions. Jot down all your thoughts and ideas, even if they seem trivial and obvious. Take a break from this task and come back to it again with a fresh perspective later. You may be surprised at how much you know about your boss that you didn't think you knew. After you finish your first-draft thinking, take a look at the right-hand side of the page. Ask yourself the questions:

- How could I help my boss correct some of these deficiencies?
- What could I do to help shore her up in some of her weaker areas?
- What are some unobtrusive things (that is, so he doesn't even know I'm doing them) I could do to assist him where he really could use some help?

If your mind is not flowing as freely with ideas as you'd like, don't hesitate to ask a close friend or co-worker to help.

Because they're not as close to the situation as you are, they may be able to come up with some fairly obvious ideas that you couldn't come up with on your own.

LIFE AND CAREER GOALS

The dictionary definition of a goal is "an object or end that one strives to attain." Like strengths and weaknesses, everybody has goals. However, while some people are very clear about what they're shooting for, others have very hazy or unclear goals. When people have clear goals, it's like they have a North Star to guide them. It's always out there, reminding them of where they're going.

The best way to find out about peoples' goals is to ask them directly, and then be a good listener when they start to talk. Listening is especially important in this context because life goals are a difficult subject to talk about clearly. A good listener can really help somebody think out loud about this topic.

We've talked briefly about the subject of listening in some earlier chapters, and we'll cover it in depth in our next chapter. For the moment, though, just imagine walking up to your boss someday and saying:

> I've been thinking lately about the subject of life and career goals and how important they are to people. One day soon, when we both have bit of extra time, I'd very much like to sit down and hear you talk about your career goals and some of your broader life goals. How do you feel about doing that?

NEEDS

We're not talking about physical needs here (like the need for food or drink) but psychological and emotional needs. All people have some basic needs, like the need to be treated with dignity and respect or the need to feel cared for by significant other people in their lives. But we also have in-

dividual or special needs that make us different from other
people.

We think of needs as a bit like driving forces in our lives.
They propel us to do things we wouldn't do if we didn't have
the need. For example, if your sense of emotional well-being
is based on having a job that pays you lots of money, then
you have a *need* (as opposed to a preference) for a high-
income job. If your sense of self-worth doesn't require making a lot of money, you don't have that need. It's that simple.

Needs become important mainly when they're not met.
When a need is unsatisfied, people feel like they're lacking
something that's important to them. Compared to *wants* or
preferences, needs seem necessary to our sense of psychological well-being. For example, let's say one of your needs
is to solve challenging problems but that need is not currently
being met by your job. If it's not, you're just not going to
feel right about yourself and how things are going for you.

Your boss has needs, too, even though it's often a little
harder to identify them than it is your boss's strengths and
weaknesses. Take the common boss need for *status*. Bosses
demonstrate this need in many ways:

• They may appear as if they're really in charge of things
  when their bosses and visting dignitaries come around the
  office.
• They may be self-conscious about their lack of formal ed-
  ucation and compensate for it by trying to impress people
  with their large vocabularies.
• They may want to play the role of "patriarch of the office
  family" even though they're much younger than many of
  the people who report to them.

To try to get a better handle on what your boss's needs
are, ask yourself the following questions:

• What does he *need* in order to feel good about himself?
• What are some of the driving forces in her life?

• What is it, when it's lacking, that tends to throw him into a funk or get him all upset?

This is another one of those areas where talking with someone else might pay off. Another person who knows your boss well may be able to identify a couple of your boss's needs you might've completely overlooked.

INTERESTS

Interests are the things people like to do, the activities they tend to gravitate toward. Interests are the kinds of things people often do in their spare time, the things that provide enjoyment, relaxation, and pleasure. It's an area where people vary immensely. Take just a few examples, such as:

• Music—There's at least country, rock, opera, classical, jazz, folk, and ethnic.
• Sports—There's group and individual, participant and spectator, contact and noncontact sports.
• Hobbies—People play chess, backgammon, camp, hike, read poetry, write short stories, paint, and do sculpture. They fly, hang glide, surf, cook, scuba dive, roller skate, bowl, ski, sew, dance, and collect all kinds of things.
• Health and Physical Fitness—People run, swim, bike, lift weights, do aerobic dancing, and care about nutrition and diet.

What are some of your boss's major interests?

VALUES

Values are the things that are important to people, the stuff they believe in and stand for. Values are what people donate their time (through volunteer work) and money to. Values are so important to people they're often willing to fight for them. (That's one of the reasons why discussions of religion and politics often end up in bitter disagreements.) If you want to get a better fix on your boss's values, spend a little time thinking about:

- philosophy and religion
- family and ethnicity
- politics and social issues

Then ask yourself questions like:

- What does my boss really believe in and stand for?
- What causes or groups does he donate time and money to?
- What causes or groups really upset her or make her mad?
- How important is family and ethnic background to him?
- What groups is she a member of? Which would she never join?

It'll take time to think about all the areas we've mentioned here, like your boss's overall operating style, strengths and weaknesses, life and career goals, interests, and values. But, once you do, you'll have completed the first step in managing your boss, which is figuring out what your boss wants and needs.

Giving Bosses Some of What They Want and Need

Let's be absolutely clear on one thing here—we're not saying that employees should give their bosses *everything* they want and need (or even most of it). What we are saying is this: If you want to manage your boss effectively, you've got to be prepared to give *something*. And our recommendation is you give them something that: (a) is going to be relatively easy for you to provide, and (b) doesn't compromise you or your integrity in any way.

When it comes to what's easy to provide, the list of potential things is almost infinite. It seems like there're a million *small* things employees can do for their bosses. We suggest you experiment with various ways to accommodate to some of your boss's characteristics, meet some of your boss's needs, and strengthen some of your boss's weak spots. For example:

If Your Boss . . .	*Then . . .*
. . . likes to appear as if he's really in charge when visiting dignitaries and big bosses come around the shop . . .	. . . respectfully refer to him as "Mr. Brown" at those times.
. . . is disorganized and a poor manager of time . . .	. . . suggest a book or seminar on time management. Ask what you can do to help her become more effective. Start doing small things on your own to help her.
. . . is self-conscious about his lack of formal education and compensates by trying to impress people with his large vocabulary . . .	. . . every now and then ask him the meaning of a big word. Buy him one of those "Page-A-Day" vocabulary-builder calendars for Christmas.
. . . has great ideas, but has trouble setting them down in writing . . .	. . . volunteer to help polish up ideas she's expressed verbally. Suggest that the two of you have a tape-recording session before she starts writing. Ask her what you can do to help in this area.

If Your Boss . . .   *Then . . .*

. . . is a S.O.B.   . . . don't challenge him
(remember, that's "Son of   when he makes a
the Boss") who likes to   reference to employees as
play the role of   members of the "family."
"patriarch" of the   Every now and then ask
company . . .   him how he feels about
                                  being the head of the
                                  company, and then listen
                                  to what he has to say.

. . . is overweight,   . . . invite her to lunch at
smokes like a chimney,   your health club (ask
and never exercises . . .   several of your attractive
                                  male friends to drop by to
                                  say "Hi"). Ask her what
                                  you could do to help her
                                  lead a healthier, less
                                  stressful life style.

THE BENEFITS OF "BOSS MANAGEMENT"

We've talked about what it is and how to go about it, now let's look at the benefits of successful "boss management":

Your Boss Will Benefit

Instead of having an adversary as an employee, your boss is going to have more of an ally and supporter. It's going to make your boss feel more comfortable and relaxed. It's also going to make your boss more effective as a boss, because you'll be helping out in areas where your boss needs help. Employees who manage their bosses well can turn normally ineffective bosses into pretty effective ones. And because they're functioning more effectively, these bosses are more likely to achieve some of their important life and career goals.

The conclusion is inescapable: Bosses who are managed well benefit greatly.

The *Relationship* between You and Your Boss Will Improve

As you'll recall from an earlier chapter, we think a relationship between two people is a bit like a living organism—it's got vital signs you can look at to see how healthy it is. For us the vital signs of a relationship are trust, respect, affection, and confidence. (Use the acronym TRAC to help remember them.) In relationships where people give each other low TRAC ratings, both people feel frustrated and dissatisfied. The higher the TRAC ratings people give each other, obviously, the more satisfying and productive the relationship is.

If you do the kind of thing we've described in this chapter, we predict your boss's TRAC ratings of you will go up, maybe even dramatically. And we wouldn't be surprised if your ratings of your boss go up as well.

You'll Benefit

You're not just doing this "managing" stuff to benefit your boss and your relationship with your boss. You're also doing it for you. Here are some of the benefits you can expect:

- Your boss will like you better.
- Your performance ratings will go up.
- You'll experience less of the stress that comes from struggling every day with a boss you're not getting along with.
- You'll get more of what you want from your boss (e.g., you're more likely to be considered positively when raises, bonuses, and promotions come around).
- You can expect some "unexpected" benefits. Since bosses have a lot of discretionary authority, they can give the worst jobs to the employees they're struggling with and the most attractive ones to employees who manage them well.

IS IT "MANAGING" OR IS IT "MANIPULATING" YOUR BOSS?

This is a good question and one a lot of people have asked us. In discussing it with people, we've discovered something very interesting: When bosses do the kinds of things we've talked about in this chapter to employees, it's called "managing." But when employees do the same kind of thing to their bosses, it comes across as "manipulating."

We're not sure why this is true. So far, our best answer is that people are used to the idea of bosses *doing something to* employees, but not vice versa. Books on management recommend a wide variety of techniques and strategies bosses should consider using to handle their employees. But similar suggestions for employees often come across as "how to stay one step ahead of your boss."

We don't see what we've described in this chapter as manipulation. Not at all. We see it as skillful interpersonal functioning. But it really doesn't matter a whole lot what you call it, managing or manipulating. What's important is its potential to improve things between you and your boss.

Another common reservation people have about managing bosses is that it sounds like "brown nosing." Is what we're describing here just fancy window dressing for an attempt to curry the favor or win the approval of bosses?

The answer depends on you. Clearly, if your primary motivation is to win your boss's favor, then doing what we're describing here would help you achieve that goal. However, it's definitely not brown nosing if:

- Your primary goal is a more effective working relationship with your boss.
- You realize that to achieve this goal you have as much responsibility to "manage" the relationship as your boss does.

• You expect both you and your boss to benefit from your efforts.

We'd like to end this chapter by admitting that managing your boss is a strategy that some people like a lot more than others. In general, the employees who like this strategy are people who've had a history of getting along fairly well with authority figures (parents, teachers, principals, etc.) by being subtle, tactful, and interpersonally adept. In fact, when we describe it to people like this, many of them feel they've been using it already, at least in part.

On the other hand, employees with a history of locking horns with authority figures generally don't like this strategy as much. It tends to run against the grain of their personalities. They're the ones who tend to see the strategy as somewhat phony and manipulative.

If you fall into this latter group, here's a thought. Maybe maintaining your hard-nosed attitude toward these authority figures has been worth all the friction you've experienced. You've got to decide that. *But*, maybe it might be worth your while to try the approach we've outlined here. Maybe this strategy will let you hang on to your sense of independence *and* avoid the bumps and bruises you normally get from struggling with the powers that be.

11

••••••••••••••••••••••

TALKING TO YOUR BOSS
ONE ON ONE

Years ago, when we got interested in the topic of problem
bosses, we thought talking to your boss one on one
would make up an entire book. We knew that most of the
problems people had with each other resulted from their not
sitting down with each other to talk about their problems. So
all we had to do was teach employees how to have an effective "talk session" with their problem bosses, and then things
would get a lot better. Right?

Well, it didn't take long for us to realize how unrealistic
a notion that was. Yes, for *some* employees and *some* problem bosses, sitting down to talk one on one made a lot of
sense. But for many more, the strategy was not only not
feasible, but actually rather dangerous. That is, for lots of
employees, talking to their bosses one on one would make
things *worse*, not better.

So in this chapter we want to teach you how to sit down
with your boss one on one to talk about how the two of you
can improve your relationship, and we also want to help you

decide whether or not your boss is a good candidate for this strategy.

We've gone into considerable depth in this chapter because this strategy is hard to do effectively. But if you pull it off, it can make a very positive difference in the quality of your relationship with your boss. And we want to give you as much help as we can.

IS THIS STRATEGY RIGHT FOR YOU?

Clearly, sitting down to talk one on one with your boss is not a strategy that all employees with problem bosses should use. There are just too many ways for things to go wrong. But how do you decide if this strategy is right for you and your boss?

In this section we'll show you how to "qualify" your boss for this strategy. We'll ask you to think about where your boss stands on six important traits in order to decide if he or she is a good candidate or a poor candidate for this particular strategy:

1. taking criticism
2. problem solving
3. vindictiveness
4. caring
5. honesty
6. ability to listen

Taking Criticism

Some people take criticism—especially the constructive kind—reasonably well. They don't get defensive or upset. They listen to what you have to say about them, think about it, and even take some of it to heart. Some people, on the other hand, don't take criticism so well. They're ultrasensitive to even the most harmless negative comment. They get hurt, upset, or all bent out of shape, and you end up wishing you'd never made the comment in the first place.

The key question here, of course, is how well *your* boss takes criticism. For example, your boss may be like Carleton Farthwell—a fellow in his late forties who runs a regional office for a national management consulting firm.

Carleton's an easygoing guy who never seems to get unduly upset over anything. He's the kind of boss who's comfortable with having you walk into his office and talk about problems. In the last several months, Carleton has even started inviting people to sit down with him in the conference room and talk about their ideas for improving things in the office. One employee recently said about Carleton, "You know, the guy is sincere about wanting to hear what we have to say, even when it's stuff that's not so positive about him."

When it comes to taking criticism, maybe your boss is like Carleton, and maybe not. Maybe your boss is more like Don Flouth, a foreman in an injection-moulding shop in a Chicago suburb. Here's what one of the toolmakers who works for Don told us about him.

What can I tell you? He's touchy. I mean you can't say *anything* critical to him without him getting his nose bent out of joint. He takes any kind of negative comment as a personal insult. I can't talk to the guy unless I'm willing to sugarcoat everything that's even a little critical of him. Frankly, talking to Don is a big waste of time.

Carleton and Don are pretty much polar opposites when it comes to taking criticism. How would you assess your boss on this important boss trait?

Problem Solving

Some bosses are problem solvers, and some aren't. Problem-solving bosses are fairly easy to spot:

- They don't waffle on decisions. They'll do *something*, even if it's wrong.
- They don't always say, "It's out of my hands," when you bring an important problem to their attention. They believe they can do something to improve most bad situations, and they at least give it a try.
- They don't bury their heads in the sand when problems come along. They attack problems. They don't ignore them and hope they'll go away.
- They are willing to rock the boat, to take a risk, if necessary, to solve an important problem.

Think about it for a moment. How much of a problem solver is your boss?

Vindictiveness

Unfortunately, there are quite a few vindictive bosses out there. These are the bosses who seek revenge on people they feel have "wronged" them. Employees who work for bosses like these run real risks in giving them honest, straightforward feedback. If vindictive bosses don't like what they hear, they can make things *very* unpleasant.

Russ Whitkins is a vindictive boss. Russ is now almost seventy, but he's more robust and virile than many men thirty years his junior. He's been the executive director of a trade association ever since it was formed shortly after World War II. Russ rules his employees with an iron hand. He demands total loyalty from his staff, and whenever he doesn't get it, "zap!" the person is gone.

Over the years, several of Russ's employees have tried to talk to him about his operating style as a manager. Each attempt has been a disaster. Just recently one of the more assertive people on his staff, Carol Matterly, a woman who's worked for him for over ten years, met with Russ. In the meeting Carol told Russ she was bothered by the way he treated people on the staff. Later Carol told us that Russ seemed to take some of the things she'd said to heart. But the next day, after sleeping on it, Russ came in and summarily fired Carol. His last words were:

> Carol, I've thought about everything you've said yesterday. I don't agree with your assessment of me, and I can't permit that kind of insubordination in this office. I'm sorry, but we're going to have to part company.

Now think of your situation. Where does your boss stand on this not-very-pleasant trait of vindictiveness?

Caring

For us, caring simply means having a genuine concern for the well-being of other people, especially people you spend a lot of time with. Interestingly enough, as critical as we are of them, we've run into a lot of *very* caring bosses over the years. A surprising number of them, many of whom at first seem like pretty gruff characters, want to do right by their employees. These bosses will go to bat for their employees to get them raises, protect them from unfair treatment from higher-ups, get them extra time off during times of personal crisis, and so on.

If you have a caring boss, there's no guarantee that talking to him or her one on one is going to make things better. But your chances will be significantly better than if you have an uncaring boss—a boss who doesn't really give a hoot about your needs, your concerns, and your well-being.

To help decide if you have a caring boss or not, you might ask yourself these questions:

IS MY BOSS A THOUGHTFUL PERSON?

Do you have the kind of boss who remembers things that are important to you, even though they're not necessarily that important from your boss's perspective? For example, caring bosses remember salary reviews, anniversary dates, and performance reviews with their employees. Uncaring bosses always seem to forget these kinds of things.

IS MY BOSS A COMPASSIONATE PERSON?

When you or other employees have experienced pressing personal problems—like a death in the family, a divorce, or the prolonged illness of a spouse or a child—how has your boss acted? Has she shown her compassion by occasionally asking about the problem in a sensitive way, or even arranging for extra time off? Or has she largely ignored the problem and maybe even gotten annoyed that your "personal problems" were interfering with your work performance?

WILL MY BOSS STICK UP FOR ME WHEN IT COUNTS?

Caring bosses are willing to go to bat for you when you need them to. Let's say you've had some heavy medical expenses that aren't normally covered by the company's insurance plan. But you know an appeal to a certain vice-president would probably get the extra money you need. Do you have the kind of boss who will go directly to that vice-president (without a lot of prompting) for you?

What kind of marks would you give your boss on the trait of caring?

Honesty

Honesty is an important trait for any boss to have, but it's especially important if you're thinking about using this strategy. In this section we'll point out some negative—even catastrophic—consequences of talking one on one to a dishonest boss. Then we'll suggest ways you can tell where your boss stands on this trait.

Let's start with the negative consequences. Here are a few of the bad things that can happen when employees talk frankly and candidly to bosses who're not very honest:

THEY MAY REVEAL CONFIDENCES

These kinds of bosses won't hesitate to reveal things you've said in confidence if they think it'll do them some good— even if it could end up hurting you. For example, imagine that while talking to your boss you make a complaint about a company vice-president you don't like and who doesn't particularly like you. A dishonest boss who wanted to curry favor with that vice-president might just go to him and seal your doom by revealing what you said.

THEY'LL ENTICE YOU INTO SAYING
SOMETHING YOU'LL REGRET LATER

A lot of dishonest bosses are fairly smooth characters. They can lull you into thinking you're opening up to a warm, sympathetic, and understanding person, one you should speak to freely. But a month or two down the line an offhand remark you made can come back to haunt you. Maybe you told your boss you don't really care that much about the kind of car you drive—then when company cars get assigned to the sales force, you end up with a piece of junk.

THEY USE WHAT YOU'VE SAID
TO HURT OTHER PEOPLE

As we've said, dishonest bosses don't always respect things you've said in confidence. Not only will they use things you've said against you, they'll also use what you've said about other people if it suits their purposes. In talking to your boss you might point out that a fellow worker needs professional help with a drug or alcohol problem. A dishonest boss might feign concern over this employee's well-being, but then use your information to get the person fired.

How do you tell if your boss is a dishonest person? At this point you may already have a good idea. But if you're not sure, here are a few brief descriptions of some of the more common types of dishonest bosses we've run into over the years:

- *The Slick (a.k.a. the Smooth Talker)*. Slicks are very good talkers who seem very sincere, and people who first meet them find it easy to trust them. Unfortunately, however, slicks are not all they seem. After you get to know them a bit, your trust and liking for them drops off quickly. You end up seeing them as self-centered people who promise almost anything to get what they want but who rarely follow through on their promises.
- *The Sycophant*. Watch out for this one. This is the kind of boss whose loyalties, devotions, and allegiances blow in the same direction as the wind. Bosses like these have just about no sense of integrity. One day you can be on the top of the heap with them because the big bosses in the company think you're the greatest thing since drip-dry shirts. But should you fall out of favor with these big shots, your sycophantic boss will forget you ever existed.
- *The Liar*. Some bosses, like some people, are chronic liars. Psychologists call them pathological liars. They'll lie about almost anything from trivial things (like when they came back from lunch) to very important things (like when they put in for your annual raise). Exactly why these people lie so much is a bit of a mystery. The important thing to remember is that their lies can often cause you big problems. If you start to catch your boss in a series of lies—no matter how harmless they might seem—watch out.

Does your boss resemble any of these three bosses, or in any other way show dishonest tendencies?

Ability to Listen

A great deal of what we do professionally involves teaching people how to listen more effectively. Unfortunately, we've found that most bosses, like most people, are poor listeners. Nobody's ever taught them how to keep quiet, pay attention, and hear what another person (especially an employee) is trying to say.

For this strategy to work, it's important that your boss be a reasonably good listener. If not, you'll find the experience frustrating and a waste of time. We've discovered some clues for gauging how good a listener your boss it.

INTERRUPTING

Does your boss frequently cut you off in mid-sentence? Does she often talk right over you when you're trying to express an important idea or thought? Does she ask another question when you're right in the middle of answering the first one?

BAD BODY LANGUAGE

There are three kinds of body language people use when listening—good, bad, and horrible. People who use good body language look you in the eye when you're talking; nod to encourage you to talk more; and use their facial muscles to express interest or otherwise indicate they're staying with you. People who use bad body language never really look you in the eye, are so stone faced or impassive that you're not sure they're still alive, or do distracting things like glancing at their watches or gazing out the window. People who use horrible body language roll their eyes to the ceiling in disbelief when they think you've said something stupid, shake their heads vigorously back and forth when they disagree with you, or throw their hands down in disgust when you say something they find threatening.

NONSTOP TALKING

It's easy to spot a nonstop talker—they *never* shut up. To use an old country expression, it seems like they're "bumpin' their gums" about something almost all the time. For them, listening is pretty much out of the question because they don't stop talking long enough to give anybody else a chance to say anything.

Being as objective as you can, how good—or bad—a listener would you say your boss is?

Does Your Boss Qualify for One on One?

Up to this point you've had a chance to get familiar with each of the six traits and to think about how your boss stacks up on each of them. Now we'd like you to "grade" your boss on each of the traits. You can give your boss a letter grade from A to F on each one. An A means your boss is excellent, as far as that particular trait is concerned. An F, of course, means the opposite—that your boss is awful as far as that trait is concerned. Go ahead and take a minute or two to grade your bosses on:

- taking criticism
- problem solving
- vindictiveness
- caring
- honesty
- ability to listen

What kind of report card does your boss bring home? Overall, does your boss look like a good candidate for this strategy, or are you finding yourself thinking, "There's no way I'm going to sit down to talk to that person!" (Just a word of caution. If you gave your boss less than a C on any one of the traits, we think there's little chance you'll be able to have a successful meeting.)

By the way, it might be a good idea for you to also grade

yourself on these traits. It's quite possible that *neither* your boss nor you are suited to holding an effective face-to-face meeting with each other.

MEETING WITH YOUR BOSS ONE ON ONE

Before we talk about *how* to meet with your boss, let's talk a little about the *purpose* of the meeting you're about to have. In our view, the purpose is reasonably straightforward: It's to talk about how the two of you can improve your working relationship. Stated a little more specifically, it's for the two of you to discuss and agree on ways you can both make each other's jobs *less frustrating* and *more satisfying*.

To help you achieve this purpose we'll be covering four important topics:

1. preparing for the meeting
2. asking your boss to meet with you
3. conducting an effective meeting
4. following up on the meeting

Preparing for the Meeting

One of the most important things you can do to prepare for this meeting—and to prepare for a lot of other important encounters with people—is to learn how to be a better listener. "Be a better listener?" you may be saying. "How about my boss? That's the person who needs to be a better listener, not me." Maybe so. But if you want to get your boss to listen to you—to really hear what you have to say—you're probably going to have to listen to your boss first. Maybe it's not right, maybe it's not fair, but it's reality.

We define listening as "helping another person to think out loud." In our opinion, being a good listener is absolutely essential if you're going to be an effective problem solver, especially when the problems have to do with how people are getting along with each other. We've already briefly exposed you to listening skills in previous chapters. But in this section, we'll go into much more depth. We'll introduce you to four basic skills that we teach people in our seminars and consulting work. These skills are straightforward and easy to understand, but they're not so easy to put into practice. But if you work at it, we think mastering these listening skills can change your life. They'll not only help you with your boss—but also with every one of your important relationships.

The four skills are:

1. attending
2. asking thought-provoking questions
3. encouraging
4. reading back

Here we'll talk about the skills one at a time. Later on we'll show you how to put them together when you talk with your boss.

ATTENDING

A little earlier in the chapter we talked about the body language people use when they listen. Well, *attending* is just another term for body language. It means the way you use your body, from the waist up, to show that you're following and interested in what another person is saying.

The important question here, of course, is how good an attender are *you*? When you listen to people, do you often use the bad body language we talked about earlier—not looking the other person in the eye, appearing stone faced and impassive, and doing distracting things like glancing at your watch or gazing out the window? And do you sometimes use the *horrible* body language we talked about? When someone says something you disagree with or find threatening, do you roll your eyes to the ceiling in disbelief? Do you shake your head vigorously back and forth? Do you throw your hands down in disgust?

If you're not a naturally good attender, then you'll have to work at it if you want to become a good listener. You're going to have to practice looking people in the eye when they talk to you. You're going to have to practice nodding to encourage the other person to keep talking. You're going to have to practice using your rich array of facial muscles to smile, to wrinkle your forehead, and to send out signs that you're listening and interested in what the person is saying

One of the best ways to find out how good an attender you are is to see yourself on videotape while listening to another person. If you can't do this, ask a friend to give you some candid feedback on your attending skills, that is, on your body language. Then practice, practice, practice until being a good attender becomes second nature to you.

ASKING THOUGHT-PROVOKING QUESTIONS
Most people are not particularly good question askers. If we're not careful, we also catch ourselves asking questions that do a lousy job of getting people to talk:

- "Do you like your boss?"
- "Is the weather always like this in August?"
- "Do you live in the suburbs or right downtown?"
- "Is the food good in this restaurant?"

We think a better kind of question to ask is a thought-provoking question. Thought-provoking questions have a couple of distinctive characteristics: They invite another person to (1) think out loud on a topic that (2) the person would really like to talk about. For example, let's assume that you're married. Imagine that your spouse came to you one day and said:

You know, dear, I've been thinking lately. We've been together for quite a while now. We have a pretty solid relationship, but I think it could stand some improvement. So I'd like to ask you an important question. After I ask it, I want to really listen to what you have to say. Here's the question. "What can I do to make our relationship a lot less frustrating and a lot more satisfying for you?

Or imagine that your boss walked up to you one day and said something similar:

Pat, you've been working for me for two years now. I think I'm a good boss, but I also think there are a bunch of ways I could probably improve. In a second, I'd like to ask you a question. After I ask it, I'd like you to be as honest with me as possible. I'll try to be the best listener I can. Okay, here's the question: "What can I do to make your job less frustrating and a lot more satisfying?"

We think you'd find these two questions very thought-provoking. They both invited you to think out loud and said they really wanted to hear what you had to say. And, more importantly, both picked a topic that you should be interested in talking about—what each of them could do to make you more satisfied and less frustrated. There aren't many spouses and employees who wouldn't love to take a crack at answering both those questions.

When you eventually meet with your boss, you'll find that these kinds of thought-provoking questions can go a long way toward making the meeting a successful and productive one. But they're also helpful tools—just like good attending—in building and improving the quality of other important relationships (spouses, lovers, children, relatives, close friends, etc.) in your life.

ENCOURAGING

We put on seminars at the annual conventions of trade and professional associations, and, since the people in attendance are generally owner-operators of their own companies, our audiences are usually almost all men. Because of this, we usually use the following husband-and-wife example to talk about the next two skills.

Imagine that you're a husband and you've asked your wife the question: "What can I do to make our relationship more satisfying and less frustrating for you?" What's going to happen when you ask this question? Is your wife going to start off by mentioning the most touchy, sensitive, hard-to-talk-about issues in your relationship with her?

We don't think so. More likely, she's going to talk about some "safe" topics, some things she's already mentioned but that you've either ignored or haven't really heard before. For example:

> Well, I can think of a few things you can do. Well . . . for one, you could stop smoking. There's all this evidence piling up now about how bad smoking is for your health. I'd really like you to quit once and for all. Ah . . . Another thing is that . . . ah . . . that rubber tire you're carrying around your midsection. You've put on about fifteen extra pounds in the last several years, and I'd like to see you lose that weight and get into a regular exercise program. Hmmm . . . and I guess another thing . . . well, you spend so much time at work . . . ah . . . I guess I'd just like you to spend more time at home with me and the kids. Ah . . . I guess that's about it. I can't really think of anything else.

Well, of course, that's not "it." There's *lots* more she *could* tell you, but she's holding back. She wants to see how you're going to react to what she's said so far. If you want her to continue to talk—to tell you more about what's on her mind—a good thing to do is simply encourage her to keep talking. For example, you could say something like:

> Honey, this stuff is very important for me to hear. Please keep going. I want to hear more.

By encouraging her in this way you send some important direct and indirect messages to her:

- "I really *want* to hear what you have to say."
- "It's *important* for me to hear what you have to say."
- "I'm not going to be a *bad* listener by doing things I might normally do—like cutting you off, telling you you're way off base, rolling my eyes to the ceiling in disgust, or any of that kind of stuff."

When you sit down to meet with your boss, you'll find that encouraging him or her to talk more will send these same kinds of positive messages. And, of course, it will increase the chances of making the meeting a productive and successful one.

READING BACK

We think reading back is one of the best tools available for helping people think out loud. That's really all good listening involves, helping other human beings get their thoughts and ideas and feelings out on the table where they can look at them, and maybe make a little bit better sense out of them.

To show how reading back works, let's return to our example:

YOU: Honey, this stuff is very important for me to hear. Please keep going. I want to hear more.

WIFE: (long pause) Well, I guess I can think of something else. You know how when we first started dating . . .

you used to bring me flowers once a week . . . we'd go out to cozy dinners in little restaurants? We don't do that kind of thing anymore. I don't know . . . maybe there are things like that you could do to bring a little of the romance back into our relationship.

YOU: (trying to encourage her to talk more) Please keep going. This is good. I need to hear more.

WIFE: (deciding this is about as far as she's prepared to go) No, really, I can't think of anything else.

At this point, to get her to open up some more, you can try a read back. That is, using your own words, you can try to *summarize the essence* of what she's been saying to you. For example:

YOU: Well, honey, I think I've heard you say four pretty important things. First, you're concerned about the effect of smoking on my health and you'd like me to quit. Second, you'd like me to lose some weight and get into a regular exercise program. I think a third thing you said is that you'd like me to spend more time with you and the kids and less time at the office. And the last thing I heard . . . you said it a little tentatively . . . is that some of the romance has evaporated from our marriage. Maybe there are a few things I could do to turn that around. (Then you pause.)

WIFE: Yes . . . (long pause) . . . well (laughing a little nervously), since I have such a receptive audience here . . . I guess I can think of a few more things you could do . . .

At this point, things are beginning to roll. Your read back has gotten your wife to start disclosing things that are a little more sensitive, a little more touchy, and therefore a little more important for her to talk about than the things she's mentioned so far. That's one of the primary purposes of a read back—to help another person explore the depths of her (or his) thinking, to dig out the really important things on her mind and express them.

A good read back also serves some other useful purposes.

- It *proves* to the person that you're really *trying* to listen. You can fake good attending, but you can't fake reading back.
- It gives people a chance to correct any misunderstanding you might have formed of what they've said. For example, after the read back you offered to your wife, she could have replied, "No, that's not really what I was trying to say. What I was trying to say is . . ."
- Like the three other listening skills, a good read back sends an important message: "I care enough about you and our relationship to try to really hear what you're saying to me."

Given that your boss is a reasonably good candidate for the one on one approach, we think these four listening skills can be extremely helpful tools in actually conducting the face-to-face meeting (and, of course, can also help you improve the quality of other relationships that are important to you).

In addition to becoming a better listener, another important way to prepare for the meeting is to do a performance analysis on your boss. This may sound a little strange because performance analyses are something that bosses usually do on employees. But we think employees should do them on their bosses, too. At any rate, doing a performance analysis on your boss will help structure and focus the feedback you give your boss when the two of you actually meet.

In chapter 3, "Taking a Look at Your Boss," you did a rather extensive analysis of your boss. If you'll recall, you did a boss history; you rated your boss on TRAC; you did an ideal boss analysis; and you took a look at your own boss in terms of five ineffective boss tendencies: avoiding, over-reacting, complaining, lecturing, and externalizing.

Now what we'd like you to do is step back from the thinking you did and answer two questions:

1. What *does* my boss do that helps make my job reasonably satisfying and fulfilling?
2. What *could* my boss do to make my job less frustrating and more satisfying?

If you have any hope of getting your boss to change, you'll need to be as clear as you can about what you like (as well as what you don't like) about how your boss treats you. Answering these questions will help you clarify the thinking you've done so far. It'll help you decide what's really important to bring up in the meeting, and what's not.

To help you answer these two questions about your boss, let's look at an example. Bob Lombardi is a forty-five-year-old fellow who works for a trade association in New York City. Bob works for Matt Ringer—a man in his fifties—who's in charge of membership and professional development for the association.

We asked Bob to answer these two questions about his boss Matt. At first, Bob was a little reluctant. He's not the most analytical guy in the world, and he seemed to enjoy complaining about Matt more than he did doing anything to improve things between them. However, after a little pushing, Bob obliged us. Here's his first shot at answering the two questions:

1. WHAT *DOES* MATT DO THAT MAKES MY JOB SATISFYING AND FULFILLING?
   • He's got a good sense of humor.
   • He sticks up for me with higher-ups.

- He cares about me as a person.
- He boosts office morale with parties and celebrations from time to time.
- He's honest and straightforward.

2. WHAT *COULD* MATT DO TO MAKE MY JOB LESS FRUSTRATING AND MORE SATISFYING?
   - Do a better job of setting priorities.
   - Do a better job of handing out compliments and praise, not just criticism.
   - Do a better job of assigning me things that I can do well and not assigning me things that I can't do so well.

We told Bob that his answers were a good start, but that he could be more specific. For the first question, we suggested he put in a few examples. That way, when he actually sat down with Matt, the things he liked about Matt as a boss would seem more solid and believable. This is what he came up with:

1. WHAT *DOES* MATT DO THAT MAKES MY JOB SATISFYING AND FULFILLING?
   - He's got a good sense of humor. At times, Matt can really get carried away and act like a fool. But he does have a good sense of humor, and in calmer moments when some of us point out dumb things he does, he actually cracks up at himself.
   - He sticks up for me with higher-ups. A couple of times he's actually gone over the executive director's head to the board to argue for raises for me and other people who work for him. I know he takes a risk when he does this, and I really respect him and appreciate him for that.
   - He cares about me as a person. A couple of times I've had some family problems that have kept me out of work beyond my sick leave and vacation allowance. Matt has always been understanding with me at those times. He's always seen that I got paid for those days I was out even though, technically, I wasn't supposed to.

- He boosts office morale with parties and celebrations from time to time. Matt likes to have a good time and celebrate. A couple of times a year he makes sure all of us who work for him go out and just have a good old time. He always picks up the tab. He claims he gets reimbursed for it, but I really think it comes out of his own pocket.
- He's honest and straightforward. Matt's a straight shooter. I can't remember once in the seven years I've worked for him that he's lied to me or misled me in any way. And I can't say that about most bosses I've known or worked for.

For the second question, we told Bob we weren't exactly sure what he wanted Matt to do differently. We figured if we were confused, Matt might be, too. Here's how Bob clarified what he wanted from Matt:

2. WHAT *COULD* MATT DO TO MAKE MY JOB LESS FRUSTRATING AND MORE SATISFYING?
- Do a better job of setting priorities. Matt has a tendency to dump an awful lot of work on me. Much more than I can possibly get done in the time he sets for me to do it. When he gives me stuff to do, I'd like him to sit down with me and help me decide what's most important and what's least important. That way I'll be able to get the most important stuff done, and I won't feel so guilty and frustrated when the less important things don't get done.
- Do a better job of handing out compliments and praise— not just criticism. Matt's kind of a faultfinder. I mean, he's good at pointing out things you've done wrong. And that's okay. But he's not so good at giving compliments and praise. A lot of times the compliments he does hand out are a little left-handed. That is, they're a mixture of praise *and* criticism. I guess all I'm asking is that he tell me when I've done something he's pleased with. Just a simple "nice job" or "well done" or "I really like that little report you wrote on member char-

acteristics.'' Something like that. It'd make a big difference.

- Do a better job of assigning me things I can do well and not assigning me things I can't do so well. This is a bit of a bone of contention between me and Matt. He *knows* that reading and writing are not my strong points. Yet he seems to insist on always giving me these useless technical articles to read and asks me to write summary reports on them. I really hate doing that. I especially hate doing it when I think my talents could be much better used out in the field helping our members solve problems that I know I can help them with. If Matt would just give a little on this point, I can't tell you how much more I'd enjoy the job.

Of course, you don't have to do a performance analysis on your boss exactly the way Bob did his on Matt. However, trying to do a thoughtful and conscientious job of answering the two questions should help make the meeting go much smoother than if you hadn't done the analysis.

One other suggestion on the topic of preparing for the meeting. Remember in chapter 4 "Taking a Look at Yourself" how Clyde Jameson, the young pathologist, interviewed Charlene Masters about his relationship with his boss Bill Gruskins. We think you ought to do basically the same thing before the meeting. Ask somebody you trust and respect to offer their perspective on the relationship between you and your boss. You're very close to the situation, maybe too close to see things clearly. Like anyone else who's struggling to get along with another person, you'll have a tendency to see things only from your point of view. Someone else who's not so involved should have a clearer, more balanced, and more objective view of the situation.

Before Bob Lombardi sat down with Matt Ringer, he met with Shirley Larousseau (who'd known both Matt and Bob for over ten years). Bob asked her this question:

Shirley, you've known Matt and me for a long time. I'd have to say that you're an expert on both of us. You know our strong points and our weak points. You know pretty well what each of us does to get in the other's hair. I'd really appreciate it if you'd tell me three things. One, how do *I* contribute to the problems that Matt and I have getting along with each other? Two, how does Matt contribute to those problems? And, three, what could *both* of us do differently to make our relationship smoother and more satisfying?

Without going into a lot of detail here, Bob told us he found Shirley's analysis enlightening and helpful. He said he was a little surprised because he expected Shirley to take his side against Matt. She didn't. Although she pointed out how Matt caused problems in the relationship, she said there were a number of things Bob did that she thought annoyed Matt, and that if Bob would just stop doing those things, the situation between the two of them would improve greatly.

We'd recommend you do the same thing with someone like Shirley before you meet with your boss.

Asking Your Boss to Meet with You

Before you actually meet with your boss, of course, you'll be *asking* your boss to meet with you. This may seem so obvious that it's not even worth mentioning. However, we've found that *how* people handle this part of the process can have a strong effect (either positive or negative) on the eventual outcome.

Here are some things we think you *should not* do when you ask your boss to meet:

DON'T JUST MAKE AN APPOINTMENT TO MEET THROUGH YOUR BOSS'S SECRETARY

If you do this, your boss will either have no idea why you want to meet, or will have to accept whatever the secretary said you said. Better to make the appointment yourself.

DON'T SEND YOUR BOSS A NOTE OR MEMO

If your boss sent you a note or memo telling you to come to a performance review session, you probably wouldn't like it. Your boss would also appreciate a personal invitation.

DON'T JUST POP INTO YOUR BOSS'S OFFICE TO HAVE THE MEETING

A lot of bosses have what they call an open door policy—a standing invitation to their employees to come in and discuss problems. If your boss has this kind of policy, fine. But use it to go in and *ask* your boss to meet—not to have the meeting right then and there. Like you, your boss needs some time to prepare for the meeting.

DON'T WAIT UNTIL YOU'RE ANGRY OR ANNOYED TO ASK FOR THE MEETING

For some people, being angry or annoyed seems like the perfect time to go in and unload on the boss. We don't recommend this. Yes, sometimes it works—sometimes it gives employees the courage they otherwise wouldn't have to get things out on the table. But more often than not, it fails. And it can easily make things worse.

Here are some things we think you *should* do when you ask your boss to meet:

APPROACH YOUR BOSS WHEN THERE AREN'T OTHER PEOPLE AROUND

Obviously you don't want employees or customers listening in when you ask your boss to meet. (You know, they're bound to be thinking something like, "What's he talking to the boss for?") It'll only make both of you uncomfortable and get things off to a bad start.

BRIEFLY EXPLAIN THE PURPOSE OF THE MEETING AND GET YOUR BOSS'S REACTION TO THE IDEA

We think you should be straightforward with your boss. Say you want to meet to talk about how the two of you can improve your working relationship. You might even say you'd like to discuss and agree on ways that you can both make each other's job less frustrating and more satisfying. After you explain why you'd like to meet, it's a good idea to simply ask for your boss's reaction to the idea.

EXPLAIN HOW YOU PLAN TO PREPARE FOR THE MEETING AND SUGGEST YOUR BOSS DO THE SAME

You're going to prepare for the meeting by writing down some things you like about how your boss manages you; but also some areas where you think your boss could stand to improve. You might also mention that you're going to get someone else's perspective on how the two of you cause each other problems and what you could both do differently to improve the situation. We think you should suggest that your boss consider doing the same—especially doing a performance analysis on you.

ARRANGE A SPECIFIC TIME, DATE, AND PLACE TO MEET

It's important to pick a place to meet where you'll both feel comfortable and that'll be free of distractions. You don't want to meet where others can eavesdrop on your conversation, and where the phone or other interruptions will get in the way. If you can't find a place like that at the office, go somewhere else—but *not* to a restaurant. Restaurants are full of distractions.

END ON A POSITIVE NOTE

After you've set a comfortable place to meet, and a time and date that's convenient for both of you, tell your boss you're sincerely looking forward to the meeting and are expecting both of you to get a lot out of it.

At this point you may be saying to yourself, "Well, this all sounds good in theory, but what do I do if things don't quite go according to plan?"

That's a reasonable concern. Like it or not, when you're dealing with human beings, things often don't go according to plan. On the other hand, you've got some new skills, *listening* skills, that can help bail you out when you run into problems. As an example, let's go back to Bob Lombardi and his boss Matt Ringer. Here Bob is encountering a little trouble when he asks Matt how he feels about having the meeting:

BOB: Anyway, Matt, that's the purpose of the meeting as I see it. Now, how do you feel about the idea of getting together to talk?

MATT: Ah . . . I don't know Bob, I'm not so sure it's a good idea for us to do that.

Obviously Matt's not completely sold on the idea of getting together to talk. What should Bob do? Should he say,

"Okay, I guess it's not a good idea then." Or maybe get assertive and try to talk Matt into meeting? We think the best thing for Bob to do is simply *read Matt back*, something like this:

BOB: Well, Matt, it sounds like you've got some reservations about getting together to talk? (pause)

MATT: A-h-h-h . . . Yeah, I guess so . . .

BOB: Uh huh. (pause)

MATT: (long pause) Well, look, Bob, let me be straight with you. I don't know if you know it or not, but just last week I had one of these little heart-to-heart type talks with Tony Sclara. And . . . ah . . . it didn't go so hot.

BOB: (waiting for about ten seconds) So you had kind of an unpleasant meeting with Tony, and maybe you're wondering if the same thing might happen with me?

MATT: Yeah, exactly . . . I mean he got all bent out of shape when I didn't immediately give him what he wanted, and he slammed the door and stormed out of here like a runaway freight train . . . I guess you could say I'm just a little gun-shy at this point.

BOB: So right now you'd just as soon avoid a repeat performance of that lousy experience?

MATT: Yeah . . . that's it. You got it.

Notice what's been happening here. Matt expressed an initial objection to the idea of getting together to talk with Bob. Since then, all Bob has done is *read Matt back*. What Matt has done is elaborate on his reasons for not wanting to meet. Now that Matt feels as though Bob really understands his reservations, Bob can try to put Matt's fears to rest:

BOB: Matt, I can understand your concern, but I can also guarantee you I'm not going to behave like Tony did. I see this as an opportunity to discuss how both of us can have a better working relationship. I certainly don't see it as a chance for me to lay any demands on you. Or storm out all pissed off if I don't get what I want.

MATT: (looking relieved) I'm sold! When do you want to meet?

BOB: Okay, let's . . .

Listening skills are a powerful tool for helping make face-to-face interactions like this go more smoothly. Whenever you run into a problem, like Bob did with Matt, just ask yourself: "How can I use my listening skills—especially reading back—to help bail myself out?"

Conducting an Effective Meeting

Up to this point you've prepared for the meeting by: (a) doing a performance analysis on your boss; (b) getting the perspective of someone who knows both of you fairly well; and (c) asking your boss to meet with you. Now it's on to the meeting itself. In this section we've broken the meeting into five stages:

1. getting things started
2. getting feedback from your boss
3. giving your boss feedback
4. forming a performance agreement
5. ending the meeting

We'll talk you through each stage using the example of Bob Lombardi and his boss Matt Ringer.

GETTING THINGS STARTED

Let's assume you and your boss have found a comfortable place to meet without phones ringing, paging systems blaring, and people knocking at the door every five minutes. Now the trick is to get the meeting off to the best start possible. To do this you need to do a couple of things: (a) warm up the atmosphere a bit, and (b) "structure" the meeting so you and your boss both know what you're doing and where you're headed.

All "warming up the atmosphere" means is doing whatever you can to make sure you and your boss feel reasonably relaxed and at ease before you get down to business. There are any number of ways to do this. Trading jokes is one way. Teasing each other is an excellent way. But if you're not a good joke teller or a natural teaser, maybe it's best to simply get your boss talking about some interest or hobby. Bob Lombardi warmed up the atmosphere by taking advantage of Matt's keen interest in freshwater fishing:

BOB: Matt, I know we should get started here in a second. But I've got a question for you. I was reading this article in *Rod and Reel* and I got a little confused. What's the difference between "dry" flies and "wet" flies?

MATT: You really want to know?

BOB: (smiling) Yeah, I really want to know.

MATT: Well, actually there's quite a difference. First of all . . .

Before he knew it, Matt was into what turned out to be a five-minute explanation. A waste of time? Not at all. By the time he finished, both guys were so caught up in the explanation that a lot of their anxiety about the meeting had evaporated.

Once you've warmed up the atmosphere with your boss, it's a good idea to *structure* the meeting. All *structuring* means is you and your boss agreeing on:

• the purpose of the meeting
• what you're going to cover in the meeting
• how the two of you can get the most out of the meeting

This kind of game plan usually helps any meeting (not just one between you and your boss) go more smoothly.

Here's how Bob structured the meeting with Matt:

BOB: Matt, before we get started, I thought it might be a good idea for the two of us to spend a little time talking about exactly what we're up to here . . .

MATT: Okay, so what *are* we up to here, anyway?

BOB: Well, let me talk about the purpose first. I think the purpose of our getting together here is to talk about and agree on some ways the two of us can improve our working relationship. I think we work together reasonably well, but I think there's room for improvement. I see this meeting as a first step toward that improvement.

MATT: Makes sense to me.

BOB: Good. In terms of how to go about this process, let me suggest an outline. I think it would be a good idea if I started off by simply asking you this question: "Matt, what can I do as your employee to make your job less frustrating and more satisfying?"

MATT: (chuckling) Now that's a question I'd enjoy answering.

BOB: (smiling) I thought you might like taking a crack at that one. And while you're answering it I think my job is to be the best listener I can. I'll try not to get defensive or interrupt you in any way. I'll try to draw you out as best I can.

MATT: (nodding) Okay, sounds good.

BOB: After I get done drawing you out, I think it'd be a good idea if we just flipped the coin over and maybe you could ask me the same question.

MATT: You mean, what could I, Matt, do to make *your* job less frustrating and more satisfying?

BOB: Exactly.

MATT: (hesitating a little) O-o-kay.

BOB: Looks like you might be a little concerned about that?

Notice what Bob is doing here? He's reading Matt back. But all Matt has said is, "O-o-kay." Here Bob is reading back the hesitation in Matt's voice and his body language as well as his simple verbal message. It looks like a great read back to us, because it's trying to capture the essence of what Matt is saying and thinking. Let's see what it yields.

MATT: Well . . . I guess I'm still smarting a bit from the experience with Tony. But I think it should go a lot smoother this time.

BOB: (smiling) I guarantee it. Well, after I draw you out and you draw me out, I think it would be a good idea for us to try to agree on a few things we could do to make the other guy's job a little easier. You know, just a few things that we can work on over the next several weeks. I think it would even be a good idea to write these things down so we can review them when we get together for a follow-up meeting.

MATT: (smiling) Oh, so now we're going to have a follow-up meeting, too?

BOB: (smiling but not saying anything)

MATT: No, I'm teasing. That sounds fine to me, Bob.

BOB: (beaming) Good. Well, the only thing I'd add is that the best way for us to get the most out of this session is to be as honest as we can with each other and also to be the best listeners we can.

MATT: And not take the whole process *too* seriously?

BOB: (smiling) Right. Not too seriously.

GETTING FEEDBACK FROM YOUR BOSS

All right, let's say you've gotten the meeting off to a reasonably good start. The next stage is getting your boss to give you feedback by posing the question: "What can I do to make your job less frustrating and more satisfying?" But before we talk about how to do that, you may be wondering why it's a good idea to do it at all. After all, isn't this meeting primarily an opportunity for you to give your *boss* some feedback in hopes your boss will change and make things a little easier for *you*?

The answer, of course, is Yes. You are meeting in the hopes of trying to get your boss to change. *But*, all our experience as psychologists and consultants points to this fact: If you want the other person to change, you better first show that *you're* willing to change. If you want your boss to listen to what *you've* got to say, it's a good idea to first listen to your boss's suggestions on how *you* could change.

What's the best way to get your boss to give you feedback? As you might have guessed, we think you should simply ask a thought-provoking question and then use the listening skills we've covered to draw your boss out. Here's how Bob did it with Matt:

BOB: Well, I guess we're ready to roll here, Matt. Okay, let me ask you what I think is an important question, and then I'll try to be the best listener I can be as you answer it. Okay?

MATT: Shoot.

BOB: Matt, you know me pretty well. We've worked together for a lot of years. As you think about me and my performance over those years, what would you say I could do to make your job a lot less frustrating and a lot more satisfying?

MATT: (thinking but not saying anything for a while) Hmmm . . . I actually have given that question a little thought in the last couple of days since you asked me to meet with you. Well . . . one thing that immediately comes to mind, and it's not really that big a deal with me, but it does bother me. Ah . . . at five o'clock, come hell or high water, you're out of here! It doesn't matter what we've got cooking, you're either gone, or you're chomping at the bit to go. I guess that kind of bugs me because I almost never leave early . . .

BOB: (nodding his head) Uh huh . . .

MATT: (looking a little warily at Bob) . . . I don't know. Instead of just bolting out of here at five, maybe you could check in with me and say that you're about to leave and ask if there's anything you could do before taking off. That way I wouldn't feel so deserted at the end of the day.

BOB: (pausing for a few seconds and then deciding to use an encourager) Keep going, Matt. I know it's a little hard to talk about this stuff, but it's important for me to hear it.

MATT: (looking a little more comfortable) Okay. Well, another thing . . .

In the next ten minutes or so, Bob was able to get Matt to bring up two more areas where he thought Bob could improve. During this time Bob didn't do any reading back. All he did was attend well and use an occasional encourager. But after this last encourager, Matt seemed like he was almost through.

BOB: (nodding) Anything else you can think of, Matt? I'm all ears.

MATT: No, that's really about it. I don't think I can think of anything else.

Now Bob decides to try a read back to see if he's heard Matt correctly, and maybe even get him to say a little more.

BOB: Matt, I think I've heard you bring up three areas
        where I could improve. The first thing you men-
        tioned was the business about my always leaving
        promptly at five o'clock. There I think you were
        saying that it bugs you, mainly because you feel
        kind of abandoned when I do that. Like you're left
        holding the fort.

MATT: (nodding) Exactly.

BOB: I think another thing you mentioned was the way I
        always seem to duck out of writing assignments.
        That seems to bother you because we all have so
        much writing to do. And you'd just as soon not get
        stuck with most of it. (pausing)

MATT: Yes.

BOB: And I think the last thing you mentioned was the fact
        that I don't seem to take the weekly progress reports
        we're supposed to fill out very seriously. Basically,
        you were saying it bothers you that I either don't do
        them, or I do them superficially. (pausing)

MATT: (looking thoughtful) Yeah . . . I . . . ah, I don't
        know. Maybe it's not that important.

BOB: Matt, it sounds like there's something on your
        mind, but maybe you're wondering whether or not
        it's worth mentioning?

MATT: Well, all right. It's a little thing, but it bugs the hell
        out of me. I'm a little embarrassed to even bring it
        up. But . . . well, it's the way you laugh when
        we're at a social function. I mean . . . it sounds
        like a horse whinnying and I can hear you clear
        across the room . . . and it makes me cringe.
        (pausing) Well, anyway, for better or worse, I said
        it. And I certainly never meant to bring it up. (look-
        ing down sheepishly)

This sort of thing happens all the time when one person
reads another person back. Here, Bob's good read back gets

Matt to mention something that he was thinking, but would've never mentioned if it hadn't been for Bob's skill as a listener.

BOB: (trying hard to cover up a smile) Matt, it's obviously hard for you to talk about this, but I think what you're trying to say is pretty clear. I have a way of laughing—maybe a better word would be guffawing—especially when some of our members are around—that bothers you and upsets you and embarrasses you.

MATT: Yeah . . . it does bother me, and I guess I should have told you about it a long time ago.

BOB: Well, I'm glad you told me about it. Is there anything else on your mind?

MATT: No, I really think that's about it. Maybe it's time for me to hear from you.

There probably are more things Bob could get out of Matt if he really probed for them. But this seems like a good transition point for the next stage of the process.

The important point here—and in the meeting you'll eventually have with your boss—is that Bob really *listened* to what Matt had to say. He helped Matt think out loud about a topic that was hard for Matt to talk about, and probably even harder for Bob to listen to. Even though there were a number of points where Bob easily could have jumped in to defend himself, he didn't. He did what we call "staying in listening mode." If you can do this with your boss—and it's *extremely* hard to do when you're getting feedback from another person—we think you'll be surprised at how smoothly the rest of the meeting will go.

GIVING YOUR BOSS FEEDBACK

In many ways, this is what you've been waiting for. You're finally getting a chance to tell your boss some things that just may make your job easier and more enjoyable.

But this is also the stage where the conversation can most easily get derailed. First, chances are you're going to be more motivated to be cooperative and effective than your boss is. Because you're the employee, not the boss, you've got less power and really have to be cooperative. Your boss has the option of pulling rank on you. Second, since you're the one with the interest and motivation to read this book and especially this chapter, chances are you're a better listener than your boss. Your boss probably doesn't have your listening skills to fall back on if the conversation starts to go sour. So, like it or not, most of the responsibility for the success of this stage is going to fall on your shoulders.

To help make things go as smoothly as possible here, we've got a few suggestions:

Start with the positive. Begin by mentioning the things your boss already does that make your job reasonably satisfying and fulfilling. By mentioning the positive things first, your boss will be more receptive to hearing your suggestions for improvement later on.

Be specific. The English language is full of words called "fuzzies"—words that sound good but don't convey a whole lot of meaning. For example, you may feel your boss is a reliable and dependable supervisor. But "reliable" and "dependable" are fuzzies. If you want to tell your boss you think she's reliable, fine. But also tell her why; give her some *examples* of how she's been reliable.

Avoid emotionally loaded words and expressions. There are lots of words and expressions in our language that have a very good chance of triggering an emotional or defensive reaction. For example, you're probably better off not referring to your boss as "fussy," "overbearing," "crude," "boring," "plodding," and a host of other terms like these that are probably only going to get your boss's hackles up.

When giving feedback, ALWAYS be prepared to STOP talking and START listening. If you forget every other principle, remember this one. Just because your boss starts out being receptive to your feedback is no guarantee he'll stay receptive. If you say something and your boss starts shaking his head or interrupting or giving you some other sign his receptivity has dipped, stop talking and let him say what he's got to say. Then read him back. That's the best way to eventually get him to start listening to you again. We'll give you an example of how to do this shortly.

Let's return to the example of Bob and Matt. Notice how Bob tries to pay attention to the suggestions we've just made:

BOB: Well, Matt, you've offered a number of suggestions about what I could do to make your job less frustrating and more satisfying. Maybe it's time now to turn the coin around and you ask me the same question I asked you earlier.

MATT: Right. So you want to go ahead and do that?

BOB: Well, before I talk about what you could do to make my job less frustrating and more satisfying, I'd like to mention some things that you're already doing that I'm satisfied with. (pausing)

MATT: (smiling) Fine by me.

BOB: Okay. To start off, one thing you do as my boss that helps make my job go smoothly is your good sense of humor. I appreciate the jokes—even the corny ones—but what I really appreciate is your ability to laugh at yourself.

MATT: (smiling a little sheepishly) Yeah?

BOB: Yeah. For example, I remember a staff meeting we had a few months back where you threw out a suggestion that, to put it mildly, went over like a lead balloon. After you made the suggestion, you

> paused and looked around the room for a few seconds and then muttered: "That was kind of a stupid thing to say, wasn't it?" Everybody cracked up and really appreciated it.

MATT: (laughing heartily, but not saying anything)

BOB: (smiling) Moving right along. Another thing you do that helps me a lot on the job is sticking up for me and the rest of the staff with higher-ups that make all the "big" decisions around here . . .

For the next several minutes Bob continued to give Matt *positive* feedback on Matt's performance as a boss. Now we'll pick up with the two of them as Bob begins to suggest some ways he'd like to see Matt change.

MATT: . . . Well, I'm glad you appreciate my honesty because I think that's an important quality in general, and certainly here in the job.

BOB: Good . . . ah . . . up to this point, Matt, I've been talking about things you do that keep me satisfied on the job. Now I'd like to shift to some of the areas where I think you could stand to improve as my boss. You know, some of the things you could do to make my job less frustrating and more satisfying . . .

MATT: (smiling) Time for the bad news, huh?

BOB: (smiling and pausing a few seconds) It's not really bad news. I just think it's going to be a little tougher to talk about this kind of stuff.

MATT: (more serious) I understand . . . go ahead.

BOB: (taking a breath) Okay, here goes. Well, one thing is . . . you could definitely do a better job of setting priorities for me.

MATT: (nodding but looking a little puzzled)

BOB: Let me be more specific. Matt, you dump an awful lot of work on me. Much more than I can possibly get done in the time you set for me to do it in . . .

Notice the mistake Bob has made here. He's used some emotionally loaded language—"dump an awful lot of work on me." Watch how Matt reacts and how Bob handles the situation.

MATT: (interrupting) Now wait a minute, Bob. Don't you think that's a little strong? First of all, I don't think I "dump" anything on you. And I certainly don't think I give you any more to do than anybody else on the staff, *or* than I give myself.

BOB: (Realizing that Matt's receptivity has plummeted, Bob shifts into listening mode and tries a read back) Matt, it sounds like you feel I'm being a little unfair to you. You're saying you don't think you dump work on me or anyone else. I think you're also saying that you don't ask any more of me than you do of the rest of the staff or of yourself.

MATT: (softening a little) Exactly . . .

BOB: (pausing, saying nothing, and maintaining good eye contact)

MATT: (softening some more) Now maybe I do have a tendency to expect too much of you and myself and the others on the staff. But I just didn't like your implication that I unload all this work on you, not leaving all that much for me to do myself. I think I work very hard, and I resent it when *anybody* implies that I'm a slacker.

BOB: (pausing some more) I think you're saying two things there. Yes, you may have a tendency to ask too much of all of us, including yourself. But you don't like being called a slacker or anything like

that given the way you're always breaking your
back around here.

MATT: You got me. That's exactly how I feel.

By the way, Matt's not even aware that all Bob has been
doing is reading him back. This is quite common. And, as
you've noticed, it's taken two good readbacks from Bob, but
Matt's receptivity seems to be back up. Now Bob can clarify
what he meant earlier. But imagine for a moment how the
meeting might have degenerated had Bob not been such a
skillful listener. Let's return now to the meeting.

BOB: Matt, let me try to clear up several points. First of
         all, I shouldn't have used the term "dumping" be-
         cause I don't think that's what you do. And I cer-
         tainly didn't mean to imply that you're a slacker.
         Nobody around here works harder than you. But I
         would like to come back to what I was trying to
         say earlier. Maybe this time I can say it more
         clearly.

MATT: And I do want to hear what you have to say. Really.

BOB: Here's all I'm trying to say . . .

Here Bob will use a feedback technique we call, "When
You . . . I Feel." This is a helpful way to give people "de-
scriptive" versus "judgmental" feedback. It's very simple.
You start off by describing some specific things that the other
person does, and then you disclose how you feel about those
things. Back to Bob and Matt:

BOB: Here's all I'm trying to say. When you give me
         work assignments, I often feel confused and frus-
         trated. I know I can't do everything you want me
         to do in the time you want it done. So I guess what
         I'm saying is I need some help from you in setting
         priorities . . . in helping me decide what's the most

important stuff to work on. Do you see what I'm trying to say?

MATT: Yes, that's a lot clearer. Okay, well, how could I do that?

BOB: Good question. How about if we hold off on that until I get more things out on the table? Pretty soon we'll be writing down what we can both do to make the other guy's job easier. Maybe that would be the best time to get specific about what exactly we can do for each other.

MATT: Sounds fine to me.

BOB: Great. Okay, moving right along . . .

In the next ten to fifteen minutes Bob covered the other two "needs improvement" items he wanted to cover with Matt: Handing out compliments and praise, not just criticism, and picking assignments that were more up Bob's alley. Bob didn't run into any more snags with Matt after this. But if he did, he would have used his listening skills to get him out of trouble.

NEGOTIATING A PERFORMANCE AGREEMENT

Now that both Matt and Bob have given each other feedback, they're at the stage of the meeting where they can begin talking about a performance agreement. All this means is that the two of them will be agreeing on—and writing down on paper—some specific things both of them will be doing over the next several weeks to make each other's jobs less frustrating and more satisfying.

Forming an agreement like this with your boss may seem like a difficult undertaking. But we've found that if you can get this far in the meeting, the tough part is really over. Most of the touchy stuff has already come out. Now the job is to bring closure to the meeting by getting both of you to commit to making a few changes over the next few weeks.

Before we rejoin Bob and Matt, here are a few things to

keep in mind about the process of negotiating a performance agreement with your boss:

Make sure there's something in it for both of you. The agreement should be a balanced one. You shouldn't agree to do much more than your boss, and vice versa. If the agreement isn't balanced, one of you is going to feel resentful, and it won't work.

Limit the agreement to a few tasks. Whatever the two of you come up with, don't bite off more than you can chew. Agreeing to change in a few small areas and succeeding is much better than agreeing to make big changes and failing.

Be specific. Whatever you write down in this agreement, it should be specific. The more specific the commitments you make to each other, the more likely they are to be lived up to. For example, a commitment that reads, "Paula agrees to give Mike criticism in private, never in front of others" has a much greater chance of being carried out than one that reads "Paula agrees to be more sensitive to Mike about giving criticism."

Go into the process with a spirit of cooperation and compromise. You and your boss are looking for common ground where you'll both feel comfortable. The more willing *you* are to be cooperative and compromising, the more likely the two of you will find that common ground.

Back to Bob and Matt, who are starting to come up with their performance agreement:

BOB: Matt, that pretty well covers all the things I wanted to talk about. Is there anything else on your mind? Any other feedback you'd like to give me?

MATT: No . . . I really can't think of anything else.

BOB: Okay . . . well, I think now it'd be a good idea for us to talk about what the two of us can work on over the next several weeks. I suggest we actually write down some things for me to work on based on the feedback you gave me. And also some things for you to work on based on the feedback I gave you.

MATT: Okay . . . ah . . . there's just one problem.

BOB: What's that?

MATT: My handwriting is even worse than yours.

BOB: (both laughing) Well, why don't I just take responsibility for the writing? (watching Matt smile and nod his head) All right, why don't we start with me? Matt, you gave me some real clear feedback a while ago. What's one specific thing you'd like me to work on over the next several weeks?

MATT: Hmmm . . . I . . . ah . . . think the business about your always leaving on the dot of 5:00 is something we could put down there.

BOB: How would you like me to word that, Matt?

MATT: Okay . . . ah . . . how about if we agree that you'd check in with me before you leave each day to see if there's anything pressing that needs immediate attention?

BOB: Okay, I think I could live with that. (starting to write) How about if I put down: "Bob agrees to check in with Matt every day to see if there's anything pressing before leaving"?

MATT: Good.

BOB: All right, how about if we put down something for you?

MATT: Okay.

BOB: Well, you know what I'd really like? I'd like to sit down with you in the next several days to go over all the projects I'm working on and have the two of us put some priorities and completion dates on each one.

MATT: Haven't we already done that?

This may *look* like a question, but it's probably a statement *disguised* as a question. The best way to deal with it—as you

may have already guessed—is simply to read it back. That's
how Bob handles it:

BOB: Matt, maybe you're feeling like this has already
          been done and you're wondering why we'd need
          to repeat the process?

MATT: Yeah . . . but maybe we haven't done it as well as
          we should. What do you think?

BOB: (noticing that Matt's receptivity is back up) Well,
          I don't think we've done it the way I have in mind
          . . . (pausing to monitor Matt's reaction) . . . but
          even if we have done it, I'd like to do it again
          because I've really lost sense of where we are on
          some of these projects. Maybe what I'm saying is
          that at this point I need a little more direction from
          you.

MATT: Fine. I'll be glad to sit down and do that.

BOB: Okay, let me get that down. How does this
          sound . . .

Bob and Matt spent the next portion of the meeting coming
up with a performance agreement. In final form, this is what
it looks like:

What Bob's Going to Work On

Bob will check in with Matt every day to see if
there's anything pressing before leaving.

If Bob feels he can't handle a particular writing assignment from Matt, he agrees to talk about it with
Matt so the two of them can work out a compromise
solution.

Bob agrees to conscientiously fill out his weekly
progress reports for the next three weeks. If, at the end
of the three-week period, he still sees them as a problem, he and Matt will discuss a way to modify the
reports to make them easier and faster to fill out.

Bob agrees to keep the "horse laughs" under control at social functions with members.

What Matt's Going to Work On

Within a week Matt will sit down with Bob to go over all the projects Bob is working on to help him put priorities and completion dates on each one.

In the next three weeks Matt will give Bob a full compliment—no "nice job, but . . ."-type stuff— whenever Bob does something that Mat thinks merits some genuine praise.

Matt agrees to make a special effort to assign tasks that really take advantage of what Bob does well—like field projects and helping members with problems over the phone. Matt will also make a special effort to hold down the writing and research tasks that Bob has so much difficulty with.

Notice some things about the agreement that Bob and Matt have come up with. One, it's not too ambitious. Given a little effort from the two of them, they ought to be able to achieve everything in the agreement within the next several weeks. Two, every item in the agreement is tied right in to something that one person said the other could do to make his job less frustrating and more satisfying. And, three, the tone and language of the agreement are light and informal. It's an important document, not a legal one. Neither Matt nor Bob has taken it too seriously.

ENDING THE MEETING

This is the home stretch. You and your boss have made a lot of progress up to this point. You've given each other feedback. You've reached a simple agreement on some things both of you will be working on over the next several weeks. Now it's time to close the meeting by setting a time and place for a follow-up meeting and ending this one on a positive note.

The follow-up meeting is important because it will give you a chance to review the progress you've both made on the performance agreement. It'll also act as a *motivator* for the two of you. That is, knowing you'll be reviewing each other's progress will make the performance agreement more of a priority than if you weren't going to have a follow-up meeting.

Before you bring the meeting to a close, though, it's usually a good idea to "process" the meeting. All this means is talking a little about how you and your boss feel about this important experience you've both been through. If you take a few extra minutes to do this, some important things may come out. For example, when Bob asked Matt the question, "Well, Matt, how do you feel about what we've done here today and what we've accomplished?" Matt's reply went something like this:

> Well, to tell you the truth, Bob, when you first mentioned the idea, I wasn't too hot on it. And this hasn't been the easiest experience for me, either. But I think doing this kind of thing is good. I guess I'm thinking it might be a good idea for me to have this sort of meeting with everybody on staff.

After your boss has had a chance to talk about the experience, it's a good idea for you to offer some of your own thoughts and feelings. You may have some new insights and come up with other things that you wanted to say to your boss but were holding back. Anyway, give it a try.

After you and your boss arrange the follow-up meeting, try to end the meeting as positively as possible. If the meeting didn't go well, we don't think you should be phony or insincere by claiming it was a great meeting. On the other hand, we recommend you do things like shaking hands, stressing the positive value of the meeting, and saying that you're looking forward to the follow-up.

Following Up

Following up on the meeting is important, but it's also one of those things that can easily fall between the cracks. Chances are you and your boss are busy people. It'll be natural for both of you to put the agreement aside (both physically and emotionally) as you jump back into your work. To counteract that tendency—to sustain the momentum you've built up so far—we have a few suggestions:

FOLLOW UP RIGHT AWAY

Even though your follow-up meeting is scheduled three weeks later, don't wait for that meeting to start following up. Get started *now*. If you notice your boss doing something from the performance agreement *the very next day*, say or do something to reinforce the change. For example, Matt Ringer had agreed to give Bob a "full" compliment, not a half-baked one, whenever Bob did something Matt thought merited genuine praise. Two days after their meeting, this interaction took place:

MATT: (ambling into Bob's office holding some papers) Bob, I just finished reading this trip report you wrote after you visited John Kruska's shop in Minnesota . . . I think you did a nice job on it. It's clear and concise and I think anybody reading it would have a good sense of the important things you learned while you were out there.

BOB: (smiling and with a touch of pride) Thanks, Matt. Thanks for the compliment. And, even more, thanks for doing what you agreed to do in our meeting. That helps a lot, and it makes me want to hold up my end of the bargain all that much more.

MATT: (a little embarrassed but obviously pleased) Well
          . . . good. Let's both keep up the good work, then.
BOB: (smiling broadly) Sounds good to me.

In addition to reinforcing your boss immediately when you
see a sign of progress, start living up to your end of the
agreement right away. For example, Bob agreed to check in
with Matt every day before leaving. It's very important for
Matt to see Bob doing that immediately. If Bob forgets,
Matt's motivation to keep to his end of the agreement is
going to drop like a stone—just like your boss's will if you
don't immediately start doing what you said you'd do.

USE YOUR FIRST MEETING AS A MODEL
FOR THE FOLLOW-UP

The purpose of the follow-up meeting is to give you and your
boss a chance to review the progress you've both made in
keeping to the performance agreement. It's also a chance to
discuss any problems the two of you ran into along the way.
If you follow the same basic format with this meeting as you
did with the first one, things should go pretty smoothly. Specifically, you should:

*Prepare for the meeting by analyzing your boss's perfor-
mance and your own in terms of what's spelled out in the
agreement*. Doing this ahead of time should make the meeting more productive.

*Even though it's scheduled, remind your boss of the meet-
ing*. You'll not only want to remind your boss of the meeting,
but also suggest that a good way to prepare for it is by reviewing the performance agreement.

Follow the same outline you used for the first meeting.
This meeting will probably be shorter than the first one, but
using the same outline as you used for the first one should
make it run smoother. For example, after you warm things
up a bit and structure the meeting, simply ask your boss the
question: "Why don't you take a few minutes to talk about

how things have been going since we last met? How have *I* been living up to the agreement we made? How have *you* been living up to it? And what problems or other obstacles have gotten in the way?'' When your boss takes a shot at this thought-provoking question, you'll try to be the best listener you can be. And when your boss finishes, you'll answer it yourself. Toward the end of the meeting the two of you might want to spell out some things that you both still need to work on. After that you might want to close by scheduling another follow-up meeting a couple months from now.

What we've tried to do in this chapter is describe what we think is a very important process. We call it a *relationship improvement process*. For our money, it's the most effective way two people who have an important relationship—whether they're boss and employee, parent and child, husband and wife, or whatever—can work on that relationship and make it a happier and more satisfying one.

12

·····················

TALKING TO YOUR BOSS
AS A GROUP

I n the last chapter we went into great detail on how to talk to your boss one on one. In this chapter we'll spend a little time covering a closely related strategy—meeting with your boss as a group.

We'll begin by pointing out what we think are some of the advantages and disadvantages of this strategy. Then we'll take you through a series of steps that should help make the meeting a success.

THE PROS AND CONS OF GOING
TO YOUR BOSS AS A GROUP

As with almost anything you do in life, there's an up side and a down side to talking with your boss as a group. These are some of the advantages:

1. *Meeting as a group can have a more powerful impact on your boss than an individual meeting.* The old adage "there's strength in numbers" has a lot of truth to it. Some bosses are much more likely to have their attention gotten by several employees than they are by one.

2. *It's the only way some employees would ever sit down to talk with the boss.* Like it or not, very few employees would even consider meeting with their bosses one on one. The prospect is too scary for them. On the other hand, many of these same employees could drum up the courage to meet with their bosses if they had other employees along for support. We think it's a strategy worth considering solely because of the opportunity this strategy offers to more timid workers.

3. *There's safety in numbers.* If there's strength in numbers, there's safety, too. Maybe the meeting will backfire. Maybe your boss will suddenly turn vindictive and try to strike back at you for being too candid. Who knows? But it'll be a lot harder to take it out on a group than a single individual.

4. *Meeting as a group may be more efficient than meeting as individuals.* Even if all employees were willing to meet with your boss individually, it'd be a time-consuming process. And it still might not have as strong an impact as the combined effect of a group meeting.

So much for the advantages. What are the disadvantages? There's only one, but it's important. If you choose this strategy, you'll be talking to your boss with fellow employees. And getting any group to act effectively isn't easy—especially when it's a bunch of employees trying to give the boss some candid feedback. If the meeting's going to be successful, you'll need a leader. And that leader's probably going to be you. That's the disadvantage. For this strategy to work, you'll have to lead a diverse collection of individuals through a difficult process. That'll be a challenge.

To help you meet this challenge, we've laid out a seven-step strategy in this chapter. Using an example from a group of employees we once worked with, we'll take you through each step:

1. deciding if your boss is a good candidate
2. identifying good candidates for the group
3. feeling out the candidates
4. planning strategy with the group
5. asking your boss to meet
6. running the meeting
7. following up

Several years ago we were working with a small printing company in the midwest. We had been called in to help the founder of the company, Henry Grothier, and his son Virgil settle some differences over how the business should be run. Not long after we started working with the company, however, Virgil got a very attractive offer from another company and decided to take it. All four of us agreed this would be good experience for Virgil. That way, when Henry planned to retire in several years, Virgil could come back and take the company over.

It seemed like a happy ending and we were ready to leave. Just before we did, however, Cathy Grant, the front-office manager, asked if she could meet with us for about a half-hour. And that's where the story begins.

Our meeting with Cathy lasted a lot longer than thirty minutes, even though it seemed much shorter. Her basic message went something like this: She and a number of other women had been working for Henry for at least ten years. Each of them really liked Henry, and they saw him as a good person and a caring boss. But they hated the way he behaved. Although well over age fifty-five, at times he showed the emotional maturity of a child. He was moody; he pouted; and he had an explosive, mercurial temper. More than once Henry had violently punched his fist through walls and file cabinets, scaring the wits out of employees standing nearby. One time

Henry even ripped Cathy's phone off the wall in her office and hurled it down the hall because she'd supposedly goofed up a customer's order.

When Cathy finally finished her story, she paused, took a deep breath, smiled broadly and said, "Any thoughts, guys?" In the next hour or so, we hatched the seven-step strategy that makes up this chapter. The rest of the chapter is devoted to how "Cathy and the Gang" carried out each step.

DECIDING IF YOUR BOSS IS A GOOD CANDIDATE

We suggested Cathy begin by looking at the six boss traits we talked about in the last chapter to decide if Henry was a good candidate for this strategy. Cathy liked the idea and jumped right into the task. These are the grades she gave Henry on each trait, along with a brief explanation:

Taking Criticism

Grade: C −

Taking criticism is definitely not one of Henry's strong points. He's not the kind of guy who's going to sit there and listen patiently to your explanation of something you think he did wrong. He's more likely to get defensive and maybe even build a case that the problem is more *your* fault than his. On the other hand—and to Henry's credit—I've seen him make personal changes as a result of some feedback I've given him.

You know his wife Alice works in the company. And a couple of times the two of them have had a real ripsnorting fight, and *not* in private. I mean, we're talking about yelling and screaming and throwing things around. After the second one of these bouts, I told him that marital squabbles at work had to cease. He got pretty hot and told me to mind my own business. But a day later he apologized and said I was right. We haven't had any more main events since.

Problem Solving

Grade: B+

Henry's a good problem solver. The fact that he had you guys come out here to help him work out his differences with Virgil is a good sign of that. Every now and then he'll sit on a decision longer than I think he needs to. But maybe I'm just a little more impatient than he is.

Vindictiveness

Grade: A

Henry's got a lot of faults, but this isn't one of them. He doesn't hold grudges. He doesn't try to get back at people or to get even. He's just not a vengeful person.

Caring

Grade: A

I think Henry really cares about the people who work here. He's a generous man. Not long ago the wife of one of our pressmen went through a long illness where she was bedridden for over five months. Henry gave the guy several months off with pay so he could take care of his wife. Also, many times he's lent his Mercedes to employees who've needed a fancy car to go to some affair. He definitely cares.

Honesty

Grade: B

I would have given Henry an "A" on this one except for one tendency he has that I don't particularly like. I don't know. Maybe it's because of his temper, but Henry doesn't come to you right away if you've done something he doesn't like. He has a tendency to keep that sort of thing inside. To let it build up. And then sometimes it all comes out like a volcano. I'd rather see him be a little more up front right away about how he feels if he thinks we've done something wrong. But otherwise he's a reasonably straightforward guy. I can't ever remember catching him in a lie.

Ability to Listen

Grade: D+/C−

Of all the six traits, I'd say this is Henry's worst. He is not a good listener. If you say something that he disagrees with, he's quick to jump in and offer his own opinion. And his body language can be very bad at times. More than once he's tried to balance his checkbook or read a memo while I've been trying to explain something to him. Henry needs a lot of work in this area.

After Cathy finished, we talked awhile about the potential advantages and disadvantages of meeting with Henry as a group. At the end of our conversation, we asked Cathy what she thought. She paused for a long time and then said:

Yeah, I think it's a go. Maybe Henry's not the best listener in the world and maybe he's touchy about criticism, but overall I'd have to say he's a good risk. I'd at least like to take the next step.

IDENTIFYING GOOD CANDIDATES
FOR THE GROUP

By the time Cathy decided she wanted to move forward, it was time for us to leave. So we did the rest of our counseling and advising with her by telephone conference calls.

In the first call, Cathy was already ahead of us. She immediately asked, "What's the best way for me to pull this group of people together?" We said we thought her next step should be to list people who might make good group members. Then she could compare everybody on the list to the same six traits she'd graded Henry on.

Two days later she called back. She told us she'd identified seven people and then, using the six traits (plus a little horse sense), narrowed the list down to four. This is a brief summary of what she told us about each person and why she included or rejected them:

Blanche Faraday (Out)

I actually like Blanche quite a bit and thought she might make a good member of the group because she's not afraid to speak her mind. But her big problem is she can't keep her mouth shut. Since this is a sensitive mission we're undertaking here, it'd be bad if she went around blabbing about the whole thing to everybody.

Jesus Carillo (In)

Obviously Jesus is not one of the women I originally told you about. He's young—only twenty-three—and has only been with the company for two years. But I thought he'd be good for the group. He's a hard worker, and I know Henry thinks highly of him. Jesus is already assistant manager in the stock room, and he'll keep moving up. He's a little on the shy side, but he's not afraid to speak his mind. I think he'll be good.

Janet Wetstron (In)

Janet has been here longer than any of us. She's maybe five years away from retirement. She's no house-a-fire, but she's a fairly solid person who does her job conscientiously and is loyal to the company. My only concern is that she's reluctant to speak up. But I'd still like to have her in the group.

Margaret Reston (Out)

What can I tell you about Margaret? At first I thought she'd be great for the group because she's a very classy lady, and I know Henry is fond of her. I don't know. It's hard to put my finger on it. I think it was the trait you guys call "caring" that made me hesitate on Margaret. I guess in my soul of souls I see Margaret as somebody who thinks she's a little better than the rest of us. A bit of a snob, maybe? Anyway, I decided not to include her.

Adrienne Gastineau (In)

Adrienne is a real character. Both she and Henry were born in Canada. They both speak fluent French, but they never use it except when they get mad at each other. Then that's *all* they speak. I don't understand a word of it, but Margaret, who was a French major in college, says it's not very "nice." Anyway, even though I'm a little concerned about her temper, I think Adrienne will be good for the group. She cares about this place. She likes Henry. She's genuine. And she says just what she thinks.

April Goodings (In)

April's only twenty-seven, but she's been with us for ten years. She started here the day after she graduated from high school. She's a little too low-key, but trustworthy. And, by the way, she's extremely attractive. I don't know how she puts up with all the catcalls and whistles and propositions she gets whenever she walks down the street. At any rate, I think she'd be good. She's mature and serious about her work. And she seems to like working here. I guess my only concern is that she seems intimidated by Henry. I know she can't stand his temper. I think it frightens her.

Ramona Truso (Out)

Ramona's been here for quite some time. At first I thought she might be good because she has a mind of her own and isn't afraid to stand up to Henry. But I think she's got a bad attitude. Frankly, she's a little lazy. And I know Henry doesn't have much respect for her and would really like to let her go. He's just too much of a softy to do it. I guess I think she'd be more of a liability than an asset.

FEELING OUT THE CANDIDATES

After Cathy finished describing these seven folks, we told her that her choices sounded good. We suggested her next step should be to talk to each of the four individually to feel them out about the idea of meeting with Henry as a group. "How do I do that?" she asked.

We spent the next twenty minutes giving her a refresher course on listening skills. (She had once attended one of our seminars, so the material wasn't completely new to her.) Basically, we recommended that she meet with each of the four people for about forty-five minutes to an hour to do two things. One, explain what she had in mind, and, two, *draw them out* on their reactions to the idea. She told us this sounded good, but she added, "What if they're reluctant to go along with the idea? Should I try to talk them into it?" We laughed and said that we didn't think that would be necessary. If she did a good job of listening, she wouldn't have to do much persuading. "Okay," she said.

Several days later we got another phone call from Cathy. "How'd it go?" we said. "Not bad!" she said. "I didn't have any problems at all with Jesus or Adrienne or April. Janet was the only one who was reluctant, but I think she's ready to do it now."

We asked her to talk a little about the problem she had with Janet. She said:

> Like I told you earlier, Janet's a good bit older than the rest of us, and she's kind of shy. I think she was a little afraid that going to Henry like this would get her in trouble. Maybe even affect her retirement. But I just listened to her and it seemed to work. She talked herself out of her concerns, I think.

When we pressed Cathy for more details on how it went, she reconstructed most of the conversation. Here's a little bit of what happened between the two of them:

CATHY: (after a little warming up) . . . Janet, as I mentioned the other day, I wanted to talk with you a little about several of us getting together to talk to Henry about improving our working relationship with him (pausing) . . .

JANET: (looking a little wary) Uh huh.

CATHY: I happen to think that Henry is a fine person, but I see him as a bit of a problem boss. I think all of us would benefit from sitting down with him to talk about things that could stand some improvement around here (pausing) . . .

JANET: (still looking wary) Uh huh.

CATHY: I've already spoken to Jesus, Adrienne, and April about it, and they like the idea. But I wanted to know how you felt about it because I think you'd make an excellent member of our group.

JANET: (still wary) Ah . . . maybe you could tell me a little more about what you have in mind, Cathy. I guess I'm not sure I know exactly what it is you're suggesting.

CATHY: You'd like me to clarify what it is I'd like all of us to do with Henry?

JANET: Yes. I mean, I'm not exactly sure this is a real good idea. I mean, Henry has a very bad temper. I could see him blowing his top at even the *thought* of doing something like this. I think it's a good idea in theory, but (shaking her head) . . .

CATHY: (pausing) Janet, I think what I'm hearing is that you like the idea of meeting with Henry, but, knowing how angry he can get, you're afraid the idea might backfire. And maybe even make things worse?

JANET: (becoming more animated) Yes, and . . .

All Cathy did was continue to draw Janet out for the next several minutes. Cathy didn't have to do any more selling of the idea. Finally, Janet put her hands on her knees, leaned forward, and said:

Okay, let's do it. I guess I'm still a little scared at the thought of meeting with Henry like this, but it *is* a good idea, and it's probably long overdue.

After Cathy finished describing her meeting with Janet, she said, "What's next?" We said we thought she was now ready to get the group together to plan the meeting with Henry.

PLANNING STRATEGY
WITH THE GROUP

As far as the strategy session with the group was concerned, we suggested that Cathy try to do four things:

1. Explain to the group what she had in mind.
2. Get the group's reaction.
3. Help the group agree on the plan.
4. Implement the plan.

Here's a condensed version of what we told her:

- Okay, once you've gotten them sitting down and loosened up with a little chitchat, take a few minutes to thank them for coming. Then say that the purpose of this meeting is to plan for the meeting with Henry. Tell them you'll begin by offering your ideas and then you want to hear what they think of your plan. After that, tell them you'd like the group to come to some kind of agreement on exactly how it is you're all going to proceed.
- Then go ahead and tell them the basic plan you have in mind. First, you'd like all of them, including yourself, to do a performance analysis on Henry—some of the things he does that keep you all satisfied, and some of the things he could do to make you feel more satisfied and be more productive. After that you'll be going to Henry to ask him to meet. And then comes the meeting itself. You plan to start off by asking Henry what you all can do to make *his* job less frustrating and more satisfying. Then you will be giving Henry some feedback on his performance. The goal of the meeting will be to reach an agreement on what everybody—all five of you and Henry—can do to make each other's jobs more satisfying and productive.
- Then just be the best listener you can. They'll probably have a lot of opinions and reactions. Your job should be to give them all a chance to speak their minds. Be patient. It

may take a while for them to sort through their feelings and reactions.

• Once you do, you'll have some kind of plan in place. Either your original plan or some modification of it.

Cathy thanked us for the suggestions and said she'd be back to us after the meeting with the group. Four days later we got another call. When we asked for an update, she was ready:

> Well, I'll tell you. I think everything turned out all right, but it didn't go as smo-o-othly as you said it would. I mean, it is not *easy* to get a group of five people to agree on something like this. Not at all.

Then she filled us in on the details. It seems that the first part of the meeting did go smoothly. Everybody listened patiently while she explained what she had in mind for the meeting with Henry. But when she asked for the group's reaction, "All hell broke loose!" It went something like this:

CATHY: . . . and that's what I think we should do to get this meeting with Henry off the ground. Okay, now what I'd like to do is get your reactions to the plan and then try to get us all to agree on exactly how we're going to proceed here.

ADRIENNE: (shaking her head vigorously) Look, Cathy, it's a good plan in theory, but I don't think it's going to work . . .

JESUS: (interrupting) What do you mean, Adrienne? What's wrong with it? It makes a lot of sense to me because . . .

CATHY: (holding up a hand) Whoa! I want everybody to have a chance to talk, but let's do it one at a time. Adrienne, you were saying . . .

JESUS: (reluctantly leaning back in his chair)

ADRIENNE: I mean I do think it's a good plan, but I really
             don't think it's going to work. Yeah, Henry's
             going to love the part where we ask him what
             we can do to make his job easier. Who
             wouldn't? But you think he's going to listen to
             what we think he can do to make our jobs eas-
             ier? Come on! He's not going to sit still for
             that. No way!

CATHY: Okay, thanks, Adrienne. Now let's hear from
             somebody else.

JESUS: (jumping right in) Well, I don't agree with Ad-
             rienne. I think it's a good plan and I'll tell you
             why. First of all . . .

For the next ten minutes or so Cathy just gave everybody
in the group a chance to offer their reactions to the plan. Then
she tried to do what we call a *group* read back. That is, she
tried to briefly summarize what each of the four people said.
It went something like this:

CATHY: Okay, I think everybody's had a chance to offer
             their reactions to the plan. Now let me try to
             catch up with all of you. Adrienne, I think
             you're basically saying that you like the plan
             in theory, but you think it's going to fall apart
             when it comes time to give Henry our feed-
             back.

ADRIENNE: (nodding but not saying anything)

CATHY: Jesus, what I heard from you is that you disa-
             gree with Adrienne. You think the plan will
             work. You think Henry's going to listen to us
             because we're going to listen to him first.

JESUS: Right. Exactly.

CATHY: And, April, I think both you and Janet thought
             the plan was a reasonably good one, but I also

	thought the two of you were saying that every-thing could fall apart in the meeting if Henry loses his temper.
APRIL:	(nodding)
JANET:	Yes, that's what I'm afraid of.
CATHY:	(pausing and making eye contact with each of the four) Okay, well, how do you all think we should change the plan to make it better?
ADRIENNE:	(now a little more thoughtful) Okay. I think what I'd like is for us to get an agreement from Henry up front that if we listen to him first, he listens to us when it's our turn to talk. Also, I think he should agree to keep his cool and not just fly off the handle if we say something he doesn't like . . .

After another twenty minutes or so of Cathy's patient lis-tening, the group reached a consensus. They'd go with the basic plan that Cathy had outlined. But when Cathy met with Henry individually to suggest the meeting, she was instructed to get two commitments from him. One, that he'd really listen when it was his turn to listen, and, two, that he'd try as hard as he could to keep his temper in check.

Cathy said they spent the rest of the meeting doing Henry's performance analysis. Apparently, this went well. When Cathy read it to us over the phone, it sounded clearly thought-out and nice and specific.

ASKING YOUR BOSS TO MEET

After she'd filled us in on the meeting with the group, Cathy said, "Okay, now we're getting to the tough part. How do I go about getting Henry to agree to have this meeting with us?"

Here we gave her the same advice we offered in the last

chapter on meeting with your boss one on one. (If you'd like, you may want to go back and review that portion of the chapter.) Cathy liked what we suggested and told us she'd call us in a couple of days.

Two days later, another call. This time there wasn't any of the usual chitchat before getting down to business. Cathy started right in: "I came *very* close to blowing it with Henry. But now everything's all right, and we've got the meeting all set up."

"What happened?" we said, bubbling with curiosity.

She filled us in on the details. Apparently, things started to get a little out of control when Cathy got to the two points about Henry listening when it was his turn to listen and not losing his temper:

CATHY: . . . I guess the only thing I'd like to add is this. We're going to be trying very hard to listen to what you have to say about what we all can do to make your job more satisfying and less frustrating. (pausing)

HENRY: Yeah?

CATHY: Well, two things. One, we really want you to listen to us when it's our turn to talk. (pausing)

HENRY: (a slight tone of defensiveness in his voice) I'm ready to do that.

CATHY: The other thing is not losing your temper if we say something you don't particularly like. Now Adrienne was particularly concerned . . .

When we "processed" this portion of the meeting later with Cathy, she agreed it was a mistake to mention the concerns of any specific member of the group. In this case, especially Adrienne's:

HENRY: (vaulting out of his chair and throwing his hands to the ceiling) I don't believe it! She's got an un-

believable nerve, that one. Talking about me losing my temper. What a joke! Why she loses her
temper twice as much as I do!

CATHY: (reaching a hand toward him) Henry, maybe it
would be better if you sat down so we could talk
about this more calmly . . .

HENRY: (wheeling around and pointing a finger at her) I
don't want to sit down and I don't want to be
calm! My temper! I can't tell you the number of
times "Madame" Adrienne has stormed into my
office and lashed out at me . . .

Cathy told us at this point she was scared and confused;
all she really wanted to do was escape from Henry's office.
But she kept her cool and remembered how we'd said that
good listening could bail you out of most tight situations. For
the next five minutes she just sat there and did nothing while
he ranted and raved around his office. When the storm had
spent its fury and Henry plopped down into his chair, she
patiently looked at him for another ten seconds or so. Then
she said:

CATHY: Well, obviously, Henry, what I said made you
feel pretty angry . . .

HENRY: (smiling sheepishly) I guess you could say that.

CATHY: (smiling back) I think what happened is that I
mentioned that Adrienne was particularly concerned about you not losing your temper, and that
really touched you off. (pausing)

HENRY: (nodding but not saying anything)

CATHY: I thought what you were saying is that it annoyed
the hell out of you that she'd have the nerve to say
something like that after she's come in here so
many times and lost her temper at *you*. That just
didn't seem fair to you.

HENRY: (sounding spent and tired) Exactly! And I guess

I did just what you're all afraid of. I lost my temper, but . . .

Cathy continued to draw Henry out for several more minutes until:

HENRY: Look . . . ah . . . Cathy . . . I realize I got a little hot over what you told me earlier about Adrienne. But I do think this meeting idea would be a good thing to do. I give you my word I'll do the best I can when it's my turn to listen. I'll *really* try to hold my temper in check.

CATHY: (smiling) Great. I think it'll be a good thing, too. Now, how about setting a time and place to meet . . .

RUNNING THE MEETING

After Cathy finished the story of her meeting with Henry, we offered some detailed advice on how to run the group meeting. What we said was almost identical to what we told you in the last chapter about meeting one on one with your boss. However, we emphasized several points:

- Cathy, the most important thing for you to remember about this meeting is that *you'll* be running it. How well it goes will depend on how well you make sure everybody has their say.
- In the beginning, when the group is asking Henry what they can do to make his job less frustrating and more satisfying, your job will be to make sure Henry really has a chance to answer this question in depth. If somebody like Adrienne, for example, starts to butt in and interrupt him, you've got to cut her off and let Henry keep going. Do the same when it's the group's turn to offer Henry feedback. Henry agreed

to be a good listener and not to lose his cool. You'll have to hold him to that.
• During the meeting, you're going to be like a cop directing traffic. If you can do that, things ought to go well.

After we finished, Cathy asked us what we thought about the idea of getting the group together for a dress rehearsal before the meeting with Henry. When we probed for a little more information, she said:

> I think it might be good to get everybody together to practice before we actually meet with Henry. We could even role play what to do if something goes wrong. I don't know. I think it might be worth the extra time and effort.

We said we thought it was a fine idea. Then Cathy hung up and promised to call us in several days with a report on the meeting with Henry.

Five days later we got the report:

> On balance, I think everything went very well. As we discussed, all five of us met for the dress rehearsal. It was a good thing to do because it gave me a chance to stress some of the points you guys had stressed to me. But, more important, we did some role playing. It was fun, and it definitely helped us prepare for the meeting with Henry.

Intrigued, we asked her to go into a little detail on what happened in the dress rehearsal:

> Well, my big fear was that Adrienne was going to say or do something that would set Henry off. Then Henry would say or do something that would set Adrienne off. Then we'd have a donnybrook on our hands. And Shirley and Janet would either sit there in terror, or just run out of the room.

So I told them that's *exactly* what I was afraid of and that maybe we could role play how to avoid that kind of situation. It worked like a charm. First, everybody was very relieved I even brought it up because they were afraid of the same thing. So we just had Jesus—who can do an unbelievably good imitation of Henry—play Henry getting mad at something Adrienne said. And, even though we were just role playing, Adrienne started to get mad. I just gave her a subtle look. She calmed down. Then I read Henry—Jesus—back and he calmed down.

It was great. Shirley and Janet said they started to feel terrified, but pretty soon they calmed down, too.

Then we asked Cathy to talk about the actual meeting with Henry. She started chuckling:

This reminds me of something my uncle, a crusty old retired marine colonel, used to say about the six P's of good preparation: "Prior planning prevents piss poor performance." I think we were all so well prepared for the meeting—Henry included—that it pretty much went off without a hitch. I was even a little disappointed because the "excitement" we'd anticipated didn't come off.

Cathy went on to tell us how the meeting unfolded. Apparently things got off to a good start. Before Cathy could call the meeting to order, Henry got up out of his chair and went over and sat in between April and Janet. He started speaking very softly to both of them:

Ah . . . Janet and April, before we get started, I wanted to mention something that I'm very concerned about.

Cathy said the two women looked wide-eyed with apprehension as Henry started to talk.

I don't exactly know how to put this, but, as you know, Adrienne and I are very *shy* people. And . . . well . . . the two of you tend to really fly off the handle at a drop of a hat. And . . . Adrienne and I would just like to ask you . . . if you wouldn't mind . . . holding down the ranting and raving in this meeting . . .

The whole time Henry was talking, Adrienne maintained a very serious expression and occasionally nodded her head. Janet and April continued to listen to Henry with a mixture of tension and disbelief on their faces. Finally, Jesus, no longer able to contain himself, roared with laughter. Any ice in the room completely broke and melted away.

After the laughter had subsided, Cathy structured the meeting by reviewing (a) the purpose of the meeting, (b) what they were going to cover, and (c) how all of them could get the most out of the session.

The group spent almost an hour drawing Henry out on what he thought they could do to make his job easier and more satisfying. Cathy said that while he was talking she made notes of the key points on a flip chart.

The only touchy spot in the meeting, according to Cathy, was not when the group was giving Henry feedback. It was when they were trying to negotiate a performance agreement. Cathy made the suggestion that one thing they could put down for Henry to do was have performance reviews on a regular basis with the people who reported to him. Henry balked at the idea, claiming he didn't have time for that kind of thing. Adrienne jumped in and said, "Henry, you have to *make* time for that. It's important." As a look of disgust appeared on Henry's face, Cathy held up both hands and simply said, "Hey, you two. Remember what you promised."

Cathy said the meeting ended on a very positive note. Before leaving, everybody got a copy of the performance agreement; they set a date for a follow-up meeting about three weeks away; and April and Janet went over and put an arm around Henry and promised to try to keep their tempers in check.

FOLLOWING UP

Before we got off the phone with Cathy, we stressed how important it was for everybody to begin working on their portions of the performance agreement right away. She agreed that this was important and told us she'd get back to us after the follow-up meeting.

About a month later Cathy called with what sounded like a happy ending to the story. She described several positive things that had happened:

- Everybody noticed a marked change in Henry. He seemed much less moody and much more cheerful. And nobody had seen him lose his temper in the last four weeks.
- A number of times during the month, Henry mentioned to Cathy what a positive experience the meeting had been. He also said he'd seen a number of positive changes in the performance of all the group members. For example, Adrienne and Henry seemed to be really clicking together when they worked on estimating potential jobs. This had been an area where they'd frequently locked horns in the past.
- The general morale of the group was high. They had all gone out to lunch together three times during the month. Each time there was a lot of laughing and teasing—and comments about what a change the meeting with Henry had made.
- A number of other employees had come up to Cathy and said things like, "I don't know what you guys did in that meeting with Henry. But whatever it was, the magic worked. What a difference."

Well, that's the story. Of course there's no guarantee that a meeting with your boss as a group will work out as well as this one did. But it just might. If you've got a boss who seems like a reasonably good candidate for this approach, then the success of this strategy is up to you. If you're willing to put in the time and effort that Cathy did, you might be able to bring about some very nice changes in the environment you work in. It's worth a try.

13
....

TALKING TO YOUR
BOSS INDIRECTLY

Our last two chapters focused on how to talk *directly* to bosses, either one on one or as a group. Although almost all employees would like to give their bosses direct feedback, most don't. Many are afraid of the consequences (some real, some imagined) if they told their bosses what they really thought of them and their management style.

Of course, bosses don't make it any easier, either. A lot of them don't want feedback (and, in fact, don't really give a damn what their employees think). As we mentioned in our one on one chapter, many bosses simply aren't good candidates for a direct approach. For a number of reasons, then, the direct approach—whether one on one or as a group—simply isn't appropriate. A good alternative can be talking to bosses *indirectly*, through what we call indirect feedback.

WHAT IS INDIRECT FEEDBACK?

Basically, indirect feedback is a method for sending a message to your boss so the boss won't be able to identify who said it and get back at you. From the employee's point of view, it's a fairly low-risk way to express disapproval of a boss's behavior and possibly even call public attention to it.

We first got acquainted with this strategy when we were in junior high school. We had one of those old battle-axe teachers who was notorious at playing favorites. It really used to bug us when her "pets" would get A's and B's on homework that wasn't any better than ours, but we got C's and sometimes worse. Determined to fight this injustice, we found an old typewriter in the basement and wrote her an anonymous letter complaining about the situation. We stuck the letter in a mailbox and waited on pins and needles for some result. For days, nothing happened. "Did she get the letter?" we wondered. "Why wasn't she saying anything?" We were getting pretty worried when one morning she walked into the classroom, obviously upset. The letter was in her hand. Waving it at the class, she said, "I don't know who sent this letter, but you know who you are." Relieved that she didn't know who sent it, we tried to look as confused as the rest of the class. But inside we were thinking, "Bee-yoo-ti-ful!" She carried on for a minute or two, tore up the letter, and threw it in the wastebasket. The storm was over as abruptly as it began. She never said another word about it. Maybe time has played tricks with our memory, but we recall that the letter had an impact—maybe not a dramatic one, but an impact nonetheless. But even if it hadn't, we still vividly remember how good it felt to *do something* to protest a situation we didn't like.

Indirect feedback is not just a juvenile thing to do. A short time ago we were watching one of those television programs that reports news from the entertainment industry. It had a story about a national group of entertainment writers and reporters who were having their annual awards ceremony. Instead of "Oscars" they gave out "Golden Apple" awards in a variety of categories to show-business personalities. It seemed like a typical Hollywood ceremony (with acceptance speeches and all), until we noticed they also had an award for the show-business personality who was the most difficult to work with in the past year: the "Sour Apple" award. In our opinion, this was a good example of what we'd call indirect feedback.

There's really no limit to the number of ways that employees can use this strategy. In general, though, it breaks down into two broad types: (a) private and (b) public. Let's take a look at each type.

Private Indirect Feedback

As the name suggests, this is a private message from an employee (or group of employees) to a boss. We heard about a good example a couple of years ago from Clara Hansen, the secretary to the executive director of a public agency in Washington, D.C.

Apparently, Clara's boss was quite a success story, having risen from a person who was once a client of the agency to its executive director. But she also had a reputation for being vicious and frequently making cutting, sarcastic, and hurtful remarks to her employees. She could be sweet as pie when talking to community leaders, government officials, and her own board of directors. But she was downright nasty to employees—not only to Clara and others who reported directly to her, but also to maintenance workers and security guards she hardly even knew.

Clara told us that one day an envelope marked "confidential" arrived in the interoffice mail. She put it with the other letters that arrived that day and placed them all on her boss's desk. When her boss came in, she walked into her office, made a few phone calls, and started opening the morning mail. After a few minutes, the boss cried out, "Clara, come in here!" When Clara arrived, her boss was visibly upset. She handed her the letter and said angrily, "What do you know about this?" Taking the letter, Clara read it. It said:

Dear Ms._____

I'll bet your mother and father are very proud of the wonderful things you've done with your career and professional life. It's too bad they're no longer around to beam with pleasure at your accomplishments.

But wherever they are, how do you think they feel about the way you treat people, especially the way you humiliate and cut down the people who work for you? How do you think they feel about their daughter's becoming an insensitive bully who pushes little people around and sucks up to those with power? I'll bet your parents are ashamed of that part of what you've become.

"A Friend of the Family"

Clara denied knowing anything of the letter or who might have sent it. At that, her boss reached for her coat and headed for the door, saying she'd be back in about an hour and a half. Clara knew exactly where she was headed—to the office of her therapist. "That note really got her attention," she told us with a half-smile on her face, "I know for a fact that she talked about that note—and everything it brought up—in many sessions with her therapist. The person who sent it may not know that. But I do."

Like her boss, we suspected Clara sent the note—or at least knew who did. But whether or not she had anything to do with it, she was clearly *very* glad it'd been sent.

We've heard of a lot of other "private" examples over the years. For instance:

- One employee sent a bouquet of flowers to the wife of his blustery boss with a condolence card and a note that said, "We only have to work with him. You have to live with him."
- The technique has also been used successfully with what we call "sexual bosses," as the following example illustrates.

In one organization, a married vice-president of a large department store chain was a real womanizer. In less than two years, he had brief affairs with about a half-dozen female employees. When the affairs ended, as they always did, the women were not-so-delicately eased out of the company. Since none were willing to go public with a grievance or a sexual harassment case, a couple of concerned employees decided to try the indirect feedback route. They sent the vice-president a series of notes over a period of weeks. The notes said that they had documented evidence (not specified in the notes) of his affairs with female employees. Further, the notes said that what the vice-president did with his personal life was his business, but his sexual appetites at work had seriously damaged the careers of several promising young women. Later notes took on a more threatening tone. They said that if he continued to play around at work the evidence would be sent to his wife and children (three teen-agers). The notes also said that they were prepared to go a second, even more severe step if he didn't stop.

From what we heard, it wasn't necessary. While the man didn't stop his womanizing, he stopped it at work.

Public Indirect Feedback

Like the "Sour Apple" award we mentioned earlier, this is a public way to give bosses feedback and draw attention to their behavior. As with the "private" examples earlier, bosses can't get back at anyone in particular because they don't know who's responsible.

A good example happened several years ago, at the time of the Iranian hostage crisis. Apparently, Richard Snyder (his real name), the president of Simon & Schuster, has a reputation for being a brilliant chief executive, but an extremely difficult man to work for. According to *Fortune* magazine, he has a "quick, flaring temper that has driven talented employees from the company, their self-respect in shreds." During the hostage crisis, a clever Simon & Schuster employee started a joke that quickly spread throughout the organization—and, of course, eventually to Snyder's office. In our view, the joke was a "public" example of indirect feedback: "What's the difference between the Ayatollah Khomeini and Dick Snyder? Answer: the Ayatollah has only 52 hostages, Snyder has 700—the number of Simon & Schuster employees."

Here are a few other examples:

- The "problem boss of the month" award. Here, employees (especially in a larger organization) surreptitiously post the monthly award on company bulletin boards. The offending boss is named as well as what he or she did to earn the award.
- Employees create stickers with appropriate messages they want to send to their bosses (like, "Watch out! I'm a volcano ready to erupt!" or "Yes, I'm the boss. But I'm so disorganized I don't know what I'm doing.") These stickers are affixed to the boss's office door, car window, briefcase, or wherever.
- The small microcassette tape recorder offers all kinds of possibilities. Let's say a general manager in a manufac-

turing firm has a nasty habit of walking out on the shop floor and chewing out employees. It'd be very easy to tape record these daily blasts and edit them in such a way that no particular employee could be identified. The tape could then be mailed to the boss with a note that said, "Listen to this tape. This is how you behave. Why don't you play it for your wife and kids and ask them what they think of how you treat employees?" Moving from private to more public, it could be mailed straight to his spouse. Or, to go really public, it could be played on the company's intercom system. The possibilities are endless.

• In many organizations over the years employees with a literary or journalistic bent have established underground newsletters that, like the company's official newsletter, talk about company management—or mismanagement—from the employee's point of view. Publications like these offer lots of possibilities for sending indirect messages *very* directly.

WHY WE LIKE THIS STRATEGY

While many people have reservations about the idea of indirect feedback (we'll talk about them shortly), we like this strategy a lot! Here are a few reasons why:

Sometimes It's the Only Real Good Alternative

Given the vengeful nature of some bosses, a lot of employees simply can't give them direct feedback. As one person said, "You'll get screwed if you do." Truer words were never spoken! It's happened to us personally and to lots of people we've known—we give our bosses a little constructive criticism and they give us the shaft. So what are people supposed to do when they've got something important to say to their bosses but can't express it directly? Our answer: Indirect feedback.

Indirect Feedback Is Better
Than No Feedback at All

We've said many times that bosses exist in a feedback vacuum. In plain English, they don't have the foggiest idea of what their employees think or feel about them and what they're doing. But that doesn't mean they don't *need* to hear what employees have to say. Sometimes, indirect feedback is all the feedback bosses are going to get. It's better than no feedback at all.

It's a Way of Delivering Bad News
without Getting Burned

It's said that in ancient times rulers killed messengers who brought them bad news. While the modern-day consequences aren't quite so severe, they can still be bad. Indirect feedback keeps you from taking unnecessary risks.

It's a Way of Holding Bosses
at Least Partially Accountable

One of the facts of organizational life is that many bad bosses are not and never will be held accountable by their bosses or the companies they work for. It may be a small consolation, but indirect feedback is a way of holding these bosses at least partially accountable.

It's a Power Equalizer

Because bosses have so much more power than employees, they can almost say anything to employees and get away with it. But as soon as employees say something critical to a boss, they're asking for trouble. Indirect feedback takes away some of this power imbalance. It gives employees the feeling they have the freedom to say what's on their minds. As one employee said, "A fight with a boss ain't a fair fight. This is a way of evening up the odds."

It Can Say Something Serious with a Touch of Lightness and Humor

A few years ago "roasts" were a popular way of giving bosses indirect feedback. Many bad habits, offensive characteristics, and ineffective tendencies could be pointed out in a humorous setting.

Another example comes from the Marine Corps Reserves summer camp experiences one of us had years ago. At the end of each year's camp there was an established ritual for the troops to deliver the "Asshole of Summer Camp" award to the staff N.C.O. or officer who was the biggest pain in the butt that summer. Whoever was selected had to come up in front of the assembled troops to receive his award—which consisted of pitchers of beer poured over his head and a roll of toilet paper, accompanied, of course, by Bronx cheers, catcalls, and verbal abuse not appropriate for publication. The award ceremony, although unofficial, had the support of company bigwigs, who saw it as an opportunity for the troops to blow off a little steam (although we wondered if they would have been as supportive if one of them had received the award). We really needed their support, too, for they established an unwritten rule that recipients of the award couldn't get back at the "selection committee."

Sometimes, Indirect Feedback Does Get the Attention of Bosses

While it's not the primary reason to do it, indirect feedback can get the attention of some bosses and be responsible for a change in their behavior.

A short time ago we heard a story about a man whose wife worked for a couple of doctors who were submitting fraudulent health insurance and Medicaid claims. Being a loyal employee, she had assisted them in their efforts, despite feeling guilty. She became tormented by fears that she'd be discovered and have to go to jail. She was anxious, couldn't sleep at night, and began to experience marital and sexual problems with her husband. But she didn't want to leave the job. Without his wife's knowledge (he felt he never would've gotten her permission if he'd asked her), the husband sent an anonymous note to the doctor's offices:

> I know what the three of you are doing with your health insurance forms and I can prove it in a court of law. Stop now and I'll say nothing. Keep it up and you're looking at BIG trouble.

When the note arrived, the doctors suspected the woman, but she swore she knew nothing and they believed her. When she came home after work she confronted her husband and he swore he knew nothing about it. She chose to believe him. Concerned that their careers were in jeopardy, the doctors stopped what they were doing.

HOW TO GIVE INDIRECT FEEDBACK

In previous chapters, we've offered detailed advice on how to implement the various strategies. Here our advice is short and simple. There are only two things to keep in mind:

1. Be creative
2. Be careful

Be Creative

People differ in their ability to come up with creative solutions to problems. Most of us, to be honest, come up with normal, typical, stable, humdrum ideas. Some people, though, are just wacky enough to see new ideas that would never occur to the rest of us. In general, these creative folks are the most interested in this strategy.

Even if you don't think of yourself as the most creative person in the world, don't worry. When we need extra creativity to solve a problem, we find a creative person, read that person in on the problem, and ask him or her to brainstorm some solutions to the problem.

You may want to try this. Let's say you're interested in this strategy, but aren't exactly sure how you'd like to implement it. Find one or two of your most creative friends, let them read the chapter, and ask them to think of as many ideas as they can on indirect feedback. You may be pleasantly surprised at the quantity as well as the quality of the ideas they come up with.

One more thought on creativity. Sometimes, when you're scanning potential ideas, you'll come up with ideas that sound zany, or even sick. That's fine. Sometimes the kernel of a good idea is lodged inside of a bad one. So don't reject an idea too soon just because you don't like it. Just say to yourself, "How would I have to change this idea to make it better?"

Be Careful

What can we say here: Being careful is critically important. If employees can sometimes get in trouble for giving their bosses direct feedback, they can get in *big* trouble if they get caught giving indirect feedback. So please use caution.

During World War II companies manufacturing products for the war effort put up signs warning people not to talk too much about what they were doing. The signs said, "Loose lips sink ships." Well, loose lips sink employees too, especially if the boss finds out. So be careful who you involve when you're hatching your plan, and be *especially* careful who you tell after you implement it.

WHY PEOPLE DON'T LIKE
THIS STRATEGY

Even though lots of people like the concept of indirect feedback, many don't. It runs against their grain. They see it as sneaky and underhanded, or immature and sophomoric. Other people secretly like the idea, but are too frightened they might get caught to ever seriously consider it.

To get in touch with your own feelings about indirect feedback, you might ask yourself, "What are my *attractions* and what are my *reservations* about this strategy?" And then list them all on a sheet of paper. When you're through, put the paper away and let it sit for a while. Come back to it after you've read through all the strategies we offer for dealing with problem bosses.

14

....

GOING AROUND YOUR BOSS: TRANSFERRING TO A NEW BOSS

I N an earlier chapter, we said that people in a relationship often find themselves at a fork in the road, facing a decision about what to do:

• stay with the relationship
• end the relationship

Most of the early strategies of the book were based on the notion that you were staying with your boss—at least for a while. These strategies included doing nothing, accepting your boss, changing yourself, and doing a variety of other things to improve—or, at least, make more tolerable—the working relationship between you and your boss. However, our final four strategies (beginning with this one) have a very different emphasis. They're all based on a decision to take the other fork in the road: to end the relationship between you and your boss.

When people decide to end a relationship, they generally

move from a collaborative or cooperative stance with each other to an antagonistic or adversarial position. It's what happens in the typical divorce—things get messy. It's also the major risk employees run when they decide to end it all with their bosses.

As you move through the next four chapters, you'll notice that the risks associated with each strategy keep going up. For example, in this chapter we talk about going around your boss and trying to get a transfer to another job in the organization. Here you risk alienating your boss and maybe even getting a new boss worse than your current one. In the next chapter, "Going Over Your Boss's Head," we up the ante. This is a much riskier strategy, especially if your boss's boss has a tight relationship with your boss. In the final two chapters—where we talk about taking a stand against your boss and "firing" your boss—the risks go up even more.

When it comes to taking risks in life, people vary enormously. Some seem to get a thrill or even a rush from things like sky diving or wagering large sums of money in the stock market. Others are conservative. To them, even the thought of blowing five dollars worth of nickels in a slot machine brings on a cold sweat. As you read through these next four chapters, pay attention to how you *feel* as you contemplate the risks involved. For example, do the strategies tend to make you nervous? Or do they get you chomping at the bit to give them a try? These feelings should help you eventually decide how appropriate any one of these strategies will be for you.

Over the years we've come to know a lot of employees who like (even love) their jobs and the companies they work for. The problem is, they can't *stand* their bosses. They dislike their bosses so much they're on the verge of quitting— even though quitting would mean giving up a good job in a good organization.

Maybe you're one of these folks. If you are, this strategy could be for you. We'll help you decide whether it is or not in the next section. After that, we'll describe some specific things you can do to (a) find a new boss in your organization and (b) get yourself hired away from your current boss. In personnel jargon, it's called a transfer.

AM I RIGHT FOR THIS STRATEGY?

Let's begin by introducing you to two employees we once worked with: Kevin Dawkins and Donna Scampi.

Kevin Dawkins

Kevin is a twenty-eight-year-old press operator in a printing company of about one hundred employees in one of the New England states. He works for Carl Overstreet, and Kevin has *had* it with Carl:

> I just can't put up with Carl anymore. There are so many things wrong with the guy I don't know where to start. First of all, he's a lot older than me, about twice my age. But he doesn't know half of what I know about running a four-color press. He really doesn't. And he's the most cantankerous individual you'd ever want to meet. With Carl, there's only one way to do things, and it's Carl's way. I can prove to him that some other way of doing a job is faster and more efficient, and he won't even listen. Maybe it sounds conceited and all, but I feel like I'm wasting my time working for Carl. He can't teach me anything, and he causes me so much aggravation that it's starting to affect my home life. A number of times I've caught myself taking it out on Rebecca and the kids. And that's got to stop.
>
> The trouble is, I really like the company. I think Brian Grisholm, the owner, is a great guy. We've got fantastic benefits. The working conditions here are excellent. This is a clean shop. I think the company is

going to continue to grow over the years. It's a good
place to work. Like I said, the only drawback is Carl.

Donna Scampi

Donna is a thirty-year-old Pacific regional marketing manager for a large computer manufacturer. For the past eighteen
months she's been working for Neil Gressner, the company's
far west region marketing vice-president. Donna hates Neil:

> What can I tell you, I find the man repulsive. He's
> the polar opposite of what I want in a boss. He's phony.
> He's insincere. He lies to customers. He lies to our
> own manufacturing people. He thinks he has a great
> deal of technical know-how, and he doesn't. And he's
> a male chauvinist to boot. If it were up to Neil, this
> company would have no female marketing reps—in
> spite of the fact that, if anything, our female marketing
> people are selling the pants off the men.
>
> I'd really like to get out from under Neil. I'd have
> quit six months ago if I didn't like the company so
> much. The benefits are great, and the profit-sharing
> plan alone is enough to keep me here. I really don't
> want to leave.

Both Kevin and Donna were very interested in this strategy. They detested their bosses but liked the companies they
worked for and didn't want to leave. If you're in a similar
situation, you need to answer this question: ''Is there a better
boss in this organization for me to go to work for?''

Let's look at Kevin and Donna's situations first. Then we'll
look at yours.

On the surface, Kevin doesn't seem to have a lot of options. He's a press operator—a highly technical job requiring
a lot of training and hands-on experience. And there's only
one boss for all the press operators—Carl Overstreet. So it

appears that Kevin is locked into working for Carl until Carl retires in about eight years.

But, let's say Kevin isn't wedded to his job as a press operator. If he isn't, a number of opportunities seem to open up. For example, we asked him:

> Kevin, imagine you were willing to do something here at the company besides running a press. Say you were willing to do almost anything as long as it paid well and you found it interesting. And, finally, if you could work for any boss in the company you wanted to, who would you like to work for?

Kevin didn't take long to respond:

> Well, I can think of several people right off the bat. First of all, I'd love to work for Brian Grisholm. Like I said, I think Brian's a great guy. I think I'd really enjoy working for him. I think I'd learn a lot about how to run a business from him. He's not really much younger than Carl, but he thinks young. He likes new ideas, and he's not the wet blanket Carl is.
>
> I'll tell you somebody else I wouldn't mind working for—Hannah Stewart. She runs the bindery, and in some respects she may be the best boss in the place. I know her people really like and respect her. I've been very impressed with how she handles herself in department meetings. Carl's a big joke at those meetings, but Hannah is always well-prepared.

Before he finished, Kevin came up with two more people he thought would be good bosses to work for. Of course, if Kevin were to work for any of these people, he'd have to do something other than work at a printing press. He might have to learn some new skills—possibly even a whole new trade. But the point is, Kevin was able to say "yes" to the question: "Is there a better boss in this organization for me to go to work for?'' He clearly saw the possibility of staying with the company without being stuck under Carl.

When we asked Donna about the possibility of working for some other boss in the company, she hesitated a bit and then said:

> I feel like I'm caught between a rock and a hard place. Yes, there are definitely other bosses I could work for in the company. After all, we have four marketing V.P.s. And if I were willing to relocate, I could probably get a transfer to any one of them. But the problem is, I don't want to relocate. I've just bought a condo here in town, and Larry, my boyfriend, and I are thinking about getting married. I know he doesn't want to leave.

After a long pause, we asked, "What about the possibility of staying with the company in this area, but doing something other than marketing?" At first Donna didn't seem too receptive to the idea:

> Oh, I don't know. I've been in marketing now for the last five years. And I've gotten pretty good at it. Somehow the thought of shifting to something else at this point isn't very appealing to me.

We decided to push her a little: "Okay, but what are some other areas in the company where you could work if you decided to make a change?" That got her wheels turning:

> Hmmm . . . well, I guess there're actually a number of areas where I could find something. There's software development . . . but I don't know how good I'd be at that. There's finance and administration. Ah . . . hmmm . . . now that you mention it, there *is* one area that has always caught my fancy—market research. They do some interesting stuff over there. Ah . . .

there's another area, come to think of it, that I might
be good at. In fact, knowing what I do about our customers' problems, I think I'd make a good service
manager . . .

In the next several minutes, Donna identified two more
areas—human resource development and training—where she
might find an interesting job working for a better boss than
Neil. Like Kevin, she was starting to see possibilities she'd
overlooked before.

Now, what about your situation? Let's assume you have
a boss you want to leave, but you don't want to leave the
organization. How would you answer the question: "Is there
a better boss in this organization for me to go to work for?"

Maybe your answer is no. Maybe you work in a company
that's so small there's only one boss—like the secretary to a
small, independent insurance agent, or a dental hygienist in
a small dental practice. Or maybe you're so high up the lad-
der already, a vice-president or a general manager, for example, that your boss is the only one in the company you
could report to. Obviously, in these cases, going to work for
another boss in the same company isn't an option.

But maybe your answer is yes. Even if you work for a
small company, there may be at least one other boss in the
place who'd be better than your current one. Like Kevin and
Donna, you may have to consider doing a different kind of
job. You may even have to put up with slightly less pay for
a while. But if you really want to stay with the organization,
you probably can at least *identify* a new and potentially better
boss.

FINDING THE BOSS YOU WANT TO WORK FOR

Once you've decided there are other potential bosses for you in your organization, your job is to figure out specifically who it'll be. To do this, you'll need to answer three basic questions:

1. What kind of boss do I want?
2. What kind of work would I like to do for this new boss?
3. How do I find candidates for my new boss?

What Kind of Boss Do I Want?

If you're very unhappy with your current boss, you'll have a tendency to give this question short shrift. For example:

- "Hey, beggars can't be choosers. Right now I'd just like to have a boss who's a decent human being."
- "At this point, I think almost anybody else would be a breath of fresh air. I mean, who could be worse than Gary?"
- "What kind of boss do I want? I'll tell you what kind of boss I want. One that doesn't yell and scream like a two-year-old when things don't go his way. Somebody who can act his age. That's the kind of boss I want."

In other words, people are often so fed up with their current bosses that almost any other boss looks good. But not taking time to think about the type of boss you'd like to work for is a mistake. The old saying about jumping from the frying pan into the fire really fits here. It doesn't make sense to go through the trouble of getting another boss only to find the new one is as bad or worse than the old one.

Probably the best way to figure out what kind of boss you want is to go back and review chapter 3, "Taking a Look at Your Boss." For example, take a look at your boss history and the TRAC ratings you gave your boss. But the section you probably ought to pay most attention is to your ideal boss analysis. This will remind you of the traits and characteristics you'll really want to see in a boss. Kevin and Donna both found it helpful to go back over this material.

Kevin came up with five traits he thought were especially important for a boss to have—intelligence, flexibility, sense of humor, energy, and openness to new ideas. He said:

> It really was helpful to go back and look at that stuff. It reminded me of why Carl is absolutely the wrong kind of boss for me. But it also helped me see why a couple of the people I was beginning to think about here probably wouldn't work out.

Donna said:

> It was a odd thing to do because I remembered how much I value "honesty" and "dependability" in a boss. I think it also got me to add in a few traits I hadn't put down the first time. Neil's sexist attitudes have made me realize how much I detest bigotry of any kind—not just discrimination against women—and how important it is for me to work for somebody who's not weighed down with a lot of prejudices.

What Kind of Work Would I Like to Do for This New Boss?

If you're not happy with your boss, you can be doing the most stimulating and exciting work in the world and still be miserable. On the other hand, you also need to pay attention to the work you'd like to do for your new boss.

Now maybe you can continue doing the same kind of work for your new boss as you're doing now. For example, if you're a salesperson in a large retail store, it's probably going to be fairly easy to transfer to a different boss in another department within the store.

On the other hand, if your situation is like either Kevin's or Donna's, you're going to have to consider doing a different kind of job. If Kevin wants to continue working as a press operator, he's got to keep Carl as his boss. If Donna wants to continue as a marketing manager in the same region, she's going to be stuck with Neil. The point is, it's important to open your horizons if you want to find a new and better boss in the same organization.

So how do you go about discovering the kind of work you might like to do for your new boss? Maybe one of the more interesting ways is to imagine you're a detective, that is, a detective whose assignment is to go and find out as much as you can about the various job opportunities in your organization.

When we suggested the detective approach to Kevin, he was a little puzzled:

> Ah . . . it sounds like an okay idea. But what's to detect? I know what the other jobs in the company are, and I know who all the other bosses are. What else do I need to do?

We admitted he might be right; maybe he really did know about all the other jobs in the company. But we suggested that, since the company was fairly small, he just go around and *interview* different people in different jobs about what they did, how they liked what they did, and so on. Reluctantly, Kevin agreed to try the approach. However, a few days later, he came back with an enthusiastic report:

> What can I say? It was a good idea. In the last two days I've learned more about this company and what we actually do here than I have in all the years I've been here. I was surprised. We've got some really interesting jobs here. Take the art department for example. There's quite a bit of room for creativity over there.

Much more than there is working on a press. There's also a lot more customer contact. One of the things I learned is that a lot of our customers only have a vague idea of how they want a job done. People in the art department can have an awful lot of influence on how we do jobs here. I've already seen several things I could help out with, given my knowledge of our presses. Now another area I learned a lot about is camera setup . . .

By the time Kevin finished, it was clear he'd identified four or five other jobs in the company he might enjoy. He'd even come up with two ideas for jobs that currently didn't exist in the company. He said:

Who knows? Maybe I can sell Brian on creating a job just for me. Anyway, I'll never know unless I talk to him about it.

Donna immediately took to the idea of becoming a detective. When we checked back with her a week later, she had a lot to tell:

Well, as you know, we're a huge company. At last count we had over 60,000 employees. So at first I wasn't sure where to start. But after I thought about it a bit, two ideas came to mind. One was simply going to our personnel department. I found a couple of people over there who were very helpful. They showed me several things that were quite useful. One was a monthly posting of job openings throughout the company that they try to fill from inside if they can. Another thing—I didn't know about it—is a whole filing cabinet full of job descriptions. They've got at least a page-long description on every job in the company from janitor all the way up to chairman of the board. I spent three hours going through them, and it was fascinating.

There's a tremendous variety of jobs in the company. I think I'd be qualified for a lot of them.

My second idea was simply to do some networking. So I had a bunch of my friends in the company put me in touch with some of their friends. Several of those people have been able to tell me a lot about job opportunities that might never get officially posted with personnel. For example, I learned about . . .

Of course, there's no guarantee that using the detective approach will yield as much useful information for you as it did for Kevin and Donna. But if you try it, you may learn a lot about jobs in your organization that could be interesting and fulfilling for you.

How Do I Find Candidates for My New Boss?

Up to this point you've taken two important steps toward getting a new boss. You've clarified your thinking about the kind of boss you're looking for, and you've located some jobs or job areas in the company you think you might enjoy. Now you need to come up with a list of "prospects," your potential new bosses.

There are no hard and fast rules on how to do this. But try to build a list of, say, five potential bosses, designating two of them as prime candidates and the other three as backups.

When we suggested this idea to Kevin and Donna, they asked for suggestions on how to do it. One of us said:

Well, you've got a reasonably good idea of what you're looking for in a new boss. And you also have a good idea of some of the areas where you'd like to work in this place. Now would be a good time to gather as much information as you can about the bosses you could work for in those areas. You should be on the look out for people who resemble your "ideal" boss. Maybe the best way to start is by asking around. Start by asking who the bosses are in those areas, and then do some interviews with people who know those bosses. Interview some of their employees if you can, and also other people who work with them or are in a position to know about them.

Both of them picked up on the suggestion right away. After a week or so, we got a report from each of them. Kevin gave us a bit of a surprise:

Well, I liked everything you had to say, but I decided to go ahead and take a risk. I went straight to Brian, the owner of the company, and said that I'd been doing a lot of thinking. I told him I wanted to grow and advance with the company, and I wasn't going to be able to do that by continuing to work as a press operator. Then I told him I'd been taking a hard look at some of the areas in the company where I might be able to contribute. I told him flat out that one of the big problems in the plant is that printing jobs, especially some of the smaller ones, had a tendency to get lost between departments. For example, a job might get hung up in the art department, the customer would call in asking for it, and nobody would know exactly what the job's status was. Anyway, I told Brian that I'd like him to think about transferring me from press operator to a new job that we might call "expediter." I'd report to Brian—who I think is the best boss in the company—and my responsibility would be to track jobs from one department to another and help push them through the system when they got bogged down.

"What did Brian think of the idea?"

He seemed interested and said he'd like to think about it. We're scheduled to meet in a few days to talk about it some more. But I've got a feeling he's going to go for it.

Donna's report was closer to what we were expecting:

> Hmmm . . . where to start? Well, first of all, I decided that there are two areas of the company where I might like to work if I'm going to stay in this region. Market research is one, and customer service is the other. I wasn't exactly sure what I could do in these two areas, but I was sure I could find something interesting. Anyway, like you suggested, I just started asking around about the bosses in those two areas. As it turned out, there are about five managers who I theoretically could go to work for.

"What did you find out about them?"

> Very interesting. One of them, I found out, is about to be canned for incompetence. The rumor is, he's got a serious drinking problem and refuses to do anything about it. Another one, from what I've heard, makes my boss Neil look like Prince Charming. I mean we're talking *major* sleaze! So those two were immediately knocked out of the running. The remaining three look like good candidates.

Here we probed for a little specificity: "How did you get all this information?"

> Okay, well, first of all I got all their names from my friend Ivan in personnel. Then I just started asking a couple of the people I work with what they knew about them. And, by the way, I really tried to pay attention to being a good listener—body language, pausing, reading back . . . all those good techniques. I learned a lot just by doing that. Each of these bosses has a little bit of a reputation in the company. So that was helpful. But to pick the "final three" I actually had lunch or a drink with employees who work for them.

This piqued our interest: "Details, please," one of us said.

Well, that's where social networking came in handy. I didn't know any of these people, but a number of my friends in the company did. So that really helped. As far as getting information from them about their bosses, it really wasn't hard. I just explained I was starting to look around the company for other job opportunities and that their area was one I was considering. I asked them to tell me about what they did, and then I asked them to tell me about their bosses—what they liked most about them, what they liked least about them, and that sort of thing. Then I just listened, and I learned a lot.

"What did you learn?" we asked.

Maybe the main thing is that there are two people in customer service—Steve Longfellow and Judith Thompson—and one person in market research—Alan Foster—who I think I'd be happy working for. All of them sound honest and dependable, and they have the reputation of treating women and other minorities fairly. I guess of the three, I'd especially like to work for Judith in customer service or Alan in market research. I understand both of them are concerned with helping their people grow and develop and advance. It sounds like they're good teachers as well as good bosses.

In this section, using Kevin and Donna as examples, we've offered advice on how you can answer three important questions:

1. What kind of boss do I want?
2. What kind of work would I like to do for this new boss?
3. How do I find candidates for my new boss?

Once you've come up with a list of candidates, the question becomes, "How do I get myself hired away from my current boss by one of these new bosses?"

GETTING YOURSELF HIRED BY A NEW BOSS

At this stage of the game, it may be helpful to think of yourself as a salesperson. You've got a product—you—that you want to sell to a customer—one of the "prospects" on your list. In this section we'll talk about four different approaches you can use to try to make your sale:

1. a formal application
2. making a direct pitch
3. making an indirect pitch
4. making a pitch to the big boss

A Formal Application

To be honest, we don't have a lot of faith in this approach. Whenever you formally apply for a job—either through an ad in a newspaper or a personnel agency or a job listing where you work—the odds are against you. Why? There are two reasons. One, because you've got lots of competition. Even if you're a fantastic candidate, lots of other talented people are going to apply, especially if it's a desirable job. Two, the job may be "wired." That is, someone has already been identified to fill the job, but the people offering the job have to make it look like an "open" position for P.R. or legal reasons. Either way, you lose. On the other hand, you may want to try this approach for yourself to see how well it works.

If you work in a large organization like Donna's, your company probably has some kind of job posting system. That is, the personnel department (or whatever it's called in your place) will post announcements of job openings throughout the company. This is done to give company employees a chance at these jobs before they get filled from the outside. While we were working with Donna, two openings—one in customer service and one in market research—were posted in her company. She immediately applied for both. As it turns out, she didn't get either one, but we liked the attitude she had toward this method:

> I know it's a long shot with these job postings. But I still think it's worth filling out an application if the job posted is one I want. I may not have a good chance of getting any one job. But if I keep applying, the odds are going to start to shift in my favor. And another thing, for both those jobs that I didn't get, I did a little investigating to find out who got the jobs, why, and why I didn't. That paid off. Both people who got the jobs already knew the bosses who hired them. Obviously, they had an inside track. That's something I'll definitely keep in mind for the next time.

Making a Direct Pitch

If you work in an organization the size of Kevin Dawkins', however, your company probably won't even have a personnel department, much less a job posting system. So in a smaller company, going directly to one of the bosses on your list to talk about a transfer may be the best thing to do.

Frankly, we like this direct approach. It's a way of taking the bull by the horns and trying to make something good happen. It's not waiting for something to happen, which is what most people do. However, the direct approach has some risks. When you formally apply for a job opening that's been posted, you're playing by the company's rules. Even if bosses don't like the idea of their employees applying for these positions, there's not much they can do about it. On the other hand, if you go make your pitch directly to a prospective boss, your current boss may find out and get very upset. He or she may even try to get back at you. So here are some things to keep in mind if you take this approach:

DO IT WHEN YOU KNOW THE NEW BOSS HAS A JOB OPENING YOU CAN FILL

Prospective bosses are going to be a lot more receptive to the idea of talking to you if they're already looking for somebody to fill a job. Also, your current boss will have less reason to object to your talking to the new boss if there actually is a job opening. If there is, you can claim you're just interviewing for it the way other interested employees are. If there isn't, think of something . . . fast!

LET YOUR CURRENT BOSS KNOW WHAT YOU'RE UP TO

Like it or not, there's a good chance your current boss will feel threatened by your going to talk directly to a prospective boss about a job. If you don't tell your current boss that you're planning to do this, expect a negative reaction if the cat is somehow let out of the bag. Bosses hate it when they think their employees are sneaking behind their backs. So let your boss know what you plan to do. If he doesn't like it and gets all bent out of shape, use your listening skills to draw him out and calm him down. Then firmly tell him you think this is a good opportunity for you and you'd like to check it out. If he remains annoyed and makes any moves to try to stop you or get back at you, what more evidence do you need that it's time to get a new boss?

DON'T RUN DOWN YOUR CURRENT BOSS TO YOUR PROSPECTIVE BOSS

Make the transfer look like something good for you and the company. Leaving one boss to go to work for another boss in the same organization is sensitive stuff—your current boss is probably going to feel threatened and resentful. The worst thing you could do is announce how unhappy you are with your boss and how much you're looking forward to a transfer. Your best policy is to tell everybody, except people you trust completely, that you look upon a transfer to a new job as an opportunity to advance. It's a good thing for the company and everybody else concerned. Remember, you may not get the new job with the new boss. If you don't, you're still going to have to live with your old boss, at least for a while longer. It'll be hard to do that if you've burned your bridges behind you.

A little earlier we said it'd be helpful to think of yourself as a salesperson during this part of the process. Here are a couple of selling tips to keep in mind when you're in there pitching:

TRY TO PUT YOURSELF IN YOUR NEW BOSS'S POSITION

Over the years we've counseled scores of people who're looking for new jobs. We've always been amazed at how few of these folks were truly able to put themselves in the position of the person who might eventually hire them. Usually their approach was more like this: "Here I am, Prospective Employer. Here's my brand spanking new resume that tells how great I am. What do you have for me in the way of a good job?" That's a little bit of an exaggeration, but not much. The point is, when you're selling, it's so much more effective to think about things from the buyer's perspective. And what's the perspective of bosses who're thinking of hiring new people? They're nervous. They want to hire somebody good, but they're *afraid* they're going to hire somebody who *looks* good but who'll turn out to be useless as you know what. If you can put some of your own needs aside and convey to prospective bosses that you've got some understanding of how *they feel*, you might just get hired on the spot.

PITCH WELL, BUT LISTEN SUPERBLY

When you go in to talk to the new boss, it's important to make a good pitch for why you should get hired. But in selling everything—including yourself—it's even more important to do a good job of listening. For example, we talked with Donna before she met with Alan Foster about going to work for him in market research. We suggested that she make her case fairly quickly and then concentrate more on listening than selling. After the interview she told us:

> I don't know whether or not I'm going to get the job, but I think your advice about listening paid off. Alan started right off by asking me to tell him a little about my background and why I thought I'd be a good market researcher. I was sort of expecting that, and I had practiced giving what I thought was a punchy, five-minute presentation on where I'd been in the company and why I'd be good for the job. Well, I didn't get even halfway through my ''spiel'' before he interrupted me and made a comment about some of the projects he was planning over the next six months. Just by being a good listener, I was able to keep him going for *forty-five minutes* nonstop. When he finally stopped and gave me a chance to talk, I put the kibosh on what I originally planned to say and talked about how I could help him with the projects he was so hot to do. He *really* liked that. I think I've got a good shot at the job.

Making an Indirect Pitch

Let's say you've got your eye on some prospective bosses, but they don't have any job openings right now. Maybe it would be pushing things to press for a job now. But it's definitely not pushing things for you to take the time and energy to get to know them and some of their problems and challenges—whether they have a job opening or not. Donna did this very effectively with Judith Thompson in customer service. She told us:

I liked what I'd heard about Judith. She seemed to really fit what I was looking for in a boss. On the other hand, I knew she didn't have any job openings at the time. But I figured, "Why wait?" So one day I just introduced myself to her in the hall. We chatted a while, and I told her I'd like to have lunch with her some time. About a week later we did just that. And it was great! I found out a lot about what she does in her job, what she looks for in employees, and what she thinks is going to happen to her department over the next year or so. Now, whenever I see her, we talk for a few minutes. Last week I popped into her office at five o'clock and we ended up talking for forty-five minutes. At the end of the conversation, she sort of half-kiddingly asked me if I'd be interested in going to work for her. She still doesn't have any openings, but I'll bet we can work something out in the near future.

Bosses are like anybody else. If you take the time to show a little interest in them and their problems, they'll reciprocate. They'll start showing a little interest in you and some of the things you want.

Making a Pitch to the Big Boss

If you work in a fairly small organization where everybody pretty much knows everybody else, making a pitch to the big boss—the person who runs the company—may be a good idea. Presidents or owners of companies usually have ultimate decision-making power, which means they usually get what they want, without much delay. So, if you can sell the big boss on what you want, you won't have to wade through a lot of red tape or put up with frustrating bureaucratic delays. An immediate decision on the part of the big boss could have you working in a new job for a new boss as early as next week.

If you decide to try this approach, however, there are some

important things to keep in mind. We've already mentioned some of them, but a little repetition won't hurt:

LET YOUR CURRENT BOSS KNOW WHAT YOU'RE DOING

You probably won't want to do this because you know what the likely response will be. But having your boss object ahead of time is better than the response you're going to get when it's discovered that you talked to the big boss without your boss's knowledge or permission.

DON'T RUN DOWN YOUR CURRENT BOSS TO THE BIG BOSS

Make the transfer look like a good thing for you and the company. This is an important point to keep in mind in any size organization, but especially a small one. If you've got a real problem boss, the big boss will know about it along with everybody else in the place. If you start complaining about your boss, even if it's completely justified, the big boss may just see you as a whiner. But if you simply say that moving to a new job will be good for you and the company, the big boss will be more likely to think: "What a class person! She never even mentioned what a major problem Snidely is. I don't know how she's hung in there as long as she has."

IT'S GOING TO BE A LOT EASIER IF YOU HAVE A GOOD REPUTATION

In a large organization it's possible to be virtually anonymous. In a small organization everybody knows everybody else. If you've got a reputation as a hardworking and conscientious employee—and your boss has just the opposite reputation—then going to the big boss to talk about a transfer makes excellent sense. Presidents of companies don't like to lose good employees. On the other hand, if you have a reputation as an irresponsible goof-off, and your boss has a solid reputation, the big boss may agree that you *should* find another job. Outside the company, that is.

DO YOUR HOMEWORK

If you want to transfer to a new boss in the organization, you'll be much more persuasive and convincing with the big boss if you prepare a case than if you don't. Remember how Kevin Dawkins spent some time finding out about various jobs in the plant? Remember how he approached the owner of the company with some well-thought-out reasons why the company needed an expediter? The owner would've been much less impressed with Kevin's request for a transfer if Kevin had simply come in and said he was unhappy in his job and wanted to do something else.

MAKE A SHORT, CONVINCING CASE
FOR WHAT YOU WANT

As we've said a number of times before, most bosses have a short attention span. They want you to get to the point right away—even if they never do when *they* talk. You should be able to say what you want and why you want it in five minutes. That's what Kevin did. He even practiced his presentation at home so he could keep it as short and punchy as possible.

LISTEN, LISTEN, LISTEN

Once you make your case to the big boss, shut up and listen. Use your listening skills to get the boss's reactions to your idea. That's what Kevin did with his boss, Brian. And at first Brian wasn't too excited about Kevin's idea. He had a number of objections: "I don't know, Kevin. I think the idea of creating an expediter position is a good one in theory, but I'm not sure how practical it is. First of all, I'm not sure I want anybody else reporting to me right now. Another thing. You're really the best pressman we've got. It'd be tough to replace you . . ." By just giving Brian a chance to think out loud about his reservations, Kevin was able to help Brian eventually talk himself out of these concerns. On the other hand, if he'd debated and argued with Brian's reasoning, he'd probably still be stuck working for good old Carl.

BE WILLING TO COMPROMISE

This is an important principle to pay attention to whenever you're trying to work out some arrangement with another person. But it's especially important when you're talking to the big boss. For example, Kevin would've preferred Brian to go along with his idea wholeheartedly and to make the switch right away. But Brian was too concerned about losing a pressman. So the two of them agreed that Kevin would begin working for Brian as an expediter as soon as they could find a replacement for Kevin. And Kevin agreed to help Brian in the search for qualified candidates.

In this chapter we've tried to give you a number of suggestions for how you can leave your boss without leaving your company by getting a transfer to a new boss who's likely to be better to work for than your current one. In the next chapter we'll talk about a closely related strategy—going over your boss's head to talk to your boss's boss.

15

···················

GOING OVER YOUR
BOSS'S HEAD

I n the last chapter we said we were beginning to introduce
  you to strategies that involved increasingly more risk for
you. That's certainly the case with this one. Going over your
boss's head to your boss's boss—or another higher-up in the
organization—is a risky proposition, no doubt about it. On
the other hand, it can be an extremely effective thing to do.
A lot depends on the boss you choose to talk to, and how
you present your case.

We'll start off by describing what we think are the major
advantages and disadvantages of the strategy. Reading
through these should help you try it on for size and begin to
see how appropriate it would be for your situation. After that
we'll talk about some things you should definitely *not* do if
you decide to go over your boss's head. We'll end with some
specific advice on how to carry the strategy out.

SOME PRO'S AND CON'S

Going over your boss's head *is* a controversial strategy. Many people think it's a lousy idea because it involves so much risk. But other people like it a lot. They think it's a forthright way to take immediate and positive action against a problem boss. Here we'll offer both views—those of the nay sayers and the yea sayers. Later on you can decide which group seems to make the more convincing argument.

Let's start with the nay sayers.

Organizations Are Not Bastions of Justice

Only a naive person would conclude that our nation lives up to the ideals of freedom and democracy and justice that were planned for us back in the eighteenth century. Think about all the organizations you've worked for over the years. Were they modeled after the democratic society we try to be? Were the rights and freedoms you had in those organizations similar to the rights and freedoms you have as a citizen? How about the right of free speech? Did you generally feel comfortable voicing your opinion about the way the place was run? Or how about having an equal voice in the selection of the people who ran the organization? Could you vote out bosses who didn't live up to their "campaign promises?" Unless they were unusual organizations, your answers have to be "No." The hard truth is that virtually all organizations in America are not democratic in nature. Someone once put it more bluntly: "When you go to work in this country, you leave your constitutional rights at the front gate."

How does this lack of democracy in organizations relate to going over your boss's head? Think about it for a moment.

WILL THE BIG BOSS GIVE YOU THE BENEFIT OF THE DOUBT?

Let's say you have a boss who's given you half the salary increase he promised you six months ago. You've complained to him, but all he's done is offer some lame excuse why you haven't got what he promised. So you decide to go over your boss's head to make your case to *his* boss. What's going to happen? Chances are the big boss will listen patiently to what you have to say. Then he'll reply: "Thanks for coming in. I'll look into it." If he's a reasonably conscientious person, he probably will look into the matter for you. He'll speak to your boss. Your boss will give his side of the story, and you won't be there to point out any lies or inconsistencies in his testimony. Will you get the raise you feel you deserve? Not likely. Because, on balance, your boss's boss will side with your boss, not with you. It's not fair. It's not just. But it's a fact of organizational life.

IS THERE A GOOD CHANCE THE BIG BOSS WON'T DO ANYTHING?

Early in the book we said that the big bosses in organizations tend not to hold problem bosses accountable for their behavior. That's what's likely to happen when you go over your boss's head. For example, think about all the women who've had to endure the embarrassment and frustration of being sexually pursued by their bosses: sleazy compliments; daily suggestions about getting together for drinks; stares that undress; and gropes, pinches, and fondles. Finally when all their subtle and not-so-subtle suggestions to stop have failed, a few have gone over their boss's heads to complain to a higher-up. Does this usually solve the problem? No. Maybe the big boss will talk to the offending boss, who'll probably deny the charge or say the female employee led him on—and then try to get back at the woman for reporting him. More often, though, the big boss will either ignore the complaint or accuse the woman of leading the boss on.

IS THE BIG BOSS BOSOM BUDDIES
WITH YOUR BOSS?

Let's say you decide to go over your boss's head because
you feel you deserve a promotion but aren't getting one because your boss feels threatened by you. So you decide to
complain to your boss's boss. Maybe your boss's boss will
take an objective look at your case and decide that you have
been unfairly treated. But, probably not. After all, who's the
person who probably promoted or hired your boss in the first
place? Who's the person who goes out drinking or plays
racquetball with your boss every Thursday night? Who's the
person who invites your boss over for dinner once a month?
Do you think you're going to get a fair hearing and just
treatment from somebody like that?

Bosses Resent Employees
Who Go Over Their Heads

Even if you go over your boss's head and get what you want
from the big boss, you still have to go back and live with
your own boss. And that can be unpleasant. Bosses resent it
when employees go over their heads. They feel threatened,
embarrassed, and stripped of their power. And, whether they
do it consciously or not, most of them try to get back at
employees who do this to them. They'll do things like:

KNOCK YOU DOWN ON YOUR PERFORMANCE
RATINGS

The ratings you're presently getting will slip from "excellent" and "outstanding" to "satisfactory" or "marginal"
even though you think your performance has actually improved.

FAIL TO RECOMMEND YOU
FOR A SALARY INCREASE

This is a very easy way for bosses to show their resentment toward you. Their thinking may go something like this: "So, Georgia thinks she can go over my head when she doesn't get her way? Well, let's just see how she likes going without a raise for a year. And if she tries to go around me on this one, I'll be ready for her. I've got all kinds of documentation to back me up."

HAND OUT THE CHOICE ASSIGNMENTS
TO SOMEONE ELSE

If you do a lot of traveling in your job, you can forget about those trips to Florida in January. Now you'll be heading to Manitoba. And you'll be off to Florida in August.

If you just listened to the nay sayers, you'd *never* think of going over your boss's head. But when you listen to the yea sayers, you realize they've got some compelling arguments, too.

It's a Good Way to Cover All the Bases

Even though going over your boss's head may seem like a bad idea, sometimes it's necessary. You'll hear more about this in the next chapter, but, for now, imagine you want to take some kind of action against your boss. For example, you may want to:

- file a grievance
- file a formal complaint with the Equal Employment Opportunity Commission (EEOC) or some other government agency
- consult an attorney about a potential civil suit
- talk to a law enforcement agency about possible criminal charges
- "blow the whistle" to a regulatory commission or a reporter

In each case, one of the first questions you're likely to be asked is: "Have you brought this matter to the attention of your boss's boss?" So, even if you think you won't get anywhere if you go over your boss's head, think about doing it anyway to cover all the bases. If you do, be sure to document the meeting by sending your boss's boss a follow-up memo, with a copy for yourself, describing precisely what was discussed. The copy for yourself could come in *very* handy several months down the line.

There Are a Lot of Decent and Effective Bosses to Go To

Many big bosses won't give you fair and equitable treatment if you go to them with a problem about your boss. *But*, that doesn't hold true for *all* bosses. In almost every organization you can go to some decent, fair-minded bosses who will help you with a problem you're having with your boss.

Take the case of Barbara Marques, who used to work for a large trade association.

Her boss, Greg Dorner, was an overbearing sort of fellow who didn't like Barbara and wanted to get rid of her. However, he knew that Barbara was popular with important members of the association and that firing her would be politically unwise. Barbara felt horribly constrained by Greg's constant "You can't do this's and you can't do that's." Several times, she even tried to talk to Greg about their problems. If anything, it made Greg more overbearing. Finally, Barbara figured she had to do something to maintain her sanity.

She decided to talk to the chairman of the association's board, Clint Dixfield. Barbara had worked closely with Clint before and knew him to be an honest person who not only cared deeply about his fellow members, but also about the well-being of the staff who served those members. She was confident Clint would give her a fair hearing on the problems she was having with Greg—and even be willing to help her solve them.

You may not be able to find someone with Clint Dixfield's concern and compassion—as well as his power and willingness to take action. But chances are good there's some boss in your company who will: (1) listen to the problems you're having with your boss and (2) try to help you solve them.

Big Bosses Want to Know What's Going on Below Them

In several previous chapters we've said bosses are insulated from feedback. Well, higher-level bosses are insulated from something else, too—*information*. Especially information on *problems* that exist below their level. Why? Because the lower-level bosses who report to them don't bring these problems to their attention.

It's understandable. These lower-level bosses don't want to look bad in their boss's eyes. So they deliver only the "good news," information that will cast them in a favorable light. And they withhold the "bad news," the problems their bosses need to know about, but also might blame them for.

To be honest, some big bosses are like ostriches. They'd rather put their heads in the sand than face up to the unpleasant problems in their companies. As one employee put it:

> They don't want to hear it. What's worse, if you happen to be the bearer of these "bad tidings," you can get your head lopped off, just like they used to do with messengers in the old days who brought bad news.

But a lot of higher-level bosses *do* want to hear the bad news, especially the problems that're going on below them.

Sometimes the only way they can hear about these problems is for employees to screw up the courage and go over their boss's heads. Bosses like these won't lop your head off. They'll listen to what you have to say. They'll *appreciate* your bringing the problem to their attention. They'll maybe even take some action to solve the problem. *And*, they'll see to it that your boss doesn't take it out on you for having the guts to come to them.

Going Over Your Boss's Head Is Not a Form of Squealing

In our society little boys and girls grow up with a code of ethics that stays with them all their lives. The code varies a little, depending on what part of the country you're raised in. But the message is the same: "Don't be a tattletale, Don't be a squealer." The implication is clear: If you go to some higher authority, like a parent or a teacher or a boss, and "rat" on someone, you're lower than low.

This principle keeps a lot of problem bosses out of hot water—their employees won't go over their heads to a higher-up simply because it's a dishonorable thing to do. It's all very understandable. But it's a lot of garbage. Going over your boss's head to report abusive, unfair, or unjust treatment is not squealing or ratting or telling stories out of school. To the contrary, it's an act of courage and responsibility more employees should be willing to take. If they did, it'd dramatically reduce the number of bosses who flagrantly abuse their power.

One other thing. Don't let a problem boss pull any guilt trips on you with this code of ethics stuff. Rosie Fortunato didn't;

> I got my boss reprimanded by his boss once for exercising some very poor judgment in his dealings with some of our customers. I'd brought the matter up sev-

eral times before with my boss, but to no avail. Anyway, as he was coming back from his boss's office, he says, "Rosie, I'm so disappointed with you. I never thought a stand-up person like you would turn into a stoolie." I knew my position was pretty solid, so I look him right in the eye and say, "Don't lay any of that stuff on me, Arnie. If you'd listened to what I told you months ago, this would've never happened. And if the shoe was on the other foot, I know what you would've done."

Now that you've heard some arguments for and against going over your boss's head, let's look at some mistakes you should *avoid* if you decide to use this strategy.

MISTAKES TO AVOID WHEN GOING OVER YOUR BOSS'S HEAD

When employees finally decide to go over their boss's heads, they're often frustrated, upset, and even distraught. Many are just plain sick and tired of trying to deal with their own bosses. So they say to themselves: "All right, I'm going over her head. I'm going to talk to her boss. Maybe that way I can get some satisfaction."

Unfortunately, when they're in this frame of mind, employees aren't thinking as clearly as they do when they're feeling calm and relaxed. So:

THEY DON'T GIVE MUCH THOUGHT TO WHO TO TALK TO

Sometimes it's a good idea for employees to talk to their boss's boss—especially if they're fair-minded, conscientious, and willing to try to help out. But sometimes it's a terrible idea. Your boss's boss may be worse than your boss.

THEY DON'T PREPARE A GOOD CASE

If you're going to have any chance at all of getting what you want when you go over your boss's head, you need to have your ducks in a row. You need to prepare a persuasive argument for getting what you want. And that's not what most employees do when they talk to the big boss. Usually they just go in and complain. Some higher-level bosses are patient and helpful people who are willing to take the time and effort to find out what the problem is, learn the facts of the case, and hear how the employee would like the problem solved. But many more won't take the trouble to do this. They'll just view the meeting as an opportunity for the employee to let off steam. Maybe they'll mention the problem to the employee's boss, maybe not. And that'll be the end of it.

So much for what you *shouldn't* do when you go over your boss's head. Let's move on and talk about what you *should* do.

HOW TO GO OVER YOUR BOSS'S HEAD

Here we'll offer three pieces of advice on how to carry out this strategy if you'd like to give it a try:

1. picking the right boss to go to
2. getting prepared
3. possibly going as a group

Picking the Right Boss to Go To

When going over your boss's head, it's extremely important to pick the right boss to go to. For example, even though going to your boss's direct boss may seem like the obvious course of action, it may not be a good idea—and it could be disastrous.

Take the experience of Andrew Butkus, a fellow in his late twenties who used to work in the corporate communications department of a large airline. Andrew had been struggling for the last eighteen months with his boss, Darlene Frank, the director of consumer relations. The two of them couldn't see eye to eye on anything. Andrew had long since developed the theory that Darlene was trying to drive him out of the department. Exasperated, he made an appointment with Ken Rogers, Darlene's boss and the director of corporate communications. Andrew went in and complained bitterly to Ken about the way Darlene had been treating him.

After the meeting, we asked Andrew how it had gone. He said:

> Pretty good, I think. I thought I made a very convincing case. And Mr. Rogers seemed attentive and interested. I don't know, I think it should do some good.

A week later when we talked to Andrew, his optimism had evaporated:

> I was very surprised, to say the least. A couple of days after I met with Mr. Rogers, he called me in to his office. I was almost bowled over when I saw Darlene sitting there as I walked in. Then Mr. Rogers said that he and Darlene had been discussing my situation. He said they had both come to the conclusion that the best thing for "all concerned" would be for me to look for another job. I couldn't believe it. I absolutely couldn't believe it.

Sadly, what Andrew didn't know—but should have—is that Mr. Rogers had long been in full agreement with Darlene that Andrew was a marginal employee who should be let go. Andrew just sealed his fate by going over Darlene's head.

So, how do you avoid the kind of disaster that befell An-

drew? Frankly, there's no guarantee this sort of thing won't
happen. But there are some things you can do to minimize
your risks and increase your chances of getting a fair hearing
and prompt action.

First of all, do a survey of the bosses you *could* go to.
Even though it's customary to go to your boss's direct boss,
you may be better off going to a boss higher up in the organization—someone who'll give you a better hearing and more
prompt and equitable action. Do a little research. Come up
with a list of bosses who might be good to talk to.

Once you've come up with a list of bosses, we think you
should "qualify" them in the same basic way you did in an
earlier chapter to decide if your boss was a good candidate
to speak one on one with. Be prepared to answer the following questions about each of them:

HOW FAIR IS THIS PERSON?

If the boss you're thinking about going to doesn't have a
solid reputation for dealing fairly with employees, think twice
before making a move.

HOW GOOD A PROBLEM SOLVER
IS THIS PERSON?

In our "one on one" chapter we said that problem solving
was one of the traits bosses should be high on before you
decide to meet with them face-to-face. Well, it's important
here, too. You can go and talk to the most sensitive and
empathic boss in the world. But if you're talking to somebody who rarely makes a forthright decision and generally
sits on problems, you're wasting your time.

WHAT'S THE BIG BOSS'S RELATIONSHIP
WITH YOUR BOSS?

One of the reasons this strategy fails is that the boss you
decide to go to may have a "tight" relationship with your
boss. That's the problem Andrew Butkus ran into when he

went to Mr. Rogers. In his exasperation, Andrew ignored the fact that Mr. Rogers and Darlene had become bosom buddies over the years. In contrast, Barbara Marques—the association employee we mentioned earlier—was smart enough to go to a boss who wasn't tied in with her boss. On the contrary, she knew that Clint Dixfield, the chairman of the board, had a poor opinion of her boss and a good opinion of her.

HOW MUCH CLOUT DOES THE PERSON HAVE?

One of the fascinating things we've learned about clout is that people who have it don't have to have all that much rank. A good example is Caroline Brogan, who works as the executive assistant to the president of a metal-working company.

Caroline doesn't make all that much money—she isn't an executive in the company. But Caroline has clout. She has the ear of the president and he really values her perspective and opinion on things. A number of times he's overruled decisions by some of his top people purely on Caroline's say-so. Caroline's not a company officer, but she's somebody we'd seriously consider talking to if we worked for a problem boss in her company.

Talking to somebody who doesn't have much clout, on the other hand, can be frustrating and a waste of time.

After looking at the various bosses you might talk to, and comparing them on the dimensions we've mentioned here, a clear choice will probably emerge. When it does, you'll need to start thinking of how to get ready for this meeting.

Getting Prepared

This is going to be a very important meeting, so it's a good idea to carefully prepare for it. In this section we'll talk about two kinds of preparation:

1. gathering evidence
2. preparing your presentation

Let's take a look at each one.

GATHERING EVIDENCE

Earlier, we said that some of our strategies required your taking an adversarial stance with your boss—and that's mainly the position you're putting yourself into when you decide to go over your boss's head. So it might be helpful for you to try to think like a prosecuting attorney who's trying to make a case to a judge or jury.

To be convincing and persuasive you're going to need some evidence, evidence that documents and specifies the problem or problems your boss has been causing you. This evidence can take a number of forms. The particular forms don't matter a whole lot, as long as they provide specific examples of your boss's problem behavior. For example, when Barbara Marques went over her boss's head to talk to Clint Dixfield, she put together a number of items to back up her case. About six months earlier she started keeping a file on the problems she was having with her boss, Greg Dorner. The file included:

• *Notes from each meeting she'd had with Greg.* Barbara typed up summaries of every meeting she had had with Greg in the past six months. These notes included the times and dates of the meetings, as well as direct quotes of things Greg had said to her, like: "I don't care what those goddamn board members say about how great you are, young lady! You work for me, not them! And (pointing his finger directly at me) don't you ever forget that!"
• *Memos and letters that cast Greg in a bad light.* Barbara put together a number of memos she'd received from Greg along with a number of letters she'd received from members of the board of directors. The letters from board mem-

bers all praised Barbara for the exemplary work she'd done on various association projects. The memos from Greg were all critical of the work Barbara had done on those same projects. In some of the memos, Greg had even directed Barbara not to do certain tasks the board had agreed should be done by Barbara. What emerged from this package of material was a picture of an insecure and jealous boss who was threatened by the praise and attention one of his employees was getting.

• *A serendipitous tape recording of Greg chewing Barbara out in an abusive manner.* Barbara was able to get this damning piece of evidence by pure happenstance. One day she was dictating a letter when Greg stormed into her office and started ranting and raving to her about some trivial error she'd made. He was so upset he didn't even notice the dictating machine was on. Barbara just decided to keep the machine running while Greg continued his tirade. We listened to the tape, which only lasted a couple of minutes. But a couple of minutes was enough.

PREPARING YOUR PRESENTATION

Once you've assembled some evidence that paints a clear picture of the problems your boss has been causing you, prepare what you want to say and how you want to say it. Thinking like a good courtroom lawyer, you know that a dynamite presentation will sway even the most difficult jury. Here are a few suggestions we hope you'll find helpful:

Try to be as clear as you can about your goals. Generally, the clearer you are about what you want to achieve, the smoother the meeting will go. You have to decide, of course, what your goals will be. But most employees who talk to their boss's bosses want to achieve the following important goals:

• Convince them that their boss is causing them major problems.

- Motivate them to take some action to make those problems go away.

Prepare an overall agenda for the meeting. You'll have to decide exactly how you want to conduct your meeting. But we'd suggest an outline that includes these six basic stages:

- *A warm-up.* In several earlier chapters we talked about the importance of warming things up before you actually get down to business. That's important here, too. A good way to do this is simply to ask bosses questions about something they're interested in—whether or not it has anything to do with work. For example, when Barbara met with Clint Dixfield, she asked him about his latest hobby—building classic cars from prefabricated kits. Clint warmed to the question and talked for a good five minutes before he finally cut himself off.
- *Structuring.* Structuring is another topic we've discussed in earlier chapters. It means beginning the meeting by briefly explaining what you think the *purpose* of the meeting is; what you'd like to *cover* in the meeting; and your suggestions on how the two of you can *get the most* out of the meeting. Structuring is especially important in a meeting like this because you may not have a chance to talk directly to the boss before the meeting. You may have to make an appointment through a secretary. Because of that, the boss may not know ahead of time why you want to meet.

This is basically what Barbara said when she structured her meeting with Clint:

> Clint, I see three purposes for this meeting. One is for me to describe for you some problems I've been having with Greg Dorner that I think you should know about. A second is for me to suggest a way you can help me solve these problems. And a third is for me to get your reactions to what I've said.

I'd like to start off by presenting some facts about the way Greg has been treating me that I think will surprise you. Then I'll tell you a little about how his treatment has made me feel and how it's affected my work performance. Then I'd like to offer a solution to these problems that will involve your help. And then I'd like to hear your reactions to everything I've said.

I'd say the best way for us to get the most out of this meeting is for me to make the best, and briefest, case I can, and for you to give me your honest and candid reactions after I do.

- *Presenting the facts.* After you've structured the meeting, make your case—lay out the evidence you've collected about the problems your boss has been causing you. The main thing to keep in mind here is to be brief, to the point, and specific. When Barbara met with Clint, she had her three pieces of evidence—the notes from her meetings with Greg, her accidental tape recording, and the memos and letters she'd received from Greg and various board members. She placed these items in three separate piles in front of Clint and said:

Clint, I've got three sets of things here I'd like to show you that I think will convince you that Greg Dorner has been making my job needlessly unpleasant.

Then Barbara took about fifteen minutes to present excerpts from her notes and the letters and memos. She stopped talking whenever she noticed that Clint seemed interested in reading something more carefully. She finished by playing the tape. If you've got some good documentation and lay out your case well, you won't need a whole lot of words to make your point.

- *Disclosing your feelings.* We think it's very appropriate, and in your best interests, to talk about the impact your boss has had on you. Two things are especially worth talking about: How it's caused you to *feel* and the effect it's had on your *work performance*. When you do this, try to be as honest and objective as you can. And when you talk about your feelings, keep the focus on how you *feel*—not on what a lousy so-and-so you think your boss is. This is how Barbara described her feelings to Clint:

> Clint, I think my notes, that tape, and those memos and letters speak for themselves about how Greg has been treating me. But what they don't tell you is the impact of Greg's behavior on me. First, when he does these sorts of things to me, I feel angry, resentful, humiliated, and . . . well, outraged. I've lost countless hours of sleep over this. It's definitely had an adverse affect on my work performance. I don't look forward to coming to work any more. I'm sure I don't get nearly as much work done as I should because I'm often so distracted by angry thoughts about him. But, mostly, I just want it to stop because I don't deserve it.

• *Offering a solution.* One of the things we frequently hear bosses complain about is that employees often come to them with problems, but not solutions. If you want this meeting to go as well as it can, think about what you want the boss to do about the problem you're having with your boss. Barbara was very clear with Clint on this point:

> Clint, I've given a lot of thought to what I'd like you to do about the situation between Greg and me. I guess this is going to sound blunt and callous, but I'd like you seriously to consider *firing* Greg or moving him to a position in the association where he won't be supervising anyone. As a manager of people, I see him as a major liability to you and the other members. If you're not willing to do that, I'd like you to consider meeting with both Greg and me for a day to see if the two of us can work things out. I don't have a lot of optimism that it'll work, but I'd be willing to give it a

try. And if you don't want to meet with us, then I'd
like you to consider transferring me to another position
where I don't have to work with Greg.

It's very helpful if you can, as Barbara did here, offer the
higher-level boss several different options to choose from.

• *Getting the boss's reactions.* Okay, you've made your case.
You've given the boss a lot of information, some of which
may come as a real surprise, some not. Now it's time to
get his or her reactions. This is perhaps the most important
part of the meeting.

Being the best listener you can be at this point will help
the boss sort out a whole complex of reactions—some agreement, some disagreement—to what you've said. Be patient.
The longer the boss talks, generally, the better for you in
terms of a helpful solution to your problem. Being an excellent listener, Barbara took an hour and a half to draw Clint
out on his reactions. To make a long story short, Clint made
it abundantly clear to Barbara that the association did not
want to lose her. He said he'd like to try meeting with Greg
and Barbara for a day if necessary to see if he could help
them work out their problems. If that didn't work, he said
he'd seriously consider moving Greg to a nonmanagerial job,
or transferring Barbara to another position. He said he didn't
want to fire Greg, which Barbara said she understood and
accepted.

Possibly Going as a Group

In an earlier chapter we talked about how a group of employees could meet with their boss. You might also want to
consider the group approach. It'll take a lot more of your
time and energy than if you do it on your own. But it's got
some advantages, too:

THERE'S LESS RISK OF RETALIATION

There's safety in numbers. Let's say you pick the wrong boss to go to or the argument you make about your boss is met with anger and irritation. It's a lot harder for this boss (or your boss) to get back at a group than a single employee.

YOU CAN MAKE A MORE CONVINCING ARGUMENT AS A GROUP

A group presentation can be pretty compelling. For example, five or six people telling a Clint Dixfield what a tyrant Greg Dorner is would probably have a lot more impact than a Barbara Marques doing it on her own.

IT HELPS MAKE ORGANIZATIONS A LITTLE MORE DEMOCRATIC

It's no secret that we don't like the authoritarian nature of most organizations we see out there. We'd like the people who spend more than half their waking hours in these places to have more say in how their organizations are run. Going over your boss's head as a group is one small way to help make that happen.

In general, going over your boss's head is a strategy that can work marvelously or fail miserably depending on a number of factors, like who your boss's boss is and how good a case you can make for yourself.

If it doesn't work, you may be forced into more dramatic action, the subject of our next chapter.

16

....

TAKING A STAND
AGAINST YOUR BOSS

As we write this chapter, the nation is still mourning the loss of the seven astronauts who perished in the space shuttle Challenger disaster on January 28, 1986. In the aftermath of the tragedy, a specially appointed presidential panel asked the questions that were on all of our minds: "Why? What happened? Could this tragedy have been avoided?" Months after the disaster, the specific cause of the explosion is still a m̶a̶t̶t̶e̶r̶ ̶o̶f̶ ̶c̶o̶n̶j̶e̶cture. We may never learn exactly what happened̶ ̶a̶t̶ ̶a̶l̶l̶.

However, what is becoming clear is an alarming story with an almost inescapable conclusion: If NASA officials and top bosses at Morton Thiokol—the company that manufactures the booster rockets—had listened to and heeded the warnings of Thiokol engineers, the launch would have been delayed and the disaster might have been averted. The story begins months before the explosion.

July 31, 1985. Almost six months before the scheduled launch, Roger Boisjoly, a Thiokol engineer, wrote a memorandum to his superiors expressing grave misgivings about the erosion of the synthetic rubber seals in the booster rockets. In his prophetic memo, he outlined what would happen if the seals were to fail: "The result could be a catastrophe of the highest order—loss of human life." At about the same time, another engineer, Arnold Thompson, also wrote a memo to top Thiokol bosses urging that all future shuttle flights be halted until actions were taken to correct the erosion problem with the seals. In front of the presidential panel, he testified that he never received a reply to this memo.

January 27, 1986. The day before the flight, engineers at Thiokol's plant in Utah—some nervous anyway about the safety of the seals—became even more concerned when they learned that Florida was having one of its January cold spells. The temperature was expected to go into the low 20s that night and was predicted to be in the middle-to-high 20s at scheduled launch time the next morning. The engineers feared that a launch in these cold temperatures would place an additional burden on the rubber seals they were already concerned about. Their fear? The cold would cause the seals to become hard and stiff, and eventually fail—with catastrophic consequences. Since space agency policy required the company's authorization before a launch, the Thiokol engineers prepared to make a case to delay the launch until temperatures rose to what they considered a safe level, the low 50s.

9:00 P.M., the evening before the flight. The engineers and four Thiokol vice-presidents in Utah hooked up on a conference call with NASA officials in Florida and Louisiana. After an exchange of technical data, the twelve engineers *unanimously* recommended *against* a launch, arguing that the temperature should be at least in the low 50s to provide an adequate margin of safety. Speaking in front of the presidential panel, Mr. Boisjoly said, "In all the discussions among Thiokol engineers the day before the launching, there was never one positive pro-launch statement made by anybody."

During the conference call, the four Thiokol vice-presidents stood by their engineers—they too opposed the launch. However, according to the sworn testimony of the engineers, NASA officials didn't really like what they were hearing. One NASA official was quoted as saying he was "appalled" by the recommendation of the engineers. Another said he wondered, "when we'll ever fly if we have to live with" recommendations like these. (Even though the NASA officials later denied applying any pressure, the engineers testified that they felt pressured to change their minds.) After a frank discussion the engineers stood firm in their unanimous opposition to the launch. Even though NASA officials didn't like what they were hearing, they said they would delay the launch if the company recommended against it.

At this point a fateful decision was made. One of the Thiokol vice-presidents suggested a five-minute recess to discuss the issues. NASA officials were put on hold and told they could expect a formal decision shortly. During the caucus, senior vice-president Jerry Mason looked to his vice-president of engineering, Robert Lund, who a few minutes earlier had opposed the launch, and suggested that Lund "take off his engineering hat and put on his management hat." (During the inquiry, a member of the presidential panel asked Mason, "Wasn't that pressure on your part to a subordinate that he should change his mind?" Mason's response: "Well, I hope not, but it could be interpreted that way.")

During the caucus, the thinking of the four management officials at Thiokol began to shift in favor of a launch. One of the engineers said, "From this point on, management formulated the points to base their decision on. There was never one comment in favor . . . of launching by any engineer or other nonmanagement person in the room before or after the caucus." Thiokol management testified later that the engineers played no part in the decision. Mr. Boisjoly—one of the engineers most adamant about the potential danger—said, "I was never asked or polled and it was clearly a management decision from that point."

Thirty minutes later, the caucus ended and Thiokol officials got back on the line with NASA officials. Reversing their original position and overruling their engineers, this time they recommended a launch. The authorization papers were signed and a thermofax copy was immediately sent to NASA headquarters. Everyone knows what happened the next morning.

We applaud each one of the Thiokol engineers for their professional integrity and their courage. We don't want to come across as second-guessing them in any way. However, after we learned of the events at Thiokol the night before the tragedy, we began to wonder *what might have happened* if those engineers had read this chapter you are about to read. You see, in this chapter, we're going to argue that sometimes it's not only appropriate, but maybe even necessary, for employees *not to go along* with a management decision that seems clearly wrong or dangerous. Sometimes it's necessary to take a stand against a boss.

Imagine for a moment what might have happened if the Thiokol engineers had said, "Hey, this is a bad decision—a *wrong* decision—and we refuse to stand by and do nothing about it." Clearly, this would've taken monumental courage and they would've been putting their careers on the line. However, imagine what might have happened if they had called an emergency press conference and blown the whistle on the gravely wrong decision they felt their superiors were making.

In our view, it's very clear what would've happened. An unprecedented event like this would've been big news—the major news media would've covered it. Like wildfire, the controversy would've spread through the night and into the early morning hours. In all likelihood, the President would have been awakened and briefed on this unusual development. Realizing that the nation would view these engineers as safety-conscious men of integrity, not "kooks" or fanatics, we believe that public opinion-conscious NASA officials would've delayed the flight. Maybe the shuttle disaster would have occurred on the very next launch—we'll never know. But it would not have occurred that morning *if* the engineers at Thiokol had done something that thousands of employees have done in the past ten years when they decided, at great personal risk, that they couldn't live with something their bosses had done. Standing up against their bosses, this dramatic form of employee action is called *whistle blowing*.

Whistle blowing is one form of taking a stand against your boss. That's what this chapter is about. It's about formally opposing your boss on actions or decisions you strongly disagree with.

We've divided the chapter into three sections:

1. When taking a stand against your boss is something to consider.
2. Why we like this strategy.
3. How to take a stand against your boss, including: direct personal action, grievances, whistle blowing, and legal action.

WHEN TAKING A STAND IS SOMETHING TO CONSIDER

We think taking a stand against your boss is a measure of last resort employees are sometimes forced to take. It's extremely risky, but it's something at least to consider when you feel:

• you've been treated unjustly or "wronged" in some way by your boss—and don't feel you can get satisfaction either by talking directly to your boss or going over your boss's head.

For example: You're a city employee and you know that your boss has been accepting kickbacks from contractors for throwing work their way. You also strongly suspect that your boss's boss knows what's going on (and may also be part of the illegal activity). What do you do?

Another example: You're a woman and your boss has made it abundantly clear that going to bed with him will get you the raise and promotion you want. You know for a fact that he's done this with several other women in the company, who've reluctantly gone along with his sexual extortion. You don't want to leave the company and you're not sure your boss's boss or any of the other men who run the company will understand your plight. What do you do?

• your boss or your company has made (or is about to make) a decision that will seriously jeopardize human life or public safety—and you feel torn between your loyalty to your company and your moral obligation to either report the problem or do something to prevent it.

For example: You're an engineer at Morton Thiokol and your bosses have made a management decision to approve what you believe is a dangerous launch. What do you do?

Another example: Your boss owns a company that's planning to manufacture and distribute a product you know to be unsafe and maybe even potentially dangerous. You fear that distribution and sale of the product will lead to serious injury of consumers, possibly even death. What do you do?

Even though it happens to only a relatively small percentage of employees—which is still a considerable number of people— every day a certain number of employees find themselves facing a moment of truth with their bosses. They're faced with a decision to *go along with* something they know to be wrong or *stand up* to their bosses and say, in effect, "I'm not going along with you on that. In fact, I'm going to fight you on it because I think you're wrong." Is it risky? You better believe it's risky! Your job *and* your career may be at stake. But, as we've tried to show above, there are times in life when taking a stand against a boss is something that should be done. As the famous abolitionist, William Lloyd Garrison, said, "With reasonable men I will reason; with humane men, I will plead; but to tyrants I will give no quarter, nor waste arguments where they will certainly be lost."

Now let's talk about why we like the idea of employees taking stands against their bosses.

WHY WE LIKE THIS STRATEGY

In our opinion, when most employees take a stand against their bosses, they do it for very good reasons. Instead of sitting on their hands and passively accepting things they believe to be wrong, they're willing to stand up and say so, even though they may be putting their jobs on the line. We've always admired people with personal courage. And it takes courage to take a stand against a boss.

There are some other reasons we like this strategy.

It's a Way of Holding Bosses Accountable

When employees make mistakes or engage in wrongdoing, we expect them to receive some form of corrective or disciplinary action, like lowered performance ratings, formal warnings, reprimands, demotions, withholding of raises, and possibly even dismissal.

But what about bosses who make mistakes or engage in wrongdoing? What happens, for example, when a boss unjustly dismisses an employee, engages in sexual extortion, accepts kickbacks, or knowingly violates public safety laws? In our opinion, the methods we'll be describing in this chapter—like direct personal action, filing of grievances, whistle blowing, and legal action—are legitimate recourses employees have. They're not only ways of holding bosses accountable, but they're ways of keeping organizations honest. They're checks in a system that needs more checks and balances than it's historically had. As one person we talked to said, "Let's face it! Bosses, like doctors and lawyers, have done a terrible job of policing themselves over the years. If employees don't hold bosses accountable, who will?"

Employees Are More Aware of Wrongdoing than Anyone Else

More than anybody, employees know what's going on in an organization—good and bad. They're especially aware of wrongdoing. In a 1981 survey of Federal employees in fifteen Federal departments and agencies, the Merit Systems Protection Board found that almost one-half (45%) of the employees surveyed claimed to have observed one or more instances of illegal or wasteful activity during the previous twelve months. In his afterword to Kenneth Lasson's 1971 book *The Workers*, Ralph Nader said:

> Workers know an enormous amount about abuses which they encounter, endorse, observe, or try to avoid every day. Moreover, they often know about them far earlier than their ultimate disclosure—or emergence as public scandals or disasters. For example . . . they know generally which factories dump what pollutants into waterways and that there is more pollution under cover of darkness. They know how car manufacturers fudge inspection on the line. They know how government inspectors tip off coal mines of their impending arrival or how co-workers smoke in prohibited areas. They know which meat and poultry inspectors are on the take or which fail to exercise their duties. They know how taxi meters and automobile odometers are rigged by design or manipulated to cheat the rider or driver. They know of violations of work safety laws. Indeed, many of the main consumer and environmental problems are rooted in secrets known to hundreds if

not thousands of workers. The value of such information can be seen by occasional acts of courage when an assembly line worker discloses evidence of defectively designed products.

It Can Right Some Wrongs and Avert Some Major Problems

Earlier, we speculated that some form of employee action like whistle blowing might have averted the space shuttle tragedy. But that was only speculation on our part. In reality, however, thousands of employees *have* exposed major fraud and corruption in government and big business, averted potentially major disasters in the airlines and nuclear power industries, and brought some long-overdue justice to some pretty bad bosses. And it all happened because ordinary employees decided to stand up against their bosses. For some of the secrets they've disclosed and the corruption they've uncovered, we owe them a big debt of gratitude.

Sometimes It's the Only Alternative Left

Most employees who decide to take a stand against their bosses have tried other measures first, like talking to their bosses directly or even going over their boss's heads. It's usually because these less drastic measures have failed—or don't look like they'll stand a chance of working—that employees turn to these measures of last resort.

It's a Way to Get Issues Out in the Open and Argue Them Publically

Many organizations, in general as well as when they're engaging in shady practices, like to keep corporate matters shrouded in a cloak of secrecy. Issues like public welfare and safety, however, need to be brought out into the open and debated in an open forum. Whistle blowers have helped us do that.

It Makes Corporate Life More Interesting

Even though it's not their purpose, there's no question that employees who stand up against their bosses make life at work more interesting. As Ronald Berenbeim points out in his book, *Nonunion Complaint Systems*:

> The conflict generated by the grievance procedure is more interesting than the monotony and boredom of the work and provides a very important distraction . . . I perceive the griping, complaining, arguing with the foreman, and filing of grievances as social activities that alleviate the boredom.

Anyone who's ever worked in an office during a grievance or a lawsuit knows what this means. It's usually *all* people talk about on their coffee breaks, during lunch, and after work at the local watering hole. Sometimes, the human interest value of this kind of thing rivals that of television melodramas.

HOW TO TAKE A STAND AGAINST YOUR BOSS

As we said earlier, there are four major ways to take a stand against your boss: (1) direct personal action, (2) grievances, (3) whistle blowing, and (4) legal action. Let's take a look at them, one at a time.

Direct Personal Action

This means confronting bosses directly and personally—and sometimes in writing—to tell them:

1. Specifically what they've done that you don't approve of or disagree with.

2. The effect the boss's actions or decisions have had on you.
3. What you want them to do differently (for example, to stop or take steps to correct the situation).
4. What you are prepared to do if they don't resolve matters to your satisfaction.

What we're *not* talking about here is the kind of cooperative and collaborative approach we described in our earlier chapter, "Talking to Your Boss One on One." Here we're talking about playing hard ball. Direct personal action is *confrontive* in nature. It sends the unequivocal message: "I don't approve of what you're doing and I'm going to tell you why. I want you to stop what you're doing or correct the situation. If you do, I'll be happy to forget about the matter. If you don't, I'm prepared to make things very unpleasant for you."

In our opinion, direct personal action may be *the* most effective strategy for dealing with one of the most pervasive problems in American organizations today—the sexual harrassment and sexual extortion of female employees by their male bosses.

For example, Elizabeth Martin is a staff writer for a popular national magazine. When she was hired, it was like a dream come true—she was doing what she wanted to do for a magazine she really wanted to write for. She was also beginning to make decent money and establish something of a name for herself in her field. Elizabeth's most obvious characteristic, though, was also her lifelong curse—she was an extremely attractive woman. As long as she could remember, men had been showering Elizabeth with attention and putting the moves on her. The principal reason she had left her last two jobs was because of sexual pressure from senior editors who were her bosses. Unfortunately, it didn't take long before Elizabeth became an object of interest to Maurice Scherling, the executive editor of the magazine. Maurice was twenty years older than Elizabeth and had a well-established reputation for, as one of the guys in the mail room said, "breaking in all the new girls" who were hired. An old friend of the publisher, Maurice felt no need to restrain himself.

Elizabeth told us she never again wanted to leave a job simply because a boss expressed sexual interest in her. So when Maurice began to make his moves, Elizabeth was ready for him.

We won't go into the details of the case here, but suffice it to say that, with a small tape recorder she kept in her purse, Elizabeth surreptitiously tape-recorded numerous sexual propositions Maurice made to her face-to-face as well as over the phone. She kept a detailed notebook documenting dates, times, and places when he attempted to fondle her or suggested taking a long weekend together.

She eventually sent Maurice (by registered mail) a long, formal letter—along with a copy of the tape—in which she: (1) documented in careful detail what he had said and done to her since she was hired; (2) talked about the emotional distress it had caused her to feel; (3) told him to cease and desist immediately; and (4) said she would let bygones be bygones if he did, adding that she was sure the two of them could have a very good *professional* relationship. She also told him what she was prepared to do if he didn't—which included filing a grievance with the EEOC for sexual harrassment; with the assistance of a local women's group, personally suing him and the publisher; and sending a copy of the tape to his wife and adult children. In the letter, she suggested a face-to-face meeting *in her office* the next day to discuss the matter.

During the meeting (which, by the way, Elizabeth also tape-recorded) Maurice was a new man. As Elizabeth told us:

> He told me that he didn't really mean to upset me and that he was sure I could understand how he got a

little out of control with me. He said he agreed that we could have a good working relationship and he said he looked forward to working with a woman who knew what she wanted and how to get it. That was six months ago, and we haven't had one problem. Of course, he knows that I still have my copy of the tape!

Obviously, direct personal action is an extremely high-risk strategy and, like high-risk strategies, it could make things worse. But Elizabeth was emotionally ready to take a stand against her boss. She was prepared to lose her job, if it were necessary. But she was also prepared to do everything she'd threatened in her letter, if it became necessary. Happily, she didn't have to.

Here are a few other thoughts about direct personal action:

IT'S CLEARLY NOT FOR EVERYBODY
If you're the kind of person who quivers and shakes at the mere thought of conflict, you're probably thinking. "This isn't the strategy for me!" Maybe it isn't. But we've got to say that we've seen many shy and unassertive people rise to the occasion when they had to. Try to remember what William Shakespeare said in *Twelfth Night*: "Be not afraid of greatness: some are born great, some achieve greatness, and some have greatness thrust upon them."

DOCUMENT EVERYTHING
What you want to do is build a case with as much evidence as you can. Keep a diary or notebook and carefully record places, dates, and times. Immediately write down precisely what you recall your boss saying or doing (this is no time for false modesty, if he put his hand on your breast or attempted to put his hand between your legs, write it down exactly as it occurred). Even though it makes people feel uncomfortable, we strongly recommend using tiny audio-cassette recorders (that are very easy to hide in a purse) to record the

actual words of bosses. While tapes may not be admissible in a court of law, they can be used in a wide variety of other ways that can be damning to a problem boss. If possible, have co-workers who are willing to serve as witnesses also keep a written record of what they've seen or heard.

DON'T LOSE YOUR COOL

When you confront your boss, stay calm. Don't become angry or insubordinate. Any loss of composure on your part can only come back to haunt you. For example, we heard of one case where a male boss sexually propositioned a female employee. She responded angrily, "Over my dead body, you will!" and slapped him so forcefully across the face that he fell down. We were told the woman was fired the next day for "assaulting" her supervisor and was eventually denied unemployment compensation in a hearing on the matter (apparently, the company brought witnesses who observed the woman striking the supervisor, but who didn't see or hear what he had said to her). So, if anybody's going to "lose it" and behave ineffectively, let it be your boss.

YOU CAN ACT ON BEHALF OF ANOTHER PERSON

We know a woman who's a senior vice-president of a bank who's become somewhat of a corporate "equalizer" to the women in her company who are being sexually hounded by their male bosses. She started out by helping just one young woman who sought her out a couple of years ago—and then the word started to spread. She has an interesting and effective *modus operandi*.

When she finds out that a male department head is making unwanted sexual advances toward an employee, she does enough fact finding to be sure it's really happening. She then takes *direct personal action* herself. She goes directly to the boss, confronts him with what she knows, advises him to stop, tells him that if he does the matter will be forgotten, and warns him that if he doesn't (or tries it with any other women in the firm), she'll immediately pull the plug on him. The president of the bank and several members of the board of directors know exactly what their enterprising vice-president is up to—and they support her completely. As she told us, they'd much rather have their bank's sexual harassment problems solved in this "quiet" way than in an embarrassing court action or civil suit.

Grievances

As you've heard us say before, for the most part, organizations in America are *not* bastions of freedom and democracy. As a matter of fact, when we look at the presidents of most organizations, they remind us of dukes and princes and counts who rule over their fiefdoms with almost supreme power. Well, maybe not supreme power—but in many cases, it comes close. In general, presidents of companies, being the biggest of the bosses, get their way, even when they're wrong, incompetent, or misguided.

Life in most organizations is not only not democratic, it can be downright undemocratic. For example, the rights we almost take for granted as citizens—like the rights of free speech and assembly—in many ways stop when you walk through your company's front door. For example, you can walk right up to the front gates of the White House and holler at the top of your lungs, "President Reagan! I think you're the stupidest president we've ever had" and nothing would happen to you. (In fact, a few of the other people who're protesting on the same sidewalk might even applaud as you asserted your right of free speech.) However, imagine what would happen if you walked into the office of your company's president and said something similar. Do you think you could claim freedom of speech there? You'll be lucky to be claiming unemployment compensation.

Freedom of speech is one thing, but fair and just treatment

is another. What happens when bosses treat employees unfairly or unjustly? What recourse do they have? What chance do they have to get a fair and objective hearing? To handle exactly this kind of problem, many companies—some because of collective bargaining agreements with unions, others on their own—have established grievance procedures.

A grievance procedure is an appeals process for employees who feel they've been wronged or treated unfairly by their bosses. They're an attempt to put some *due process* into organizations, in effect, to give employees the right to fair treatment. For the most part, grievances have to do with differences of opinion between bosses and employees about what is fair and what is just. They're usually disputes over things like performance appraisal ratings, vacation and personal leave, dismissals, raises and bonuses, disciplinary action, promotions and demotions, and so forth.

Grievance procedures vary widely from company to company. Unfortunately, most of the small companies in America, and even some fairly large ones, have no grievance procedures at all. Employees in these companies are virtually at the mercy of their bosses. If they work for humane and enlightened bosses, they're lucky. If not, it's their tough luck.

Companies that do have grievance procedures have one of two types: informal or formal.

INFORMAL GRIEVANCE PROCEDURES
Smaller companies, especially family businesses, closely held corporations, and owner-operated firms, tend to have informal grievance procedures. Very often, they're not much more than an open-door policy on the part of the owner or president, who serves as a kind of final arbiter of disputes. When written up in an employee's handbook or personnel policy manual, they might be described like this:

> XYZ Company is committed to fair and just treatment of its employees and will objectively review any

and all grievances. Employees who feel they have a grievance should first discuss the matter with their immediate supervisor. If this doesn't resolve the matter to the satisfaction of the employee or the employee's supervisor, the matter will be settled in a meeting of all relevant parties conducted by Mr. McNulty, XYZ Company's president.

In informal systems, the president or owner *is* the court of last resort for the employee. If employees lose at this stage, it's as good as over (unless, of course, they want to consider whistle blowing or legal action). Unlike formal grievance procedures, informal systems almost never include a provision for the arbitration of disputes by an independent party.

FORMAL GRIEVANCE PROCEDURES

Formal systems tend to be found in larger organizations and in companies whose employees are represented by a union. As a matter of fact, the establishment of grievance procedures is generally considered one of the major achievements of trade and labor unions over the years. Formal systems have a quasi-legal feel to them and usually spell out the exact procedures to be followed at each step of the grievance process. Some of the formal systems lead to binding arbitration by an outside party if the matter is not settled within the company.

Here's how a formal grievance procedure might be presented in an employee's handbook:

All employees who feel they have been wronged or treated unfairly in some way may avail themselves of the following grievance procedure:

Step 1: Discuss your complaint with your immediate supervisor.

Step 2: If the matter is not resolved by your immediate supervisor, bring your complaint to the attention of your immediate supervisor's supervisor.

Step 3: If the matter is not resolved to your satisfaction in your meeting with your immediate supervisor's supervisor, you must file a written grievance with the Personnel Director within five working days of this meeting. Within five working days of receiving the grievance, the Director of Personnel will meet with you, your supervisor, and any other relevant parties in an attempt to settle the grievance.

Here are a few other things we've learned about grievance procedures:

The commitment to them varies widely from company to company. Top executives at some companies are so committed to a fair and just grievance process that employees can get almost as good a hearing in their companies as they could in a court of law. However, many other companies have established them only because collective bargaining has forced them to. And in some nonunion companies, the principal motivation to establish grievance procedures seems to be to take away one of the principal arguments of labor organizers. In some companies, grievance procedures are a farce and a joke. In these companies, employees have such little faith in them that grievances are never filed, even in the face of blatant mismanagement by bosses.

In companies where the grievance procedure is simply the open-door policy of the owner or president, grievance systems can be good or bad, depending on who's in charge. We've seen many owners and presidents who're fair, even-handed, and just. But we've seen others who're devious, capricious, and unbalanced. Like they say, a chain is only as strong as its weakest link.

They're great in theory and often not-so-great in practice. Grievance procedures are a great idea, and they sound *so good* when we see them described in personnel policy manuals. Who can argue with the idea that an unfair or bad decision by a lower-level boss can be overturned by an appeals process or a higher authority in the company? You'd also predict that the mere existence of a grievance procedure would prevent some bosses from behaving badly, that is, if they knew they could be taken to task for bad behavior, they'd be less inclined to behave in that way. However, reality often runs smack up against theory. Employees who're supposed to get a fair hearing don't; things that are supposed to be confidential aren't; and bad boss behavior that should be overruled or reprimanded isn't.

If you're thinking about filing a grievance, we'd suggest that you:

1. Assess your case. How strong is it, really? Don't assume others will see things your way. Get objective opinions about the merits of your case before filing.
2. Document your case. Just as bosses are advised to carefully document their decisions to fire or demote people, you should also carefully document (letters, previous appraisal forms, attendance records, witnesses, etc.) your case.
3. Be prepared for a case to be made against you. Your supervisor is not going to roll over and play dead or say, "Forgive me for I have sinned." Be prepared for a fight, possibly an unfair fight. Just because you're playing by the rules of fair play, don't assume your boss is, too. Be prepared for things to get messy—an attack on you, your performance as a worker, and maybe even your qualities as a person. Expect some mud to be slung your way, as well as falsehoods, inaccuracies, and distortions of the truth. Since it's not a court of law, you won't have Perry Mason there to holler, "Objection! Not relevant."
4. Be prepared to feel overwhelmed. Bosses often go into a grievance procedure with the support of the entire organization on their side. One company we heard of routinely

had a company lawyer accompany bosses to grievance hearings, just to intimidate employees. You may feel like Daniel walking into the lion's den.

5. Expect things to change dramatically after you file your grievance. You may have been the fair-haired person before the grievance, but be prepared for cold shoulders, subtle or not-so-subtle retaliation, unpleasant work assignments, and a variety of other negative consequences after you file.

6. Be prepared to lose. Even though you think you have a good case, there's no guarantee you'll win. One study showed that 40% of college professors won their grievances and 60% lost. But even if you think you're guaranteed to lose because of an unfair grievance process, be prepared to go through with it anyway. If you ever decide to take your case to another level (for example, a government agency or a court of law), it may be important to show that you tried to do it "their" way.

7. Be prepared to win. But it might be a Pyrrhic victory. You might win, but the price you pay may not be worth it. Grievance procedures are often long and difficult ordeals. Sometimes there's retaliation. Especially if it's a long, drawn-out affair, people begin feeling depressed, consumed, distracted, and preoccupied. Your home and personal life may also suffer.

Whistle Blowing

Employees who go through a grievance process are working within the system. But many employees have discovered that working within the system doesn't always work so well. Many employees who've filed grievances have experienced retaliation, even though it's wrong or even illegal. Others have been transferred to the boonies, had their jobs reorganized, been demoted, neutralized, and even fired. So, whether they've tried to work within the system and failed, or simply don't have any confidence that working within the system will help them, many employees decide to go public with their grievances and complaints. As we said earlier, it's called whistle blowing.

In general, whistle blowers are employees who try to stop their bosses from engaging in serious wrongdoing—illegal activity, unethical conduct, or behavior that's potentially dangerous to other employees or the general public. Almost always, whistle blowers begin by working within the system, generally by going to their bosses directly, going to their boss's boss, or filing grievances. When the problem isn't corrected by these means, they "blow the whistle"—usually by turning to government agencies, law enforcement officials, or the media. People who've done research in this area say that whistle blowers almost always get fired by their bosses, who view their behavior as disloyal, demented, and sometimes even dangerous. While some whistle blowers are eventually reinstated, most aren't. And those who finally "win" pay a heavy emotional and psychological price.

Whistle blowing is the most dramatic and highly popularized strategy for dealing with problem bosses. Look at what "Deep Throat" was able to do by blowing the whistle on his boss, Richard Nixon. Or Daniel Ellsberg with the "Pentagon Papers." Hollywood has dramatized the lives of other famous whistle blowers, like Frank Serpico of the New York City Police Department and Karen Silkwood, the Kerr-McGee employee who many people believe was killed for her whistle blowing efforts.

But most whistle blowers aren't famous. Like those people Shakespeare talked about in *Twelfth Night*, they're ordinary people who're thrust into extraordinary situations. They're people like:

Billie Garde [her real name]. In 1980 she was hired to work in the office of the U.S. Census Bureau in Muskogee, Oklahoma. Soon after she was hired as an assistant to the director and a personnel recruiter, Billie discovered what her "real" job involved. In charges that were later filed—and verified—Billie said she was pressured to go to bed with her boss, hire women who would do the same with local politicians who were buddies of her boss, and alter scores of civil service examinations at the request of her boss. Billie started by reporting the situation to Bureau higher-ups and even a local congressman's office. After four months of complaining, no action was taken. However, word of her disloyalty got back to her boss, and she became the victim of a massive retaliation campaign (only part of which was to get her fired). After painful self-deliberation, Billie agreed to talk to a local newspaper reporter. Apparently, several other female employees had leaked word to the newspaper and said that Billie could confirm what was going on. Billie also went to the Department of Commerce and the EEOC, which moved so slowly she decided to go to a Washington, D.C., whistle blowing group, the Government Accountability Project. Then began a year-long ordeal that culminated in her boss being indicted and convicted on several criminal counts. He was sentenced to a year in jail and three years probation. His dreams of a future political career were dashed. Billie is now a law student and works for the Government Accountability Project.

Irwin Levin [also his real name], an employee in New York City's massive human services agency. After seeing supervisors ignore case after case of reported child abuse and patient abuse, Irwin did what most whistle blowers do, he went up the chain of command. He made thirty formal complaints, all of which were ignored. He brought the matter to the attention of the city council president, but not much happened. He wrote a letter to the governor, but got no reply. Finally, he wrote an anonymous letter to the Children's Aid Society, with documentation of caseworker negligence. Incredibly, somebody at the Society sent the material back to Irwin's superiors, who used a handwriting analyst to identify him. Brought up on charges, he was found guilty by the department of breaching confidentiality laws and he was demoted, fined, and finally suspended. Even his union and the professional association he belonged to sided *against* him. Two years later, after the matter was taken up by local newspaper reporters, Irwin was vindicated. An independent investigation found that negligence and gross abuse had occurred in seventeen of the twenty-two cases cited by Irwin. Irwin has been reinstated (he says he's been "kicked upstairs") and the investigation into possible criminal charges goes on. The past several years have been a nightmare for Irwin, who sought a therapist to help him through the ordeal. But he says he'd do it all over again to "right the wrong" he saw in the agency.*

There are now hundreds of cases of whistle blowing that've been documented in books and magazine articles. In fact, the practice is being written up with such frequency that the *Reader's Guide to Periodical Literature* has a special index for whistle blowing. If you'd like to read some fascinating— and frankly unbelievable stories—we'd recommend that you take a look at the following:

• Greg Mitchell's *Truth . . . and Consequences*. New York: Dembner Books, 1981.
• Alan Westin's *Whistle Blowing*. New York: McGraw-Hill, 1981.
• William McGowan's *New Age Journal* article that we mentioned below.
• David Ewing's *Do It My Way or You're Fired!* New York: John Wiley, 1983.

Even though the strategy has been around for a while

---

*The information regarding the cases of Billie Garde and Irwin Levin was drawn from newspaper and television coverage as well as the article, "The Whistleblowing Game," by William McGowan, *New Age Journal* (September 1984).

(Ralph Nader, for example, has been advocating it for years), we hadn't heard much about it until we began writing this book. What we found was eye-opening and exciting. Here are a few other ideas resulting from our research that we'd like to pass on to you:

WHISTLE BLOWING

This is a strategy that can dramatically expose and ultimately correct unconscionable practices far too many bosses have been allowed to get away with. But it's a strategy fraught with danger and risk, too. *Everybody* says that people who're thinking about blowing the whistle on a boss should *expect* to be fired. It's truly a "high-risk" strategy.

WHISTLE BLOWING IS GAINING MORE RESPECTABILITY

Once considered to be a radical act of disloyalty, whistle blowing is actually being encouraged by many government officials and the heads of private corporations. For example, the Civil Service Reform Act of 1978 held that whistle blowing was "essential to the improvement of public service" and, for the first time, gave statutory protection to Federal employees who blew the whistle on illegal or wasteful activities. We've also heard presidents of some of America's major corporations say that they supported the idea of employees' blowing the whistle on illegal or dangerous company practices.

LAWS NOW PROTECT WHISTLE BLOWERS

There are many Federal, state, and even some city "whistle blowing laws" that make it illegal for an employer to retaliate against employees who go public with information about illegal conduct on the part of their bosses. These laws probably won't stop bosses from retaliating against whistle blowers, but it'll eventually make it a lot easier to press criminal charges against them when they do.

MANY EMPLOYEES PUT PROFESSIONAL LOYALTY BEFORE COMPANY LOYALTY

Many people are employees *and* members of professions as well (e.g., researchers, doctors, scientists, engineers, accountants, and so on). They belong to professional associations that each have their own codes of conduct. Most professional codes clearly indicate that the professional's *primary loyalty* is to "the public welfare" or "the good of society." We take that to mean that a professional's duty to society takes priority over what a boss wants—especially when the boss is doing something illegal, dangerous, or just plain wrong.

PREPARE YOURSELF BEFORE YOU TAKE THIS STEP

Everything we've said about documentation and the way to prepare for a grievance applies here. We'd also say that no employee should even consider it without carefully thinking about what's at stake, both positive and negative. If you're thinking about it, we'd strongly recommend you read some of the books and articles on the subject. They'll probably give you the best idea of what you can expect. You might also want to consult some of the many whistle blowing support groups that are springing up around the country (many are identified in books and articles on the subject). You may even want to talk to a whistle blowing counselor (generally, former whistle blowers who're now devoting their lives to helping other whistle blowers).

Most whistle blowers don't want to take such a dramatic stand against their bosses. The pain is great and the cost is high. But they feel it's their only alternative, so they reluctantly do it. In the next section, we'll talk about our fourth— and last—method for taking a stand against your boss.

Taking Legal Action

Earlier, we said that most organizations are not bastions of freedom and democracy. We live in a democracy, it's true. But, we don't *work* in one. In many ways, most companies are like little islands of autocracy in this great sea of democracy we live in. In a country that has begun to take *civil* rights very seriously, we've only recently begun to attack seriously the problem of *job* rights.

For most of our country's history, the government has taken a laissez-faire attitude toward business. The result? For almost two hundred years, bosses have had a free hand when it came to hiring, paying, promoting, and firing employees. If they didn't want to hire Catholics or Jews or women or Blacks, they just put a sign on the front door that said so. If you were a member of an unwanted group, you "need not apply." If they wanted to get rid of people—*for any reason*—they had an equally free hand. They just had to say, "We don't want you around here any more."

Based on the doctrine of *employment-at-will*, companies had an absolute right to fire workers at will. When employee dismissal cases were brought before them, judges almost always found in favor of bosses, basing their decisions on "Wood's rule." Named after a nineteenth-century legal scholar named Horace G. Wood, the rule was:

• Unless employees have a specific contract that says otherwise, they can be fired *without cause*.

Job rights? There was nothing *right* about it.

During the 1930s, the trade union movement began to pick up steam and at least helped *their* members gain a semblance of job security. If you belonged to a union, you were working under a "contract," so Wood's rule did not apply: You had to be fired *with cause*. Understandably, a union contract looked good to workers who weren't organized, and union membership grew dramatically. By the early 1950s, unions had organized over 32 percent of the work force, up from 13.5 percent in 1935. There's been a sharp drop since then, and today less than 20 percent of employees belong to unions. Some experts estimate that it will dwindle to between 10 to 15 percent by the year 2000.

However, in the past twenty-five years, something of a revolution has occurred in both *civil* rights and *employee* rights. In stark contrast to most of our nation's history, no longer do bosses have the freedom to do whatever they please with employees. Many employer practices that were standard operating procedure before the 1960s are now illegal. People entering the work force today take for granted legal protections their parents never dreamed of. For example, bosses can no longer hire or fire people on the basis of race, color, sex, age, ethnic origin, or religion. In the ten-year period from the mid-sixties to the mid-seventies, Congress passed a number of antidiscrimination and labor laws of monumental importance:

• The Equal Pay Act of 1963
• The Civil Rights Act of 1964
• The Age Discrimination in Employment Act of 1967
• The Occupational Safety and Health Act of 1970
• The Federal Privacy Act of 1974

With laws like these, the government abandoned its traditional laissez-faire approach to business and took a major step toward regulation of the work place. A major blow had been struck for employee rights.

Today, with diminishing union strength and a conservative mood in the country, some would think the employee rights pendulum has begun to swing back to where it's been most of the time, in the camp of *employer* rights. But not likely. As a July 1985 cover story in *Business Week* said:

. . . employee dissatisfaction with the boss-worker relationship in many companies is showing up clearly in polls, surveys, and a growing volume of court suits. In today's nonunion climate, the courts and state legislatures are becoming the most effective champions of employee rights.

And are they ever! Congress took the lead in the 1960s, and judges and state legislators are carrying the baton of employee rights in the 1980s. For example, in the past few years, many state legislatures (and some large city councils) have passed laws:

- protecting whistle blowers and employees who refuse to obey bosses who order them to do illegal acts
- making it illegal for employers to also discriminate on the basis of marital status and sexual orientation
- giving employees a "right to know" if they're working near or with hazardous substances
- prohibiting mandatory retirement
- requiring employers to give employees advance notice of plant shutdowns and offering severance pay to affected workers
- protecting employee privacy by limiting the use of lie detector tests in the screening and hiring of job applicants
- giving employees access to information in their personnel files

Despite all these gains, there is still no law on the books, state or federal, that protects employees from the employer action they fear most—unjust dismissal. In legal language, it's called "wrongful discharge." And if you don't think this is a big problem, experts estimate that every year up to *half a million* employees are unjustly dismissed by their bosses.

We don't think it's a question of *if* it's going to happen. It's just a case of *when*. Again, the state legislatures and the courts are taking the lead. Bills prohibiting the firing of employees except for just cause are pending in a number of states. Experts predict many other states will follow suit, with some predicting a Federal unjust-dismissal law within the next ten years.

Even without state laws on the books, employees are filing wrongful discharge suits in unprecedented numbers, and they're winning. In California alone, according to the *Business Week* article we mentioned earlier, over a recent five-year period, employees won forty-eight of seventy-four wrongful discharge suits that were taken to juries. Six plaintiffs were awarded damages in excess of one million dollars each.

Perhaps the biggest blow to be delivered in the employee rights struggle, however, will be the one that delivers the knockout punch to Wood's rule and the doctrine of *employment-at-will*. That blow may have already been struck by the Supreme Court of New Jersey. It's the case of Richard M. Woolley (his real name) versus his employer, Hoffman-LaRoche, Inc.

In 1978, engineer Richard Woolley got some bad news. After working for Hoffman-LaRoche for nine years, he was informed by his boss that he'd "lost confidence" in him and wanted him to resign. When he refused to resign, he was fired.

Given Wood's rule and the history of court decisions in similar cases in New Jersey and elsewhere, Richard's case looked pretty weak. After all, without a contract that says otherwise, companies in New Jersey had a right to fire employees at will. And Richard had no contract.

But Richard felt wronged, and he decided to stand up against his boss by taking legal action. Richard claimed that the company's personnel handbook said that employees could only be fired *with cause*—and only after certain procedures had been carried out. In court, the company took the position that the language in their handbook could hardly be considered a promise and, even if it was, it could hardly be considered a legally binding contract.

On May 9, 1985, the high court agreed with Richard and found against the company. The implication? Companies that say things to their employees in their personnel handbooks—such as, you can only be fired with cause—may be stuck with enforceable obligations.

Other state high courts in influential states like California and Michigan have taken a stand similar to the New Jersey court. It'll probably take a Supreme Court decision to settle the matter once and for all. But the trend is clear: Courts all over America are placing restrictions and limitations on the power bosses have to fire employees. And it's helpful to remember that each and every *court* decision began with a *personal* decision on the part of an employee to take legal action against a problem boss.

WHAT DOES ALL THIS MEAN FOR YOU?
Before the 1960s, very few employees tried to sue or take other legal action against their bosses. All that's changed. Today, thousands and thousands of employees have taken some kind of legal action against the unfair and unlawful actions of bosses and organizations. According to *Business Week*, in 1983 the EEOC and state and local human relations agencies received 120,000 complaints of job discrimination, a 30 percent increase over the previous year.

In civil suits, the judgments awarded to employees have often been sizeable: hundreds of thousands—even millions—in damages or back pay. It doesn't always work out so well, however. In many other cases, all the plaintiffs got were hefty legal fees, unemployment, and years of frustration and stress.

But the trend is clear. Taking some form of legal action is becoming a well-established strategy for dealing with bosses who engage in wrongdoing. More and more dissatisfied employees will be using it to correct and repair the wrongs they feel their bosses have done them. Maybe you, too.

We're not lawyers, and talking specifically about legal matters is not something we feel comfortable doing. But we do have a few thoughts we'd like to offer:

First you've got a lot of legal options, probably more than you think. On your own, you can't be expected to know what they are, but they're there. Every year new legislation is being passed, and new court decisions are being handed down, limiting the power of bosses to do as they want, and broadening the ever-expanding base of employee rights.

Second, everything we said earlier about documentation, personal courage, retaliation, persistence, frustration, and being prepared to lose applies here. Only here it applies even more.

Third, there are a variety of resources you can turn to for information and help. For example, there are dozens of private organizations (women's rights groups, minority organizations, the Government Accountability Project mentioned in the previous chapter, and industry watchdog groups like Nader's Raiders) that provide advice and counsel to employees who are thinking of taking legal action. Sometimes these groups will even help employees initiate legal action. There are also numerous public agencies (commissions against discrimination, human rights agencies, legal aide societies, equal opportunity commissions) that employees can go to if they feel their rights have been violated. And, there're a multitude of private lawyers out there who are more than willing to sit down with dissatisfied employees to talk about the possibility of a civil action.

Well, that's it! Four methods for taking a stand against your boss: direct personal action, filing grievances, whistle blowing, and taking legal action. Now let's turn to our final strategy, "firing" a problem boss.

17

....

"FIRING" YOUR BOSS

Several years ago, the popular country-and-western singer Johnny Paycheck wrote a song that leaped to the top of the charts. On occasion, when we're out in some honky tonk, a local band will try their hand at the song. When they do, something interesting happens. As soon as the chorus begins, *everybody* in the place puts on a big smile and joins in to sing:

> "Take this job and shove it!
> I ain't workin' here no more."

Part of the reason for the song's enormous popularity is that it responds to a powerful, deep-seated fantasy most employees have—telling a problem boss where to go.

In this chapter we'll offer our final strategy for dealing with problem bosses. We could have called it "quitting" or "resigning," but we didn't like the negative connotation of those

338

words. We thought, "If a boss can fire an employee, why can't an employee fire a boss?"

Specifically, we'll:

1. Explain why we think "firing" your boss is an excellent strategy.
2. Talk about why people who *should* use this strategy *don't.*
3. Offer some suggestions about how to do it.

WHY IT'S A GOOD STRATEGY

Millions of employees work in jobs they dislike for bosses they detest. Yet they continue to go to work day after depressing day (sometimes year after depressing year). Often these employees have highly marketable skills and years of valuable experience. With a lot less effort than they think, most of them could find new jobs with better bosses, better pay, and better working conditions.

These are three great reasons for getting rid of a problem boss. Here are a few more:

It's a Major Stress Reducer

When an unhappy employee decides to pack it in and take a new job, that person's tension, frustration, and unhappiness usually take a plunge. One person we interviewed said, "It feels like a big weight has been lifted from my shoulders." Another said, "It's like a new beginning. I haven't felt so exhilarated in years."

It's Another Excellent Way to Hold Problem Bosses Accountable

In several previous chapters we talked about the importance of holding bosses accountable. Firing problem bosses is one more way to do this. Think about it for a moment. Once you leave, your boss will have to replace you. This process is so time-consuming and frustrating that most bosses dread it. There's the advertising, the screening of job applicants, the interviewing, the reference checking, the mistakes while the new employee is learning the ropes, and so on. Plus, there's no guarantee new employees will be any better than old ones (and a fifty-fifty chance they'll be worse). Finally, there's also the damage to your boss's reputation if enough employees say, "Take this job and shove it." In personnel jargon it's called "high turnover." If it gets bad enough, eventually your boss's boss may take notice, wonder what the devil is going on, and *fire* your problem boss.

It Generally Leads to an Increase in Self-Respect

Employees who continue to work for problem bosses year after year almost always suffer an erosion of self-confidence. When they finally do something like fire the boss, they invariably feel better about themselves. A dental hygienist we talked to said,

> I worked for this real turd for about five years, but I didn't have the guts to leave. He was an extremely critical, fault finding type of person. Being around him every day almost destroyed my self-confidence. I began to think I couldn't do anything well. It got so bad I *had* to do something. When I finally told him I was leaving it was like a monkey off my back. I couldn't believe how much better I started feeling about myself.

Family Members and Loved Ones Appreciate It Greatly

Employees aren't the only ones who suffer at the hands of problem bosses, so do their families and loved ones. Every day, millions of employees who work for problem bosses bring their pain home with them from work. Distracted, anxious, depressed, or angry, the time they eventually spend with their spouses and children certainly isn't "quality" time. We've seen many marriages severely strained, and some even fail, because one spouse came home every night and did nothing but complain about the boss. Kids, especially the younger ones, become innocent victims. They don't believe that dad's or mom's irritability or short temper has to do with problems at work. They think it has to do with them. When a problem boss is finally fired, it can be a liberating experience for the whole family.

It Feels So Good to Do It

As we said at the beginning of the chapter, telling a problem boss to take a hike is one of the most common and pleasant employee fantasies. Why? Mainly because employees are in a one down position when it comes to bosses. It's just them against the boss and all the power and authority bosses have. Firing a problem boss causes a dramatic shift in power between boss and employee. Instead of being a passive recipient of the boss's abuse, an employee who fires a problem boss takes charge of the situation. When you say, "No more!" it's almost like ripping off your chains and setting yourself free. That feels *real* good.

WHY DON'T MORE EMPLOYEES FIRE THEIR BOSSES?

If firing problem bosses is such a good idea, why do so many employees avoid it? If employees with problem bosses are so miserable, why do they stay? There are a number of reasons:

Laziness

How many times have you heard someone say, "Finding a job is a full-time job." Whether or not this is literally true, finding a new job does take time and energy. Many people just aren't willing to put out the necessary effort. Think of all the disgruntled employees you've known over the years who've talked about firing their bosses, but who keep putting it off. It's almost as if they expect a new job to find them.

Inertia

Inertia is the tendency to settle into a rut and do nothing to get out of it. It's a little like being in a bad marriage. Sometimes, as bad as it is, we get used to the pain and find it easier to stay than to leave.

The more years people put into a job (and the older they get), the more likely it is for inertia to set in. As one man in his mid-forties told us, "If I were ten years younger, I'd leave in a minute. But ten years ago I was a lot more courageous. Plus, I have a lot of obligations now that didn't concern me when I was younger, like a mortgage, child support payments, and saving for the kids' college expenses."

Anxiety

For most people, the thought of changing jobs is scary, even when they want to get out of the jobs they're in. They may be unhappy, but they choose the unpleasant certainty of their present job over the anxiety-laden uncertainty of the future.

Sense of Inadequacy

Sadly, many employees don't have very positive views of themselves. They don't feel valuable and think they're *lucky* to have their jobs. They labor under the impression (almost *always* inaccurate) that they'd never be able to find a better job, only a worse one. Who wants to go from bad to worse?

Security Needs

There are two kinds of security needs that keep employees
in jobs they ought to leave: emotional security and financial
security. Let's look briefly at both.

EMOTIONAL SECURITY

As home and family have declined in importance over the
past fifty years, work—and the relationships we form with
people at work—has become more and more important to
people. As writer Lynn Hirschberg said in her recent article
on "The Office" in *Esquire* magazine, "But these days . . .
the office becomes at least *something* to belong to. Perhaps
it begins to take on some of the emotions, both good and
bad, usually attached to small-town life, or even to the family
itself."

These days, our closest friends are often the people we
work with every day. To fire our bosses and take new jobs
someplace else means losing contact, perhaps forever, with
people who mean a lot to us. A woman in her mid-thirties
told us: "I'm not married, I have no children, and my nearest
relatives are 500 miles away. I may not like my boss, and I
may think about leaving every now and then, but I can't bear
the thought of not seeing my friends every day."

FINANCIAL SECURITY

A couple of months ago we were talking to a thirty-seven-year-
old art director in an advertising firm. She'd been struggling for
a few years with her boss, a very tense and hard-driving man.
When we asked her why she didn't leave, she said. "You've
heard of a golden parachute, haven't you?"

"Sure," we said, "Doesn't that refer to the lucrative financial arrangements some top executives write into their
employment contracts in the event they *leave* a company?"

"Right," she said, "They literally bail out in a golden
parachute."

"So what does that have to do with your situation?" we asked.

She replied:

> I'm bound to this job by golden handcuffs. In three years I'll be fully vested in my company's profit-sharing plan. If I stay, that'll mean a big pile of money for me. If I leave before then, I can kiss all that cash goodbye. That's why I'm staying.

Whether or not you see them as golden handcuffs, there are many benefits and perks that companies offer their employees: company cars, health club memberships, stock options, tuition reimbursement, free parking, company-sponsored child care, medical and dental insurance, retirement plans, and so on. Some of them are worth lots of money, and most of them are pretty hard to walk away from. Because employees don't want to lose them, they stay in jobs they'd rather leave.

We don't want to bad-mouth security needs. Everybody's got them, us included. But too many people stay in bad situations solely because of their security needs. When this happens, it's important to ask if the price you're paying for that security is really worth it.

Pessimistic Thinking

Some people are pessimists. They stay in their jobs because they don't think that they'll ever be able to find anything better. As one employee told us, "I know what I've got here isn't any good, but what guarantee do I have that it's going to be better somewhere else. With my luck, it'd be worse."

The trouble with pessimists is they don't take the positive action necessary to make things better. On the other hand, some of the pessimism of the average worker is understandable. There are millions of people who've never had a satisfying job or a half-decent boss. Having never experienced it, it's easy for them to conclude it doesn't exist.

Irrational Thinking

We often talk to employees who justify their decision to continue working for problem bosses with irrational beliefs, like, "Well, I'm really needed here," or "I'd feel disloyal to look for another job."

We're not sure where these thoughts come from, but we do know bosses love to hear employees talk this way. We've seen more than one boss talk a disgruntled employee out of leaving because the employee was "really needed around here." Unfortunately, after employees who are "really needed" decide to stay, most bosses don't change the reasons why the employee wanted to leave in the first place.

So far we've talked about why firing your boss is a good idea, and we've offered reasons why employees who should use this strategy don't. Now let's talk about how to do it.

HOW TO FIRE YOUR BOSS

When it comes to firing your boss and finding a new job, there are only two ways to do it: with a new job waiting for you, or not. The best way is with a new job waiting in the wings. The problem is even though it can be logistically difficult, the best time to look for a job is when you already have one. Almost everybody agrees that it's much harder to find a new job when you're unemployed. So, even though you may have the urge to do something precipitous—like telling your boss where to go—it's probably not a good idea. And don't make the mistake of leaping to the first thing that comes along. We've known lots of employees who've "jumped out of the frying pan right into the fire."

Unless you're sitting on a family fortune or have won the

lottery, you'll probably be better off doing something a little less risky: *exploration* of your alternatives. A good way to begin this exploration is to become a student of the career development process.

Let's talk about what that means.

Career Development in Brief

This is an important topic, and we can't do justice to it in the few pages we have here. Briefly, though, the essence of the career development process can be expressed in three questions:

Step One: "Who am I?"
Step Two: "Where do I want to go?"
Step Three: "How do I get there?"

When people answer these questions fully and completely, their chances of finding new and better jobs increase dramatically. Let's look at each question in a bit more detail.

STEP ONE: "WHO AM I?"

Effective career decision making begins with self-assessment, which means taking a candid look at ourselves in the mirror—who we are, what we're like, what we want, and so forth. It means answering the general question, "Who am I?" as well as more specific questions, like:

- What are my *interests* (the things I like to do)?
- What are my *abilities* (the things I'm good at)?
- What are my *values* (the things that're really important to me)?
- What are my career and job *needs* (the things I must have in my job or career to feel satisfied and fulfilled)?
- What are my *preferences* (the things I'd like to have in a job or in life, but that aren't absolutely essential)?

- What are my *life goals* (the things I want to achieve or do with my life)?

To answer these questions, you don't have to lay out hundreds of dollars on a battery of psychological tests. These tests don't "tell" you what you should do or what you'd be good at. However, if you have the money and want the "objective" feedback, it won't hurt to give it a try. Since it's a lot cheaper, you may want to consult a career development book—there are dozens of good ones around, and almost every one has a chapter devoted to the topic of self-assessment. Self-assessment exercises like these are helpful, but you don't even have to do them. All you really need to do is some honest soul-searching and reflecting.

This is one of those areas where thinking out loud in the presence of a good listener is a very useful thing to do. To do it, ask a close friend to help. Have your friend read the section on listening skills in chapter 9 and then draw you out in response to questions like the ones above, or these below:

- Think about your hobbies and favorite spare-time activities. What do they have to say about the kind of person you are? What kind of *paid* work do they suggest?
- Over the years, what have you learned about what you *need* in a job and a boss to make you feel happy and satisfied?
- As you think about each job you've had, what would you say are your strengths? What would you say are your weaknesses or major drawbacks?
- What are some of your job and career fantasies? That is, if you could do anything you wanted, what would it be? Why?
- Put yourself in the shoes of the bosses you've had. How would they describe you? What would they say are your major assets and liabilities as an employee?

If you'd like to go one step further, find one or two people who are "experts" on you. This time, ask *them* the questions above, *as they see you*. Use your listening skills to get them to speak candidly. Undoubtedly you'll learn some new and important things about yourself. Plus, doing this will help you avoid the one major problem associated with *self*-assessment: the problem of self-deception.

STEP TWO: "WHERE DO I WANT TO GO?"

A lot of people go through life without clear goals—not knowing what they want to do and where they want to go with their lives. They drift along for years with no specific notion of where they'll finally end up. It reminds us of that old saying that was popular a few years back: "If you don't know where you're going, how will you know when you get there?"

Answering the question, "Where do I want to go with my life?" helps people set career goals and objectives. For us, a career goal can be likened to the North Star. It not only gives you something to aim for, but it's also a helpful guide along the way. For example, when people with clear goals are faced with a tough choice or decision, all they need to do is ask themselves, "Will this get me closer to, or further away from, my goal?"

While some people have unclear goals, other people have inappropriate ones. Because their goals are not based on an accurate assessment of who they are as people, they work in jobs they're not suited for. The result is frustration and dissatisfaction. Instead of trying to fit a square peg into a round hole, the solution is to adjust career goals to the characteristics of the person.

That's what Paul Gleason did. Paul told us he decided to become a doctor mainly because his father and grandfather were doctors. However, after receiving his M.D., Paul had to face up to something about himself he'd been avoiding for years. As he put it, "I know it sounds weird, but I hated touching people." After reexamining his career goals, he decided he could remain a doctor if he adjusted his plans.

He's now happy as a research pathologist and partner in a group practice in California.

A second example is Debbie Eden, a woman in her late twenties who'd been struggling for years doing bookkeeping and accounting work. When we met her, she told us she'd worked for a succession of problem bosses, all C.P.A.'s who owned small accounting firms. In our first conversation, we asked Debbie about her career fantasies. She replied, "I know this sounds kind of silly, but I'd like to have Julie's job on the *Love Boat*." She went on to talk about how she liked working with people and how she'd love to travel. Given her answer, it didn't take a genius to figure out that Debbie was in the wrong field. She began to explore career alternatives that were more suited to her interests. Today, she's a flight attendant for a major airline—and very happy at it.

When it comes to career goals, we think people have two basic choices in front of them: (1) going off on their own, and (2) finding a new job. Almost everyone, for one reason or another, opts for the second choice. You'll probably go that route, too. But since we chose to go off on our own and it's worked out so well for us, we'd like to offer a brief commercial for becoming your own boss.

Why not become your own boss? In our opinion, becoming your own boss is the best way to ensure you'll never again work for a problem boss, in effect, to become boss-free. It's also the best way to build the kind of career and job environment *you* want. When you're working for someone else, you're always going to have to do it—more or less—*their* way.

So, if you're an independent cuss, you're probably always going to struggle in your role as an employee. But you're also going to have to struggle to become your own boss. As enjoyable as it is, it's not easy to do. Almost everyone who goes off on their own says the same thing: Be prepared to work much harder than you ever did as an employee. Someone once humorously defined self-employed people as men and women who work eighty hours a week for themselves so they don't have to work forty hours a week for someone else. Humorous or not, often it's true. But we think all that work is worth it, because you're doing it for *you*. End of commercial.

As we said earlier, after self-assessment comes goal setting. To do it, try to answer clearly and precisely questions like "What do I want to do with my life?" and "Where do I want to go?" Have a friend interview you in depth as you explore your thinking about these two questions as well as those below:

- "What kind of work would you really like to do? What kind of work would bring you a feeling of satisfaction and a sense of fulfillment?"
- "How important are things like money, challenge, variety, responsibility, and independence in your work?"
- "What kind of organization would you like to work in? Large or small? Structured or unstructured? Old and established or new and developing?"
- "What kind of boss would you like to work for?"
- "What are your thoughts about going off on your own and becoming your own boss?"
- "What things would have to change to make your working and personal life more satisfying and less frustrating?"

STEP THREE: "HOW DO I GET THERE?"

The most comprehensive self-analysis and the clearest career objectives aren't worth anything unless they're carried out. So, once your career goals are set, it's time to think about what you're going to have to do in order to achieve them. It means mapping out and then doing what's necessary to get where you want to go.

To be frank, this is where most people screw things up. They end up not really *doing* anything. To avoid this, here are a few suggestions:

Make this a priority. It's easy to talk about what you're

going to do—and just leave it at that. A few years ago one of us was stuck in the wrong job in the wrong organization working for the wrong boss. Every day, *at least* one hour was devoted to griping and complaining to co-workers about what a rotten place it was to work in. Finally, someone said, ''Hey, if you'd spent half as much time doing something to get out of here as you have complaining about being here, you'd be long gone by now.'' The guy was right, and things changed then and there. Just like that, getting out became a priority. Two months later it was good-bye.

How will you know when getting out's a priority? As we said in an earlier chapter, it's a priority when it's right at the top of your daily list of things to do—when you do this before all the other things that are competing for your time and attention.

Read books and articles on the subject. As we suggested earlier, become a student of the process. There've been hundreds, maybe thousands, of books and articles written on the subject. But you don't have to lay out one red cent to read them. Just go to your local library and talk to the reference librarian. Say you're interested in books and articles on career development, and you'll get steered in the right direction. You'll find more books on the subject than you'll ever have time to read. Try to read one or two of them. After all, it is your life we're talking about here and it's probably worth your while to do a little research on the subject.

Your library research may also take you to what librarians call ''the periodicals,'' which are mainly the magazines the library subscribes to. When you get to the periodical room, concentrate on the women's magazines, even if you're a man. Compared to men's magazines, women's magazines have been much more aware of the career needs of their readers. You'll probably find at least one relevant article in every issue.

Reading books and articles should prove very thought-provoking. You'll get all kinds of ideas and insights you wouldn't have gotten if you hadn't read them. Even if you read this kind of material years ago, do it again. Now that you're motivated, it'll be a lot more salient and a lot more helpful.

Interview people who've done what you want to do. For every person who's written a book or article on the subject, there are many who've actually done it—gone off on their own or found a new job with a better boss. You probably know people like this already. They've traveled down the road before you, so find out what it was like for them. Think of yourself as a reporter or talk show host and interview them. Ask them what they did, what mistakes they made, what they learned, how they'd do it again, and what they'd recommend to you. They have an enormous amount of valuable information to share, especially if you're a good listener. So use your listening skills to get them talking about their experiences. You'll benefit enormously.

Use your social network. We read once that anywhere from 50 to 75 percent of all jobs are never advertised or listed, but are filled through something called "the social network." You can take advantage of this by using your own social network. Here's how.

Most of us have a fairly large circle of friends and acquaintances. But what we fail to realize is that our friends and acquaintances also have a large circle of friends. And, most important, our friends know many people we don't know—people who may be in a position to help us or hire us when we're looking for a job. When *we* embark on social networking, we say to ourselves, "I may not know the person I'm looking for now, but one of my friends (or a friend of one of my friends) probably does." The social networking concept looks something like this:

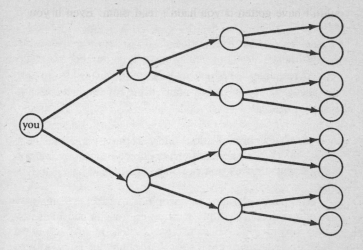

Seen in this way, your contacts to the outside world are limitless, even if you have only a few friends and acquaintances. So make a list of the people you know *who may know* someone else who has a good lead on a job. Don't overlook anyone who could possibly help. Call each of the people on your list and tell them you're looking for a job and would appreciate any *information* they can give you, either in the form of job leads or people who might know about job leads. Since most of the people you call at the beginning won't have any leads, they'll want to be helpful and will give you the names of one or two other people. Your list will start to grow rapidly.

When you call people you *don't* know, say you're calling at the suggestion of the person who gave you their name. That should open the door for you. Tell them directly what you're up to. If they can't come up with any job leads, ask them who else you might call. You'll be surprised at how many people you'll be referred to. Not everybody will be helpful. Some people will be downright *un*helpful. But don't let one or two rejections derail you. Most people will be very helpful. One or two of them may even have a job waiting for you.

Use the wide variety of career resources in your community. Almost every community has a large number of career-related resources designed to help people who are making job changes. Try to use as many different resources as you can. For example:

- Social service organizations and community agencies (like the YM/YWCA) generally have career counseling and job placement services that can help. Many also have job listings.
- Special-interest groups (for women, members of minority or ethnic groups, people with unique needs and interests, etc.) also provide career services. Plus, they often put on job fairs and career clinics for their clientele. These groups are especially fertile territory for social networking.
- Business, trade, and industry groups can provide formal assistance through job listings in their publications, and even placement services. Going to their regular meetings and conferences also can be a great place to do social networking.
- Depending on your situation, employment services, job placement agencies, and executive recruiters can be a very important component of a comprehensive job-hunting campaign.
- Local community colleges often sponsor workshops on job hunting and sometimes provide free or inexpensive career counseling.

If you run into trouble locating services, your local reference librarian may be able to help you identify career resources in your community. Or ask other people who know about community affairs, like a high school guidance counselor; a priest, minister, or rabbi; or a social worker.

Think about what a prospective employer NEEDS in an employee. Many job seekers make the mistake of thinking only of themselves and what they want when they're looking for a job. They ignore the wants and needs of the person who may hire them. That is, they don't think about the employer's perspective. When they do walk in the shoes of a prospective employer, what do they see? Often, they see employers who have job openings for competent, dependable people. But they also see employers who are nervous because they've been burned before—by employees who looked so good when they were first hired. Try to convey your understanding of this reality to prospective employers when you're talking with them.

It *is* important to be clear about what you want and need in a job. But if that's *all* you do, you're only doing half the job. Also think about what kind of employee your prospective boss is looking for. Even more important, think about the *needs* of your prospective boss. Once you do this, organize your job-hunting campaign around what you can do *for* them, not what you want *from* them. You'll be much more successful if you do.

When you're successful in your efforts to find a job, you'll be in a position lots of employees would like to be in, saying good-bye to a problem boss. We'll end the chapter with a few thoughts on how to part company.

MAKING AN EXIT

You're now ready to "fire" your boss, or, in their terms, to quit, resign, or leave to take another position. The question is, how to do it. In our experience, employees tend to fall into one of two camps when it comes to leaving an organization: (1) those who play it cool, and (2) those who let it all hang out.

Playing It Cool

This is the method most people choose and the one most recommended by people who give advice about such matters. Basically, it's like an attempt to have a civilized divorce. It means saying some things you may not really mean (like, "It's not that I was so unhappy here, but I just couldn't pass up this great opportunity that came my way") and not saying some things you'd probably like to (like, "Now that I'm leaving, here's what I really think about the kind of boss you've been").

People who recommend this approach argue that it's best to leave on a positive note. They also say that leaving on a sour note can come back to haunt disgruntled employees at the most inopportune time in the future. On the other hand, some employees find this approach a little phony or artificial. In addition, we've talked with people who chose this method and said that several years later they regretted not saying how they honestly felt when they left.

Letting It All Hang Out

Employees who choose this method tell their bosses (as well as others in the organization) exactly why they're leaving, which may include their profound dissatisfaction with their boss. Obviously, this method is risky, but it's more likely to lead to some form of accountability for a problem boss.

For example, after a very promising young designer left her firm for another one, she told the president of the company exactly why she was leaving—because her boss was a notorious credit taker who constantly "borrowed" the ideas of the younger designers and passed them off as his own with company higher-ups. She also warned the president that he was in danger of losing other talented people if he didn't resolve the problem. Within a week of her departure, the credit-taking boss was reprimanded by the company president and told to shape up. He didn't, and several months later left the company—involuntarily.

We heard of another story where an angry employee, a highly skilled printer, let it all hang out about his former boss in the exit interview with the company's personnel director. A week later, when he was supposed to start his new job, he was told that budget cutbacks had eliminated it. Even though he couldn't prove it, he strongly suspected that his former employer had leaked word to the owner of the new company that he was a complainer and a troublemaker. Being a skilled printer, he was able to find another job within a few weeks. But, in hindsight, he told us he thought it was a mistake to let it all hang out about his former boss when he left.

Exactly what to do is a bit of a judgment call. It depends on a number of factors: the kind of person you are, what kind of boss you've had, the organization and maybe even the industry you're in, and so forth. There are pros and cons to each decision, and we've seen both work out well (and badly) for people.

Well, that's it, our final strategy for dealing with problem bosses—"firing" your boss. In this chapter we've talked about why it's a good idea to consider it, offered some reasons why employees who should do it don't do it, and made some suggestions about how to get rid of your boss by making a career move.

18

•••••••••••••••••••••

WHERE DO YOU GO
FROM HERE?

Well, there you have it! Twelve different strategies for dealing with problem bosses. Our intent has been to stimulate your thinking about how to solve a problem that affects you and millions of other employees around the world—how to deal with a problem boss.

We've squeezed our minds and wrung out as many thoughts, ideas, and suggestions as we could. In the process, we've thrown a tremendous amount of information at you. At this point, you're probably thinking, "All right, but what do I do with all this information? Where do I go from here?"

We've got three suggestions.

THINK ABOUT IT

Almost every book or article we've read on creative problem solving talks about how important the principle of "incubation" is. This is the process where our minds work on problems at a level below our conscious awareness. So we recommend you put this book down for a few days and turn your attention to other matters. When you come back to it, your thoughts and ideas on where to go from here should be much clearer.

TALK IT OVER WITH SOMEONE ELSE

From time to time throughout this book, we've suggested sitting down and talking with someone you trust and have confidence in. This is another one of those times. Tell your friend several things:

- Tell them why you bought this book. If it was because of a problem boss, go into some detail about the situation: Who your boss is; what your boss does that bothers you; that sort of thing.
- Tell them about this book. Talk about your overall reactions to it; what you liked and didn't like about it; and any specific ideas it's given you for taking some action. You might even suggest your friend read the book, too, before you have this discussion.
- Ask your friend to give you some reactions to everything you've said. Before you respond to those reactions, of course, we'd like you to use your listening skills to draw the person out as fully as possible. This won't be easy, for your mind will be loaded with thoughts and feelings. But it's always surprising how someone with a fresh perspective can come up with ideas and suggestions that you—the person so close to the problem—would never have considered.

Armed with the information we've given you, we wish you success with solving *your* problem of the problem boss.

DO SOMETHING

You've heard this refrain from us before. Lots and lots of employees with problem bosses *never* take any effective action to improve their difficult situations. They just live with their "quiet desperation" year after painful year.

Well, a big reason we wrote this book was to motivate people to *do something* to make things better between themselves and their bosses. And that's what we'd like you to do. Something. You'll feel better about yourself if you do. And you might even resolve the problem that led you to pick up this book in the first place.

One last request.

We may not know you personally, but we feel we've got a little relationship going with you here. We've done our best to give you as much help as we could. Now we'd like you to do something for us:

Give us some feedback!

Bosses aren't the only people insulated from feedback. Authors are too. So we'd very much appreciate your letting *us* know what you thought of the book and, *especially*, how any of the strategies have worked out for you. Just write to us in care of the publisher.

Good-bye and the very best of luck to you!

INDEX

ABOUT THE AUTHORS

Dr. Mardy Grothe and Dr. Peter Wylie both received their doctorates in psychology from Columbia University. They are partners in Performance Improvement Associates, a management consulting firm based in Boston and Washington, D.C. Crothe is the father of two children and lives in Lincoln, Massachusetts and Wylie is married and lives in Washington, D.C.

Taking Care of Business...